Brilliant
HTML & CSS

James A. Brannan

PEARSON
Prentice
Hall

Harlow, England • London • New York • Boston • San Francisco • Toronto • Sydney • Singapore • Hong Kong
Tokyo • Seoul • Taipei • New Delhi • Cape Town • Madrid • Mexico City • Amsterdam • Munich • Paris • Milan

Pearson Education Limited
Edinburgh Gate
Harlow CM20 2JE
United Kingdom
Tel: +44 (0)1279 623623
Fax: +44 (0)1279 431059
Website: www.pearsoned.co.uk

First published in Great Britain in 2009

© Pearson Education Limited 2009

The right of James A. Brannan to be identified as author
of this work has been asserted by him in accordance
with the Copyright, Designs and Patents Act 1988.

ISBN: 978-0-273-72152-9

British Library Cataloguing-in-Publication Data
A catalogue record for this book is available from the British Library

Library of Congress Cataloging-in-Publication Data

Brannan, James A.
   Brilliant HTML & CSS / James A. Brannan.
      p. cm.
   ISBN 978-0-273-72152-9 (pbk.)
 1. Web sites--Design. 2. HTML (Document markup language) 3.
Cascading style sheets. I. Title.

   TK5105.888.B7243 2009
   006.7'4--dc22

                                                  2009002154

10 9 8 7 6 5 4 3 2 1
13 12 11 10 09

Typeset in 11pt Arial Condensed by 30
Printed and bound in Great Britain by Ashford Colour Press Ltd, Gosport, Hants

The publisher's policy is to use paper manufactured from sustainable forests.

Brilliant guides

What you need to know and how to do it

When you're working on your computer and come up against a problem that you're unsure how to solve, or want to accomplish something that you aren't sure how to do, where do you look? Manuals and traditional training guides are usually too big and unwieldy and are intended to be used as end-to-end training resources, making it hard to get to the info you need right away without having to wade through pages of background information that you just don't need at that moment – and helplines are rarely that helpful!

Brilliant guides have been developed to allow you to find the info you need easily and without fuss and guide you through the task using a highly visual, step-by-step approach – providing exactly what you need to know when you need it!

Brilliant guides provide the quick easy-to-access information that you need, using a table of contents and troubleshooting guide to help you find exactly what you need to know, and then presenting each task in a visual manner. Numbered steps guide you through each task or problem, using numerous screenshots to illustrate each step. Added features include 'Cross reference' boxes that point you to related tasks and information on the website or in the book, while 'For your information' sections alert you to relevant expert tips, tricks and advice to further expand your skills and knowledge.

In addition to covering all major office PC applications, and related computing subjects, the *Brilliant* series also contains titles that will help you in every aspect of your working life, such as writing the perfect CV, answering the toughest interview questions and moving on in your career.

Brilliant guides are the light at the end of the tunnel when you are faced with any minor or major task.

Publisher's acknowledgements

Every effort has been made to obtain necessary permission with reference to copyright material. In some instances we have been unable to trace the owners of copyright material, and we would appreciate any information that would enable us to do so.

Author's acknowledgements

Thanks to Adobe, for allowing screen shots of Adobe Kuler. Thanks also to FreeCSSTemplates (www.freecsstemplates.org); Rock Racing, and other websites who were gracious enough to permit me to include screenshots of their website. I am indebted to the creator of Vista Inspirate icons, by Saki on KDE-look.org; the website www.w3schools.com provided references on HTML and CSS, both of which are invaluable online resources. And thanks to the editorial team at Pearson, and my book agent, Neil Salkind at StudioB.

About the author

James A. Brannan is a consultant in Washington, DC, in the United States. He's developed websites, using everything from AWK to CSS to Enterprise Java, and lives off government spending. Other than that he lives a pretty boring, but reasonably fulfilling, life. He has two kids and a wife but no dog. Like a true American, rather than bike commuting, he drives his car – correction, Sports Utility Vehicle – an hour each way to work every day, but then turns around and rides his bike so hard his eyes pop out for two hours or so near his home. Like a true computer book author, he has a pipe-dream that someday authoring technical books will lead to writing the 'Great American Novel'.

For Dr. Rosemary Conover. Thanks, I followed your advice and never looked back after making my decision. Now I'm doing it again…

Introduction

HTML & CSS

Welcome to *Brilliant HTML & CSS* a visual, quick reference guide that will teach you all that you need to know to create clean, forward-looking, standards-compliant, accessible websites using HyperText Markup Language & Cascading Style Sheets. It will give you a solid grounding on the theory, coding skills, and best practices needed to use HTML & CSS to build sophisticated Web pages – a complete reference for the beginner and intermediate user.

Find what you need to know – when you need it

You don't have to read this book in any particular order. We've designed the book so that you can jump in, get the information you need, and jump out. To find the information that you need, just look up the task in the table of contents or Troubleshooting guide, and turn to the page listed. Read the task introduction, follow the step-by-step instructions along with the illustration, and you're done.

How this book works

Each task is presented in two distinct columns: with tasks listed in the sidebar and example screenshots and HTML or CSS code displayed on the main part of the page.

Every example follows a set of Task Steps which are numbered (2) to indicate a screenshot, feature or function.

The HTML and CSS examples within the main text are displayed alongside a numbered list, to help you identify any particular piece of coding mentioned in a Task Step. Just refer the to bracketed numbers at the end of a Task Step with the list beside the code.

Numbers are coloured according to chapter. Please note: the numbered list does not form part of the code!

What you'll do

Find what you need to know – when you need it

How this book works

Step-bystep instructions

Troubleshooting guide

Spelling

Completed Task examples can be found at: **www.pearson-books.com/ brillianthtml**

Wherever you see a '**Cross reference**' box, just log onto the website and select the appropriate link to view an example of the task.

Please note:

'HTML' and 'CSS' are initialisms, so are capitalised throughout this book, for style and consistency. The actual code written inside HTML tags is not case-sensitive, but for best practice it is advised to be consistent throughout. Document extensions however, (.html for example), should always be lower case!

Step-by-step instructions

This book provides concise step-by-step instructions that show you how to accomplish a task. Each set of instructions includes images that directly correspond to the easy-to-read steps. Eye-catching text features provide additional helpful information in bite-sized chunks to help you work more efficiently or to teach you more in-depth information. The 'For your information', 'Timesaver tip' and 'Jargon buster' features provide tips and techniques to help you work smarter, while the Cross-reference URLs show you completed examples of the task. Essential information is highlighted in 'Important' boxes that will ensure you don't miss any vital suggestions and advice.

Troubleshooting guide

This book offers quick and easy ways to diagnose and solve common problems that you might encounter, using the Troubleshooting guide. The problems are grouped into categories.

Spelling

We have used UK spelling conventions throughout this book, with the exception of all code, which ALWAYS uses US spellings. You may also notice some inconsistencies between the text and the software on your computer which is likely to have been developed in the USA. We have however adopted US spelling for the words 'disk' and 'program', within the main text, as these are commonly accepted throughout the world.

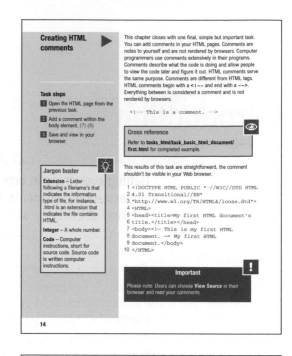

Contents

Introducing HyperText Markup Language (HTML)

Introduction

HTML is a markup language. A markup language is a language where you add instructions to text. The instructions tell the computer how to display the text enclosed by the instructions.

```
<browser do this>Text to act upon.</end
browser do this>
```

In the mid to late 1990s the only good way to write HTML was by hand. You typed the text and then added the HTML tags. These days, however, you almost don't even need to know HTML or CSS (Cascading Style Sheets). For example, Apple's iWeb application makes publishing a website easier then ever before. Choose a template, change the stock photos with your own, and add your own text. Easy, no HTML required, and certainly no CSS. With products such as DreamWeaver, almost nobody creates a professional website by hand using a text editor. So why this book? And why countless other HTML books on the shelves of your local bookshop?

True, these tools do make Web development easier. But suppose you've just developed your website using iWeb, you've pointed and clicked, and dragged and dropped, but now you wish to add your favourite YouTube playlist to your website using YouTube's embedded video player. There's no drag-'n'-drop control for that, what to do? You must add what iWeb calls an 'HTML snippet'. An HTML snippet allows you to write some HTML and embed it directly in your iWeb page. Just one

What you'll do

Get everything in order – text editors and Web browsers

Understanding elements, tags and attributes

Look at the basic structure of an HTML page

Creating a basic document – document declaration, header, metadata and body

Creating HTML comments

problem, though. Inserting an HTML snippet requires knowing some HTML. If you didn't take the time to learn basic HTML and CSS, you probably won't have much luck inserting an HTML snippet.

Knowing HTML and CSS will free you from being a slave to the tools – allowing you to use the tools when appropriate and fall back on a text editor when needed. In this book, I assume nothing more than a simple text editor and Web browser. By the end of the book, you will have the HTML and CSS skills necessary to view HTML source code and, if necessary, fix it yourself. If you plan on continuing to learn more on Web development after finishing this book, then I would recommend learning Adobe's DreamWeaver. DreamWeaver is the standard in Web development tools. Besides, it seems everybody nowadays uses DreamWeaver, and it's a skill in great demand in the information technology field. A good book for learning is *Brilliant DreamWeaver* by Steve Johnson, but before you rush out and buy his book, do yourself a favour: take the time to learn basic HTML and CSS first. Trust me, you will be glad you did when confronted with an 'HTML snippet' or something similar.

In this chapter you get organised for the future exercises. You also learn basic HTML document structure. If you want to actually do the tasks, be sure to understand this chapter's tasks. You must have a text editor and you must know how to load the finished page in your browser. Pretty basic tasks but very important. If you just want to read along, I have good news. Completed examples for all tasks are available via this book's website. Every task references the finished example, so all you have to do is look at the finished example. Of course, if you don't even want to do that, as with all Brilliant series books, the steps are clearly numbered in supporting code and figures. If you already know how to edit, save and view an HTML page, just skim this chapter. If you don't, be sure not to skip this chapter. You need these basic skills before you can complete the examples in this book.

Before getting started, you need to ensure that you have everything needed for accomplishing the tasks to come. You must identify an HTML editor, create a folder for storing your work, select a Web browser for viewing the resulting HTML page, and obtain some online reference material.

4
```
<!DOCTYPE HTML PUBLIC "-//W3C//DTD HTML
4.01 Transitional//EN"
"http://www.w3.org/TR/html4/loose.dtd">
<html><head></head><body>Hello
World!</body></html>
```

Task steps

1 Choose an HTML editor. The first thing you need is a simple text editor. If working in Windows, use TextPad. If using a Mac, use TextEdit.

2 Create a folder for storing your work.

3 Identify your browser. Choose the browser you normally use to surf the Web. I use Safari, so you will notice many Safari screen shots in this book.

4 Start your text editor and type the text above, left.

5 Save the document. Give it an .html extension.

6 Notepad users. When saving, click on **File**, **Save As**, and then **Select All Files** from the **Save As Type** drop-down, when saving your file. If you don't, Notepad appends a .txt extension to your file and your browser interprets the file as plain text rather than HTML. You must add the .html extension yourself, so type index.html when saving.

Getting everything in order – text editors and Web browsers (cont.)

7 TextEdit users. Before saving, change TextEdit's settings so it saves documents as plain text. From the **TextEdit** menu, select **Preferences**. In the dialogue box that appears, select the **New Document** tab and choose the **Plain text** option. On the **Open** and **Save** tab, ensure the **Add ".txt"** extension to plain text files check-box is not checked. Also, ensure the **Ignore rich text commands in HTML files** check-box is checked.

Important

Note: HTML document extensions (.html) are Lower Case!

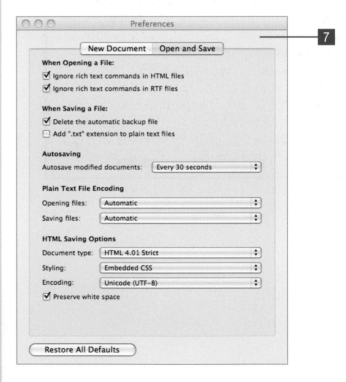

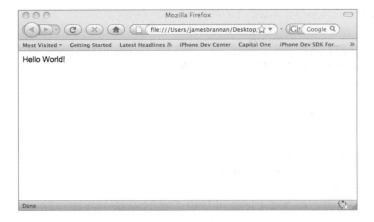

8 After saving, open your browser and open the file. For example, in Safari choose File – Open File – and then navigate to the file. After selecting the file, you should see 'Hello World' in the main browser window.

9 Bookmark or download some HTML/CSS references. This book isn't a comprehensive reference. You may need a comprehensive reference to consult while completing the tasks in this book.

10 Navigate to **www.w3schools.org** and bookmark the page.

11 Navigate to the Web Design Group's (WDG) website – **www.htmlhelp.com** – and bookmark the page.

12 Navigate to **www.w3c.org**, the World Wide Web Consortium's website. Bookmark the page.

For your information

The World Wide Web Consortium, W3C, is the World Wide Web's governing body. Although it has no legal authority, it is a consortium of all the major players: IBM, Microsoft, Apple, Hewlett Packard and other major companies. What the W3C does is get together and get everyone to agree on standards. It researches, meets and publishes specifications for different Web-related languages. Standards to come out of W3C include XML, HTML and CSS, among others. HTML 4.01 is a W3C recommendation. You can download the specification at the W3C website: **www.w3c.org** and review it if you desire. The reading is dry, but it is *the* source on HTML. The CSS specification is also available online at W3C's website.

Getting everything in order – text editors and Web browsers (cont.)

Timesaver tip

Your computer probably automatically opens HTML files using your favourite web browser. Double click on the page created in this task (index.html) and it should appear in you browser. If it doesn't, right click on index.html and choose Open With and be sure to select Always Open With check-box if on a Mac. If on Windows choose Open With, Choose Program and check the Always use the selected program to open this kind of file check-box.

For your information

Browser selection

You can choose from several browsers. Opera, Internet Explorer, Safari and FireFox are the most popular browsers. If using Windows, the chances are you have Internet Explorer. If using Mac, you certainly have Safari. As you are reading a book on HTML and CSS, I'm going to take a leap of faith and assume you already have a browser and know how to use it. The only caveat I'd add, is that if you have been holding off on updating it to the latest version, now is the time to do it. This book uses HTML 4.01 Transitional and CSS 2.01. If your browser is outdated beyond a version or two, there is a very good chance that some examples are not going to work in your browser.

For your information

Web hosting

If you want others to see your site you will eventually need to publish it. There are ample Web hosting companies on the Internet, both paid and free. But before going out and paying for space on a Web host, the chances are that you already have some free space as part of your account with your service provider. BT, the United Kingdom's largest Internet service provider, provides subscribers 15 megabytes of personal Web space. I have an **earthlink.net** account, with which comes 10 megabytes to create my own personal website; and if you are a student, you almost certainly have space to host your personal website. For more information, check with your service provider or school's IT department. It is worth your while to check and find out if you have free space.

An HTML document is comprised of elements. Elements exist for things such as headings, paragraphs, tables and other objects that comprise an HTML document. An element consists of a start tag, content and end tag.

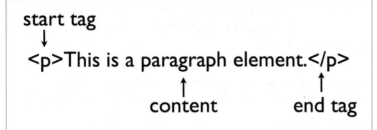

HTML elements are constructed by a start tag marking the element's beginning, one or more attributes, some optional content and an end tag. Tags are instructions that tell browsers to format its content a certain way. Tags are enclosed in two angle brackets (**<tag>**). For example, as your browser loads an HTML document, when it reaches the **<body>** tag, it knows that everything it loads until it reaches the closing **</body>** tag is part of the body element.

Attributes define an element's properties. Consider attributes as adjectives. For example, the image element contains a source attribute.

```
<img src="./site/images/mypicture.jpg"
alt="My picture"/>
```

A table element often contains a border attribute.

```
<table border="1"></table>
```

Attributes are name/value pairs that provide browsers with further instructions on rendering elements. The table tag with a border attribute tells the browser to not just create a table, but to create a table with a border. Moreover, make the border one pixel wide. The values an attribute can have vary depending on the attribute. Some attributes can take text, for example the

Understanding elements, tags, and attributes (cont.)

image tag's src (source) attribute. The browser cannot know in advance all the possible values for a source, so the attribute is not constrained. However, the table tag's border value is constrained. You can't have a border of 'Sam' or 'Frank', only an integer value that specifies pixels. Other attributes are similarly constrained. Some attributes only allow one of several predefined choices. For example, the input element's type attribute accepts the values: button, check-box, file, hidden, image, password, radio, reset, submit and text.

For your information

Few people bother referring to elements and instead just call everything tags. For example, you will see written: 'the paragraph tag', 'the body tag', 'the HTML tag'. In common web vernacular, tag and element mean the same thing. This book is no different, but I do use both terms throughout to remind you that they mean the same. Hopefully it doesn't distract you.

An HTML document consists of two parts: the header and the document's body. The header, specified by the **<head>** **<head>** tag, contains data not actually displayed by browsers. The head element is where you place the document's title, any metadata describing the document and other data pertaining to the document. The body element is where the Web page's content is placed.

The first line in an HTML document should be the document type definition (DTD). A document type definition declares the HTML version. There are three HTML 4.01 DTDs: HTML 4.01 Strict DTD; HTML 4.01 Transitional DTD; and HTML 4.01 Frameset DTD. In this book we use HTML 4.01 Transitional. You don't really need to know too much about the doctype, other than that it is good form to add this to an HTML document's first line. This line tells your browser to expect an HTML document that conforms to the HTML 4.01 Transitional DTD.

```
<!DOCTYPE HTML PUBLIC "-//W3C//DTD HTML
4.01 Transitional//EN"
"http://www.w3.org/TR/html4/loose.dtd">
```

After the DTD, the first element is the HTML element. The HTML element is comprised of the **<html>** opening and **</html>** closing tags. The browser views everything between these tags as an HTML document.

```
<!DOCTYPE HTML PUBLIC "-//W3C//DTD HTML
4.01 Transitional//EN"
"http://www.w3.org/TR/html4/loose.dtd">
<html></html>
```

HTML documents contain two sections, defined by the header and body elements. The document's header adds basic information about the document, such as its title, metadata, scripts, styles, etc. The body is the document's content. Everything appearing in the body appears as the document displayed in the browser's window, and is where you place content and formatting HTML tags.

Looking at the basic structure of an HTML page

1

Important

If you do not specify a DTD your browser will revert to 'quicks' mode, and make its best guess in how to render the page!

Looking at the basic structure of an HTML page (cont.)

Task steps

1 Open your browser and navigate to the **www.onlinebikecoach.com** website.

2 If using Safari, go to the menu and select **View** and then **View Source**. If using FireFox, select **View** and then **Page Source**.

3 Note, the document's DTD is HTML 4.01 Transitional.

4 Notice the document is comprised of two sections, the head and the body.

5 Within the `<head>` tags, there are several other tags. For example, notice the title, metadata, script and link tags.

6 The `<link>` tag is particularly important, this element tells browsers to get a CSS stylesheet from the location specified and apply that style to the document. You'll learn more on this element later.

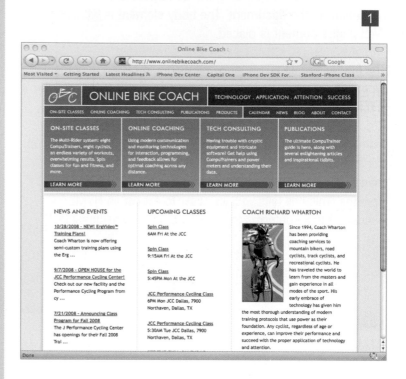

Looking at the basic structure of an HTML page (cont.)

```
<!DOCTYPE HTML PUBLIC "-//W3C//DTD HTML 4.01 Transitional//EN" "http://www.w3.org/TR/html4/loose.dtd">
<html>
<head>
<title>Online Bike Coach : </title>
<meta http-equiv="Content-Type" content="text/html; charset=iso-8859-1">
<meta name="description" content="">
<meta name="keywords" content="">
<link rel="stylesheet" type="text/css" href="/includes/style.css">
<script language="JavaScript" type="text/javascript" src="/includes/scripts.js"></script>
<script src="js/lib/jquery.js"></script>
<script type="text/javascript" src="js/jquery.validate.js"></script>
        <script type="text/javascript">
try {
var gaJsHost = (("https:" == document.location.protocol) ? "https://ssl." : "http://www.");
document.write(unescape("%3Cscript src='" + gaJsHost + "google-analytics.com/ga.js' type='text/javascript'%3E%3C/script%3E"));
</script>
<script type="text/javascript">
try {
var pageTracker = _gat._getTracker("UA-6528155-1");
pageTracker._trackPageview();
} catch(err) {}</script>


  <script>
  $(document).ready(function(){
    $("#test").validate();
  });
  </script>
</head>
<body class="onecol">

  <div id="outer">
        <div id="top">
            <h1><a href="home.asp">Online Bike Coach</a></h1>
            <h2>Technology . Application . Attention . Success</h2>
            <ul>

            <li id="navclasses"><a href="classes.asp">On-Site Classes</a></li>
            <li id="navcoaching"><a href="coaching.asp">Online Coaching</a></li>
            <li id="navconsulting"><a href="consulting.asp">Tech Consulting</a></li>
            <li id="navpublications"><a href="publications.asp">Publications</a></li>
            <li id="navproducts"><a href="products.asp">Products</a></li>
```

7 The body contains the HTML you see in the page as viewed in your browser.

8 Scroll through the document and view the different tags. It's okay if you don't understand everything, the important thing to take away from this task is the document's basic structure.

Creating a basic document – document declaration, header, metadata and body

Task steps

1 Open your text editor and create a new document.

2 Before you forget, choose Save As, and save the document. Be sure to give it a .html extension, and don't forget to set up your editor correctly, as instructed earlier in this chapter.

3 Add an opening **`<html>`** and closing **`</html>`** tag. (4,8)

4 In the HTML element, add the header element's opening and closing tags. (5,6)

5 Below the header element, add the body element. (7)

6 Within the body element, add some text. (7)

7 In the header element, add a title in the header. (5,6)

8 Save the document and view in your browser.

In the last task you reviewed an HTML document's layout. In this task you will learn to create a simple HTML document.

Table 1.1 Tags used in this task	
Tag	**Function**
<DOCTYPE .../>	Specifies the HTML document's DTD.
<html></html>	Specifies an HTML document.
<head></head>	Specifies an HTML document's header.
<title></title>	Specifies an HTML document's title.
<meta></meta>	Specifies metadata about an HTML document.
<body></body>	Specifies an HTML document's body.

This results of this task are straightforward. Your document's title should appear at your browser's top. You should also see the text you typed now displayed in your browser's window.

```
1 <!DOCTYPE HTML PUBLIC "-//W3C//DTD HTML
2 4.01 Transitional//EN"
3 "http://www.w3.org/TR/html4/loose.dtd">
4 <html>
5 <head><title>My first HTML document's
6 title.</title></head>
7 <body>My first HTML document.</body>
8 </html>
```

Important

Remember: the numbers beside the code are an indicator and should not be included within your document!

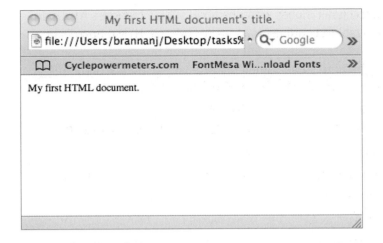

For your information

Create an informative title. Use descriptive titles such as 'James Brannan's HomePage' rather than 'My HomePage'. What appears as the link in Google is your title. When a user bookmarks your page, the title is the default name given the bookmark. Make it descriptive and interesting, and your site will get more visits.

Timesaver tip

Create a template for the rest of this book and save it as template.html. Use this file repeatedly as your task's base file.

```
<!DOCTYPE HTML PUBLIC "-//W3C//DTD
HTML 4.01 Transitional//EN"
"http://www.w3.org/TR/html4/loose.dtd
">
<html>
<head><title>insert title
here</title></head>
<body></body>
</html>
```

Creating HTML comments

This chapter closes with one final, simple but important task. You can add comments in your HTML pages. Comments are notes to yourself and are not rendered by browsers. Computer programmers use comments extensively in their programs. Comments describe what the code is doing and allow people to view the code later and figure it out. HTML comments serve the same purpose. Comments are different from HTML tags. HTML comments begin with a **<!--** and end with a **-->**. Everything between is considered a comment and is not rendered by browsers.

```
<!-- This is a comment. -->
```

Task steps

1 Open the HTML page from the previous task.

2 Add a comment within the body element. (7) (8)

3 Save and view in your browser.

Cross reference

Refer to **tasks_html/task_basic_html_document/ first.html** for completed example.

This results of this task are straightforward, the comment shouldn't be visible in your Web browser.

```
1 <!DOCTYPE HTML PUBLIC "-//W3C//DTD HTML
2 4.01 Transitional//EN"
3 "http://www.w3.org/TR/html4/loose.dtd">
4 <html>
5 <head><title>My first HTML document's
6 title.</title></head>
7 <body><!— This is my first HTML
8 document. —> My first HTML
9 document.</body>
10 </html>
```

Jargon buster

Extension – Letter following a filename's that indicates the information type of file. For instance, .html is an extension that indicates the file contains HTML.

Integer – A whole number.

Code – Computer instructions, short for source code. Source code is written computer instructions.

Important

Please note: Users can choose **View Source** in their browser and read your comments.

HTML text layout tags

Introduction

Despite the popularity of viral video sites such as YouTube, the Web remains comprised primarily of text. Web pages are most akin to printed magazines. Magazines are text with photos. Formatting magazines, or Web pages, at its most basic, is formatting text. There are many more mundane formatting tasks you must do before adding eye-catching graphics. Text requires breaking into paragraphs, long quotations need to be set apart from other text and sections distinguished by headings. Key phrases require emboldening, shorter quotations require quotation marks and key points should be displayed as lists. This basic text formatting makes the Web page easier to navigate, summarise and understand.

In this chapter you explore basic HTML text formatting. You should understand basic text layout before applying cool backgrounds to your page, dazzling fonts and adding interesting photos. Don't worry though, soon enough, in the second section of this book, you will learn how to make brilliant Web pages using CSS. The tasks in this chapter provide you with more mundane but highly important fundamental text layout HTML elements.

HTML provides several tags for marking up text into appealing paragraphs. The most fundamental is the paragraph element. The paragraph element consists of the opening `<p>` tag and closing `</p>` tags, and any content between them. The browser knows that all text occurring between the paragraph element's opening and closing tags form a cohesive paragraph.

What you'll do

Create HTML paragraphs

Add headings to your document

Create ordered and unordered lists

Create a definition list

Format ordered and unordered lists

Format quotations

Mark up other text elements

Insert special characters

The heading elements – represented by the tags: **`<h1></h1>, <h2></h2>, <h3></h3>, <h4></h4>, <h5></h5>, <h6></h6>`** – are equally fundamental. Heading elements allow you to easily add section headers to your paragraphs so you can divide your page into hierarchical topics. Headers are hierarchical, where **`<h1></h1>`** is the topmost heading (with the largest heading font), and **`<h6></h6>`** is the bottommost heading (with the smallest heading font).

HTML also provides several other basic text formatting tags. There are three tags to create lists. The ordered list element – represented using the **`<ol></ol>`** tags – allows you to easily create a numbered or ordered list: the unordered list element, **`<ul></ul>`**, an unordered list; and the definition list element, **`<dl></dl>`**, a definition list. You can specify quotations using the quotation element, **`<q></q>`**, for shorter quotations and the blockquote element, **`<blockquote></blockquote>`**, for larger quotations that you wish to set apart from a paragraph. There are also tags for making your text look like computer terminal printout, emphasising keywords and other basic formatting tasks you would expect of any decent word processing, or magazine layout software. This chapter explores these basic tags and their use in your HTML pages.

!

Important

Remember the discussion about elements versus tags in Chapter 1? Although technically different meanings, you can use the terms element and tag interchangeably. An element is the logical unit or the meaning. Tags are the physical markup, the opening and closing text that distinguishes an element's beginning and ending. For example, the paragraph element consists of the opening **`<p>`** and closing **`</p>`** tags and anything between the two tags is the element's content. But in Web vernacular, tag and element are equivelant. You can refer to the paragraph tag or the paragraph element and most people will understand you mean the **`<p>`** tag. Remember, this book uses both terms interchangeably.

With the HTML 4.01 specification's release, the W3C deprecated most formatting; CSS simply does a better job. For example, when laying out a paragraph in the past you could specify an align attribute in the paragraph element's opening tag, **<p>**, and give it a value of left, right, centre or justify. For example: **<p align="right">**. This attribute formatted the paragraph as you would expect, right aligned the text to the right, centre centred the text, left aligned the text to the left and justify the text.

Although most browsers still accept the align attribute, it is deprecated. There is no guarantee that the align attribute will display correctly in the future. Most other formatting attributes for basic HTML tags have likewise been deprecated. In this chapter, and in future chapters, I omit deprecated tags and attributes from the tasks. As a result of this omission, the task results in the next couple of chapters will seem, well, a tad ugly. But don't worry, in future chapters you apply CSS styles to them, making them appear as modern Web pages.

2

Creating HTML paragraphs

A paragraph element consists of an opening **<p>** tag, a closing **</p>** tag and any text between the two tags. This element defines paragraphs. When rendered, text inside a paragraph element appears as a single paragraph, with extra space before and after the paragraph's text, much like a paragraph in Word or OpenOffice Writer.

HTML paragraphs are left-aligned by default and the first line is not indented. You can align a paragraph using its align attribute. For example, **<p align="right">**. But note, this formatting attribute is deprecated and shouldn't be used. Use CSS instead. Trust me, you'll see, it's easier and more robust to use CSS. Oh, one final thing you should know about paragraphs. You cannot hit your [Return] key and expect the browser to render the linebreak. Web browsers handle paragraph wrapping automatically. To override this behaviour you must use the **
** tag (covered in a later task).

For your information

Using a closing **</p>** tag when using the paragraph element is not required. Browsers recognise **<p>** *some text* **<p>** *some more text* as two distinct paragraphs. But not closing your paragraph forces the browser to guess where the paragraph ends and could possibly lead to unpredictable results. It's also just plain sloppy. Be safe and tidy, always end your opening paragraph tag with a closing paragraph tag.

Table 2.1 Tag covered in this task	
Tag	**Function**
<p></p>	Specifies a paragraph.

Cross reference

See **tasks_html/task_html_paragraphs/paragraph.html** for the finished example.

Cross reference

The task 'Aligning elements' in Chapter 12 covers aligning elements using CSS.

The results of this task are straightforward: the paragraph tags separated the text into three distinct paragraphs.

```
 1 <html>
 2 <body>
 3 <img src="wonder3cc.png" width="150"
 4 height="150"/>
 5 <p>SeguroImpulso Software and Consulting
 6 ---snip--- consulting services.</p>
 7 <p>SeguroImpulso Software and
   Consulting
 8 ---snip--- under development.</p>
 9 <p>On this site you will find
10 information ---snip--- track racing, or
11 even cyclocross.</p>
12 </body>
13 </html>
```

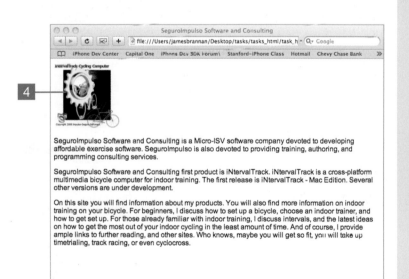

Task steps

1 Open the template and save with a different name.

2 Add three sets of **<p></p>** tags to the body element. (5, 7, 9)

3 Type some text in all three paragraph elements.

4 Save and display the page in your browser.

Adding headings to your document

Headings on a Web page are like headings in a Word or OpenOffice Writer document: they allow users to browse the page and determine what sections, if any, they are interested in. Headings also reinforce comprehension by providing a summary of a page's content. HTML headings go six levels deep, where each heading level denotes decreasing emphasis. Headings use the following tags: **\<h1>\</h1>**, **\<h2>\</h2>**, **\<h3>\</h3>**, **\<h4>\</h4>**,**\<h5>\</h5>** and **\<h6>\</h6>**. Browsers render headings larger and bolder than normal text, with **\<h1>** rendered the largest and **\<h6>** the smallest. As with the paragraph element, headings have an optional – but deprecated – align attribute that shouldn't be used.

Task steps

1. Open the template and save with a different name.

2. Add three sets of **\<p>\</p>** tags to the body element and type some text in all three paragraph elements. (6, 9, 13)

3. Add **\<h1>\</h1>** tags above the first paragraph and add some text to the element. (3)

4. After the **\</h1>** tag, but before the first **\<p>** tag, type the **\<h2>\</h2>** tags. Between the tags, enter some text. (8)

5. Repeat step 4, only place the second-level header between the first and second paragraphs, and the second and third paragraphs. (12)

6. At the bottom of the page (but before the **\</body>** tag) add **\<h3>\</h3>**, **\<h4>\</h4>**, **\<h5>\</h5>** and **\<h6>\</h6>** tags. Between each tag set add appropriate heading text. (16, 17, 18, 19)

Table 2.2 Tags covered in this task

Tag	Function
\<h1>\</h1>	Specifies a first level heading.
\<h2>\</h2>	Specifies a second level heading.
\<h3>\</h3>	Specifies a third level heading.
\<h4>\</h4>	Specifies a fourth level heading.
\<h5>\</h5>	Specifies a fifth level heading.
\<h6>\</h6>	Specifies a sixth level heading.

Cross reference

See **tasks_html/task_html_headings/heading.html** for the finished example.

As with the previous task, this task is also straightforward. The heading tags added headings to the HTML page. The **\<h1>** added the largest heading text, while **\<h6>** added the smallest.

```
 1 <html>
 2 <body>
 3 <h1>Seguro-Impulso Software and
 4 Consulting</h1>
 5 <h2>Seguro-Impulso's Mission</h2>
 6 <p>Seguro-Impulso Software and
 7 Consulting ---snip--- services.</p>
 8 <h2>SeguroImpulso's Products.</h2>
 9 <p>SeguroImpulso Software and Consulting
10 first product ---snip--- under
11 development.</p>
12 <h2>What's on the Site?</h2>
13 <p>On this site you will find ---snip---
14 fit, you will take up timetrialing,
15 track racing, or even cyclocross.</p>
16 <h3>test3</h3>
17 <h4>test4</h4>
18 <h5>test5</h5>
19 <h6>test6</h6>
20 </body>
21 </html>
```

Adding headings to your document (cont.)

7 Save your work and display it in your browser.

For your information

Don't leave this task thinking that headers are a catch-all formatting for making text larger. They really should only be used for bona fide headers. Bona fide headers, together with paragraphs, provide basic document structure. You should use CSS for formatting text that isn't a bona fide header.

7

SeguroImpulso Software and Consulting

SeguroImpulso's Mission

SeguroImpulso Software and Consulting is a Micro-ISV software company devoted to developing affordable exercise software. SeguroImpulso is also devoted to providing training, authoring, and programming consulting services.

SeguroImpulso's Products.

SeguroImpulso Software and Consulting first product is iNtervalTrack. iNtervalTrack is a cross-platform multimedia bicycle computer for indoor training. The first release is iNtervalTrack - Mac Edition. Several other versions are under development.

What's on the Site?

On this site you will find information about my products. You will also find more information on indoor training on your bicycle. For beginners, I discuss how to set up a bicycle, choose an indoor trainer, and how to get set up. For those already familiar with indoor training, I discuss intervals, and the latest ideas on how to get the most out of your indoor cycling in the least amount of time. And of course, I provide ample links to further reading, and other sites. Who knows, maybe you will get so fit, you will take up timetrialing, track racing, or even cyclocross.

test3

test4

test5

test6

Creating ordered and unordered lists

A list is an easy way to summarise information. You probably use two list types extensively in your everyday life. When you create a numbered, heirarchical list, you are creating an ordered list. When you create a list without numbering – a list of items – you are creating an unordered list. In HTML, there are three list types: ordered lists; unordered lists; and definition lists. In this task you learn to use ordered and unordered lists. In the next task you learn definition lists.

Ordered lists present data, when order is important. For example, my top three favorite bike brands (in order):

1. Fuji

2. Huffy

3. Serotta

Unordered lists present data where order is unimportant. For example, current programming languages I'm using at work (in no particular order):

- Java
- C
- JavaScript

You present numbered, or ordered, data using the **<ol></ol>** tags and unordered lists use the **<ul></ul>** tags. List elements in ordered and unordered lists are inserted in the list using the **<li></li>** tags.

```
<ol><li>Fuji</li><li>Huffy</li><li>
Serotta</li></ol>
<ul><li>Java</li><li>C</li><li>
JavaScript</li></ul>
```

Ordered lists are particularly valuable for presenting ordered instructions, such as the tasks in Brilliant series books. List elements are given their own text line and their own number. Unordered lists are are also useful by providing emphasis to distinguish each element in a group of items. List elements in the unordered list, like the ordered list, are each given its own text line.

Table 2.3 Tags covered in this task	
Tag	**Function**
<ul></ul>	Specifies an unordered (bulleted) list.
<ol></ol>	Specifies an ordered (numbered) list.
<li></li>	Specifies a list element.

Cross reference

See **tasks_html/task_html_lists/ordered_unordered .html** for the finished example.

Cross reference

In the Using hyperlinks – absolute URLs task, in Chapter 3, you use an unordered list to organise a list of links to other websites.

2

Creating ordered and unordered lists (cont.)

Task steps

1. Open the template and save it with a different name.

2. Type an **\<ol\>\</ol\>** tag pair in the body element. (6, 32)

3. Type three or four **\<li\>\</li\>** tag pairs in the ordered list element. Place text between each pair's opening and closing tags. (7, 10, 14, 26, 29)

4. Type another set of **\<ol\>\</ol\>** tags between the opening and closing of one of the list elements. (16, 24)

5. Place a couple **\<li\>\</li\>** tags in the nested ordered list element and enter some text in each. (17, 19, 20, 21, 23)

6. Below the outermost **\</ol\>** tag, type the **\<ul\>\</ul\>** tags. (35, 41)

7. Type a few **\<li\>\</li\>** tags in the unordered list element and enter some text in each. (36, 37, 39, 40)

8. Save your work and display it in your browser.

```
1 <html>
2 <body>
3 <h1>iNtervalTrack QuickStart</h1>
4 <h2>QuickStart Steps (Assuming Sensors,
5 DVD Playback, and M3U Playlist)</h2>
6 <ol>
7 <li>Start the Mac DVDPlayer, navigate to
8 where you wish iNtervalTrack to start
9 playing, and press pause.</li>
10 <li>Activate iNtervalTrack's DVDPlayer
11 plugin, check fullscreen, check mute
12 sound, then click the Finished
13 button</li>
14 <li> Configure the QuickTimePlayer Music
15 Player plugin.
16 <ol>
17 <li>Select the QuickTimePlayer Music
18 Player plugin.</li>
19 <li>Select Play a Playlist.</li>
20 <li>Click the browse button.</li>
21 <li>Select the M3U playlist to
22 play.</li>
23 <li>Click Finished.</li>
24 </ol>
25 </li>
26 <li>From the Window menu, select View
27 All Horizontal. Move the window to
28 desired location and size.</li>
29 <li>Click Start, jump on your bike, and
30 start pedaling (the software gives you
31 a ten second countdown.)</li>
32 </ol>
33 <h2>Prerequisites for Running
34 iNtervalTrack QuickStart</h2>
35 <ul>
36 <li>iNtervalTrack Software</li>
37 <li>SerialPort speed and cadence
38 sensor.</li>
39 <li>A M3U playlist already created.</li>
40 <li>A DVD in your DVD drive.</li>
41 </ul>
42 </body>
43 </html>
```

After completing this task you should see a numbered list. In one of the numbered list's items, you should see a nested list. This nested list should be a numbered list, indented from the outer list. Below the outermost ordered list you should see an unordered list. This list should be a list where each line begins with a bullet.

8

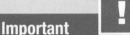

Important

Overlapping tags
As the task illustrates, you can nest lists within other lists. Any list type can be nested in any other list type. But be careful, you can get unpredictable results when nested list tags get mixed with the containing list. This mixing is called overlapping tags. For example, **`<h1>My Heading<p></h1>My Paragraph text</p>`** is an overlapping tag example. The results of such a mistake in a browser are unpredictable. Avoid overlapping tags!

Creating a definition list

In the previous task you learned the ordered and unordered list types. In this task you will learn about definition lists. Definition lists present term definitions. For example, consider Serotta's definition. The definition consists of a definition term, Serotta, and an actual definition: A manufacturer in the United States of high-end, custom bicycles. You wrap the definition's term in **<dt></dt>** tags and the term's definition in **<dd></dd>** tags. Using a definition list, you can quickly create a formatted glossary using HTML.

> **Cross reference**
>
> See **tasks_html/task_html_lists/definition.html** for the finished example.

The results of this task are straightforward. You should see two terms aligned with the left margin. On the line below each term, you should see the term's definition indented by five spaces. Note that terms with multiple line definitions are wrapped and indented to align with the previous five-space indented line.

Task steps

1. Open the template and save it as a new page.
2. Type a **<dl></dl>** tag set in the body element. (5, 17)
3. Type two **<dt></dt>** tag sets in the definition list. (6, 9)
4. Type a word to define in each definition term element.
5. Just below the definition term element, type a **<dd></dd>** tag set in each definition list. (7, 10)
6. Type each term's definition in the corresponding **<dd></dd>** tag set.
7. Save your work and open it in your browser.

```
1 <html>
2 <body>
3 <img src="./kfind.png"/>
4 <h1>Glossary of Terms</h1>
5 <dl>
6 <dt>Serotta</dt>
7 <dd>A manufacturer in the United States
8 of high-end, custom bicycles.<dd>
9 <dt>Time trial</dt>
10 <dd>A cycling event where the athlete
11 races against the clock to get the
12 minimum time possible. It can be a team
13 event or individual event. Common time
14 trial types are the 40K road time trial
15 and the 1K track event - affectionately
16 called "the kilo".</dd>
17 </dl>
18 </body>
19 </html>
```

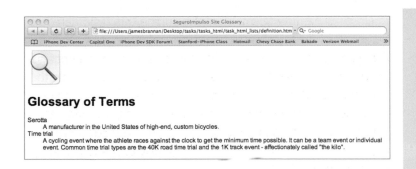

Formatting ordered and unordered lists

Against my better judgement, I'm including this task. Personally, I feel it safest to treat deprecated elements and attributes as non-existent. Nobody ever created a page that was rendered incorrectly, or a program that didn't run, because they didn't use deprecated language features. However, formatting a list is something that is still commonplace. For example, maybe you wished to use Roman numerals to number your list. Or maybe you wanted to use square rather than round bullets. Although CSS is now the recommended way to implement such formatting, you can do it directly in the HTML tag. Although it is deprecated, so your really shouldn't: you can specify an ordered list element's value.

Task steps

1. Open the template and save it with a different name.

2. Add an ordered list with three list items. (14)

3. Add a header just below the ordered list. (16)

4. Create another ordered list with three list items. Only for the first number add a value attribute and give it a value of four. (18)

5. Create an unordered list with a type of square. (21)

6. Save and open in your browser.

Table 2.4 Deprecated formatting attributes for ordered and unordered lists	
Ordered lists	
type="1"	1, 2, 3 …
type="a"	a, b, c …
type="A"	A, B, C …
type="i"	i, ii, iii … (lowercase Roman numerals)
type="I"	I, II, III … (uppercase Roman numerals)
Unordered lists	
type="disc"	disc
type="circle"	circle
type="square"	square

Cross reference

See **tasks_html/task_deprecated_list_formats/ordered_unordered.html** for completed example.

The results are straightforward. The ordered list should go from one to three and then the second list from four to six. The unordered list should be squares rather then round bullets.

```
1 <!DOCTYPE HTML PUBLIC "-//W3C//DTD HTML
2 4.01 Strict//EN"
3 "http://www.w3.org/TR/HTML4/strict.dtd">
4 <html>
5 <head>
6 <meta http-equiv="Content-Type"
7 content="text/HTML; charset=UTF-8">
8 <title>Deprecated List
9 Attributes</title>
10 </head>
11 <body>
12 <img src="./kfind.png"/>
13 <h3>The steps to take.</h3>
14 <ol><li>Step one.</li><li>Step
15 two.</li><li>Step three.</li></ol>
16 <h3>This is an interruption in the
17 list.</h3>
18 <ol><li value="4">Step
19 four.</li><li>Step five.</li><li>Step
20 six.</li></ol>
21 <ul type="square"><li>Item
22 one.</li><li>Item two.</li></ul>
23 </body>
24 </html>
```

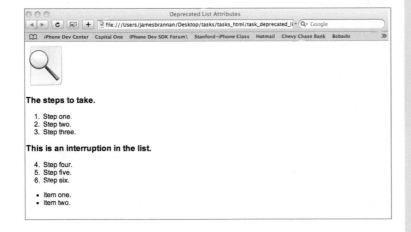

Formatting quotations

Quotations in HTML pages are just like quotations in print. Just remember what you learned when learning how to write a term paper. You should attribute your sources – when you take verbatim text from another source you must quote the source. Like writing an essay, shorter quotations are displayed in your paragraph's body and simply enclosed in double quotation marks. Longer quotations are separated and indented to distinguish it from your text.

The blockquote and quote elements display quotations in an HTML page. You format larger quotes using the **`<blockquote></blockquote>`** tags. For shorter quotes use the **`<q></q>`** tags. The resulting formatting is as you would expect – the same as what is expected in word processors or printed pages. The blockquote element is a separate indented paragraph. The q element is a shorter quote, displayed in-line with the rest of the text, but enclosed in opening and closing double-quotation marks.

Important !

Don't abuse the blockquote element. You should only use it when creating a bona fide quotation, not for general paragraph indentation. First, vision-impaired people use reading devices to read a Web page. They are going to mistakenly think your page is filled with long quotations. Second, CSS does a much better job at aligning paragraphs. CSS is the easy and correct way to indent general text.

Important !

Internet Explorer does not support the <q> tag.

Table 2.5 Tags covered in this task

Tag	Function
<q></q>	Specifies a short, in-line, quotation.
<blockquote></blockquote>	Specifies a long quotation (a separate, indented quotation).

Cross reference

See **tasks_html/task_html_quotations/whyrollers.html** for the finished example.

After completing this task you should see the quotation displayed in-line with the paragraph's text. The only difference is that a double quote is added to the beginning and ending of the quotation. The blockquote, in contrast, is displayed beginning on its own line. The text in the blockquote is indented from normal paragraphs.

```
1 <html>
2 <body>
3 <img src="./rollers.jpg" width="150"
4 height="150"/>
5 <h3>Rollers - The Key to Smooth
6 Cycling</h3>
7 <p>It is a well-known fact that rollers
8 are the quickest path to smooth bike
9 handling. My coach used to say,
10 <q>overcorrect your steering and you
11 fly right off the rollers, you gotta
12 learn to steer gently if you don't want
13 to fall.</q>
14 </p>
15 <p>
16 Wikipedia defines bicycle rollers as:
17 <blockquote>Bicycle rollers are a type
18 of bicycle trainer which makes it
19 possible to ride a bicycle indoors
20 without moving forward. ---snip---
21 bicycle's wheelbase. Generally, the
22 front roller is adjusted to be slightly
23 ahead of the hub of the front
24 wheel.</blockquote>
25 </p>
26 </body>
27 </html>
```

For your information

You can embed **<q></q>** tags in another set of **<q></q>** tags. The embedded quotation is rendered as a single quote. At least it is supposed to be rendered this way. Different browsers may render it differently. You can also embed standard formatting tags within blockquote elements.

Formatting quotations (cont.)

2

Task steps

1. Open the template and save with a new name.

2. Enter a paragraph in the body element. (7)

3. Somewhere in the paragraph, identify a sentence to make a quote.

4. Just before the quotation, type the opening **<q>** tag. At the end of the quotation, type the closing **</q>** tag. (10)

5. Below the paragraph's closing **</p>** tag, type an opening **<blockquote>** tag and a closing **</blockquote>** tag. (17, 24)

6. Enter some text in the blockquote element.

7. Save and display in your browser.

Formatting quotations (cont.)

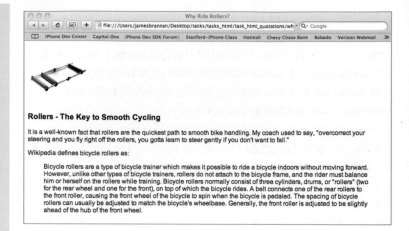

Rollers - The Key to Smooth Cycling

It is a well-known fact that rollers are the quickest path to smooth bike handling. My coach used to say, "overcorrect your steering and you fly right off the rollers, you gotta learn to steer gently if you don't want to fall."

Wikipedia defines bicycle rollers as:

> Bicycle rollers are a type of bicycle trainer which makes it possible to ride a bicycle indoors without moving forward. However, unlike other types of bicycle trainers, rollers do not attach to the bicycle frame, and the rider must balance him or herself on the rollers while training. Bicycle rollers normally consist of three cylinders, drums, or "rollers" (two for the rear wheel and one for the front), on top of which the bicycle rides. A belt connects one of the rear rollers to the front roller, causing the front wheel of the bicycle to spin when the bicycle is pedaled. The spacing of bicycle rollers can usually be adjusted to match the bicycle's wheelbase. Generally, the front roller is adjusted to be slightly ahead of the hub of the front wheel.

For your information

The blockquote element has an optional cite attribute. If the quotation's source comes from another website, you can enter the URL in this attribute. Your browser doesn't display the cite attribute's value, but it is useful for the metadata it provides.

There are many other elements used to mark up HTML text. Covering each one separately would add 16 more tasks to this chapter. But each element doesn't warrant its own task, as the elements covered in this task are quite easy to grasp. Still, this task explores 16 elements, so pay attention! Note, in this task I only cover elements that are not deprecated, so don't worry that you're learning an irrelevant element. There really is no reason to learn deprecated HTML formatting tags when CSS is so much more powerful for layout.

The elements covered in this task are the b, br, i, big, small, em, strong, sub, sup, del, ins, code, samp, kbd, var and cite elements.

Tag	Function
Table 2.6 Basic text formatting tags covered in this task	
<b></b>	Emboldens text.
 	Places a line-break in text.
<i></i>	Italicises text.
<big></big>	Enlarges text.
<small></small>	Makes text smaller.
<em></em>	Emphasises text.
<strong></strong>	Emphasises text, with more emphasis than the em tag.
	Subscripts text.
	Superscripts text.
<del></del>	Specifies enclosed text as deleted.
<ins></ins>	Specifies enclosed text as inserted.
<code></code>	Specifies enclosed text as computer code.
<samp></samp>	Specifies enclosed text as sample computer code.
<kbd></kbd>	Specifies enclosed text as keyboard text.
<var></var>	Specifies enclosed text as a variable.
<cite></cite>	Specifies enclosed text as a citation.

Marking up other text elements

Task steps

1 Open the template and save it with a new name.

2 Type opening and closing **<b></b>** tags. Type some text between them. (4)

3 Type another sentence and place a **
** tag in the line's middle. Don't forget to make the tag self-closing, as the linebreak element has no closing tag. (7)

4 Type a line of text and place an opening **<i>** tag before and closing **</i>** tag after a few words in the line. (11)

5 Type a **<big></big>** tag pair and enter some text between them. (14)

6 Type a **<small></small>** tag pair and enter some text between them. (15)

7 Type an **<em></em>** tag pair and enter some text between them. (16)

8 Type a **<strong></strong>** tag pair and place text between them. (17)

9 Type a line of text, then place an opening **<del>** and a closing **</del>** tag around one word. (19)

Marking up other text elements (cont.)

10 Select another word and place **`<ins></ins>`** tags around it. (20, 21)

11 Type a sentence, select a word and place the **`<sub></sub>`** tags around the word. (23)

12 Select another word in the sentence and place the **`<sup></sup>`** tags around the word.

13 Type some text and enclose the text in a **`<pre></pre>`** tag pair. (26)

14 Type another line and do the same using the **`<code></code>`** tags. (28)

15 Type some text and enclose several words in **`<samp></samp>`** tags. (31)

16 Type some more text and enclose in **`<kbd></kbd>`** tags. (33)

17 Type a letter and enclose it in **`<var></var>`** tags. (35)

18 Finally, type some text and enclose in **`<cite></cite>`** tags. (37)

19 Save and display this work in your browser.

Before beginning the task, note that I do not cover the very important div element. I also omit the span element. Because they are more useful when discussing CSS, I cover both elements in Chapter 8, in the CSS section of this book. The div element is covered in the task 'Aligning text', see p. 159, and the span element in the task 'Setting an element's font weight and size', see pp. 152–3. Also, note that I don't cover the underline element. It's deprecated and achieving the same affect using CSS is covered in Chapter 8, in the task 'Decorating text and changing case', see p. 157. Finally, if you are really astute, you'll notice I don't discuss common HTML tag attributes such as id or class. These attributes are most useful for CSS layout and are discussed in Chapter 7, in the task 'Understanding CSS rules', see p. 128.

> ### Cross reference
> See **tasks_html/task_html_other_text_elements/other. html** for the completed example.

The **`<b></b>`** tags should have emboldened any text between the two tags. The **`<br/>`** tag should have broken the line in its middle with a hard-return. The **`<i>`** tag's text should be italicised, the **`<big>`** tag's text larger then normal text, the **`<small>`** tag's text smaller then normal text, and the **`<em>`** tag's text should be emphasised (italics and/or emboldened). The **`<strong>`** tag should have emboldened its text, while the **`<del>`** tag should have drawn a line through its text. The **`<ins>`** tag should have underlined its text, the **`<sub>`** tag should have subscripted its text and the **`<sup>`** superscripted.

The **`<pre>`** tag should have displayed its text as preformatted text. Most browsers translate preformatted text to be courier monspace text. The **`<code>`** tag should have displayed its text as code, usually translated to courier monospace. The **`<sam>`** tag should have displayed its text as sample text, usually translated to courier monospace. The text enclosed in the **`<kbd></kbd>`** tags should be displayed as keyboard text, also usually translated to courier monospace. Finally, the text enclosed in the **`<cite></cite>`** tags should be displayed as a citation, usually translated to be italicised.

```
 1 <html>
 2 <body>
 3 <img src="./kwrite.png"/>
 4 <b>This is bold.</b>
 5 <p>
 6 This sentence has a line break
 7 here<br/>which means its on two lines.
 8 </p>
 9 <p>
10 This line of text has several
11 <i>italicised words</i> in it.
12 </p>
13 <p>
14 <big>Some big text</big> that I wish
15 was <small>very small</small> but I
16 <em>emphasise the text</em> to make a
17 <strong> strong point </strong> in this
18  contrived example. I wish to delete
19 these words: <del>hello world</del> and
20 insert these <ins>goodbye cruel
21 world</ins>.
22 </p>
23 <p>This is not the <sub>final</sub>
24 example. There are the <sup>code</sup>
25 and pre tags remaining.</p>
26 <pre>y=mX + b;</pre>
27 <br/>
28 <code>for(int i = 0; i < 20; i++)
29 sum(t);</code>
30 <br/><br/>
31 <samp>while(i < 100) sum(r);</samp>
32 <br/><br/>
33 <kbd>Hello World</kbd>
34 <br/><br/>
35 <var>y</var>
36 <br/><br/>
37 <cite>The Lord of the Rings</cite>
38 </body>
39 </html>
```

Marking up other text elements (cont.)

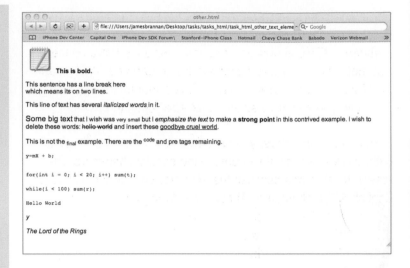

For your information

Logical tags vs physical tags

The tags in steps eight and nine of the task illustrate the use of logical markup tags. These are in stark contrast to physical tags such as **`<i></i>`** or **`<b></b>`**. Rather than instructing a browser how to render text, logical tags instruct browsers what type of text the tags contain and lets the browser decide how to display the element. Logical tags instruct a browser on the enclosed text's meaning. For example, placing text in **`<strong></strong>`** tags instructs the browser the enclosed text is important. Likewise, the **`<em></em>`** tags instruct a browser to emphasise the enclosed text. In contrast, the physical **`<b></b>`** tags simply instruct a browser that the enclosed text should be emboldened. It's a subtle but important difference. There is nothing inherent in the **`<samp></samp>`** tags that instruct browsers to use a courier monospace font. The browser sees that the text is enclosed in **`<samp></samp>`** tags and knows it is sample text. Usually browsers display text in the **`<samp>`** element using courier monospace. But you can change that behaviour using a CSS style sheet.

Some characters, such as the ampersand or multiplication and division symbols, cannot be easily entered using your keyboard. HTML allows you to use codes as a convenience. But, note that you must represent the ampersand (&) symbol in HTML using the **&** code. This requirement is because & is how you specify a special character code in HTML.

In the Web's early days, you were forced to enter non-English characters and special symbols using special characters. The reason for this was because the Web started with a small set of English ASCII characters. These days, though, HTML is much less provincial and supports all languages using something called UNICODE. But if you are typing in English and still want to type one or two words or sentences in a foreign language, note that you can still use special characters to represent the foreign characters. Table 2.7 summarises the more common special character codes.

Table 2.7 Common special characters		
Code	**Character**	**Meaning**
&amp;	&	ampersand
		non-breaking space
&pound;	£	pound sterling character
&cent;	¢	cent character
&copy;	©	copyright character
&reg;	®	registered character
&deg;	°	degree character
&plusmn;	±	plus or minus character
&times;	x	multiplication character
&divide;	÷	division character
&quot;	"	quotation mark
&lt;	<	less-than sign
&gt;	>	greater-than sign

The results of this task are pretty straightforward, you should see each special character displayed in your browser rather then the code typed in the HTML.

Inserting special characters

Task steps

1. Open the template and save it as a new page.

2. Between the body tags, enter **&**, **£**, **¢**, **©**, **®**, **°**, **±**, **×**, **÷**, **"**, **<** and **>** text. (4–7)

3. Now, between each special character code, type the ** ** code. (4–7)

4. Add a definition **list**, **dl**, after the previous step's line and enter the following text for the definition term: **automação** and then enter "**Portuguese for automation**". as the definition. (8–11)

5. Save and display the work in your browser.

Cross reference

See **tasks_html/ task_html_special_ characters/special .html** for completed example.

Inserting special characters (cont.)

```
1  <html>
2  <body>
3  <img src="./wp.png"/>
4  &amp;   &pound;   &cent;   &cop
5  y;   &reg;   &deg;   &plusmn; &n
6  bsp; &times;   &divide;   &quot; &nb
7  sp; &lt;   &gt;
8  <dl>
9  <dt>automa&ccedil;&atilde;o</dt>
10 <dd>Portuguese for automation.</dd>
11 </dl>
12 </body>
13 </html>
```

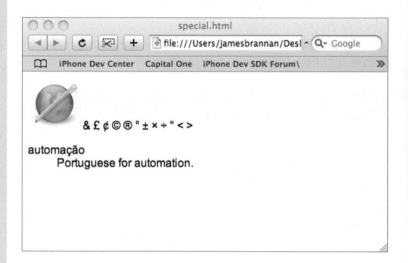

For your information

Unicode and languages other then English

Unless you live in the most rural of areas, chances are you hear at least one or more languages other than English spoken on any given day. It's a multilingual world. Chances are you speak at least a little of a language other than English. Setting up your computer's default character set for languages other than English is beyond the scope of this book; but you should note that you can specify the character encoding of your page. Refer to the W3C's website for more information (**www.w3c.org/International**).

Don't leave this task thinking you must use special characters if you wish to create a website in a language other than English. You don't; special characters are for single words or short sentences.

Jargon buster

Viral video – Video shared over the Internet. This sharing leads to the video becoming popular.

Deprecated – Replaced software features that should no longer be used. A replaced element or attribute that is outdated by a newer element, attribute or construct. For instance, most HTML formatting features were replaced by CSS, so these HTML formatting features are deprecated.

For your information

Within the body element, there are two HTML tag types: block-level and in-line. A block-level tag formats blocks of text, and causes browsers to render a new line following the element's closing tag. Block-level elements may contain other block-level elements and in-line elements. Block-level elements are used for holding larger amounts of data. For instance, the paragraph element is a block-level element. Think of block-level elements as your page's building-blocks.

In contrast, in-line elements are for applying formatting to smaller data structures such as hyperlinks, images and other tags. In-line elements may only contain other in-line elements and cannot contain block-level elements.

Table 2.8 Block-level elements

<p></p>
<h1></h1>...<h6></h6>
<blockquote></blockquote>
<ol></ol>
<ul></ul>
<dl></dl>
<div></div>
<form></form>
<table></table>
<fieldset></fieldset>

Understanding hyperlinks

Introduction

The World Wide Web as we know it is founded on hyperlinks. A hyperlink is a location in a resource that links to another location in that resource or links to another resource. When you click on the link in your browser, your browser knows where to go through the uniform resource locator, or URL. A URL is the address that identifies a resource. Usually that resource is another Web page, although it might be something else, such as an image or video.

When you view a Web page in your browser, you're actually viewing text mixed with one or more URLs. Before being displayed by a browser, an HTML page consists of text, nothing more, nothing less. All the images, movies, sounds and other multimedia are text hyperlinks to the actual resource. As a browser reads the page's HTML, it finds the resource by using the resource's URL, downloads it and places the resource in the appropriate location in the page. If the resource is an image, it displays the image. If the resource is Flash, or some other multimedia, it loads the appropriate plugin and loads the resource into the plugin. If a browser doesn't know how to handle the resource, the browser usually raises a dialogue box either asking you to choose the application to open the resource with, or if you wish, to save the resource. When you physically click on a hyperlink with your mouse, you are instructing your browser to find the resource the hyperlink points to and load it. If it is an HTML page, your browser replaces the current page with the page newly retrieved.

What you'll do

Understand uniform resource locators (URLs)

Using hyperlinks – absolute URLs

Using hyperlinks – relative URLs

Adding targets to hyperlinks

Creating anchors

Linking to an email address

The technical information behind a URL is beyond the scope of this book. Anyway, you don't need to know all the technical information; if you are interested, just google it and you will find more than you ever wished to know about the subject. For our purposes, however, just think of it as a unique, global address. More on URLs in the first task.

For your information

Most websites these days are dynamic. Rather than serving static HTML pages, there is an intermediate layer where a programming language actually dynamically writes the HTML page and sends the results to a Web server that delivers the page to your browser. For example, if you go to **ebay.co.uk** and navigate the listings, these listings are dynamically generated, you will not see static page names such as **listing.html** in your browser's address bar.

If you have any experience surfing the Web, you probably already understand uniform resource locators (URLs). URLs are addresses, much like the address to your house. Actually, a better analogy would be an apartment complex. An apartment's main address – or base address – points to the apartment complex.

```
127 Garden Grove Apartments
```

The apartment's address then points to the apartment's actual unit number in the complex.

```
Apt #27
```

But URLs take it one step further. A URL can point to a room and even a location in the room.

```
Master Bedroom/left corner
```

So the complete URL would be:

```
/127 Garden Grove Apartments/Apt
#27/Master Bedroom/left corner
```

A complete URL begins with the protocol identifier. You almost never enter the protocol when typing an address into your browser. You usually simply type the domain name rather than the protocol followed by the domain name. For example, you would usually just type **uk.yahoo.com** rather than **http://uk.yahoo.com**. Your browser guesses that you mean the hypertext transport protocol (http) and prepends it to your URL.

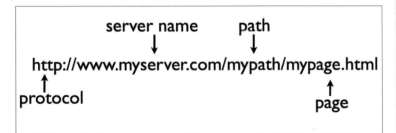

Http is the primary protocol used by the Web. It is transparent to you, though. Just know that, behind the scenes, http is the way computers understand that they are sending Web pages to one

Understanding uniform resource locators (URLs)

Task steps

1. In your browser, type: **www.webopedia.com** into the address bar and hit [Return]. This takes you to the online resource: Webopedia.

2. Add: **/TERM/d/domain_name.html** to the address and hit [Return]. This takes you to the static page **domain_name.html:** a definition of domain name.

3

3. Now type the address **www.paypal.com** in your browser's address bar and press [Return]. As your browser navigates to PayPal, it changes the protocol from http to https. The https protocol, adds an encryption layer to http so that hackers cannot eavesdrop on the information being sent to your browser.

Understanding uniform resource locators (URLs) (cont.)

4 Finally, type: **http://theocacao.com/** into your browser's address bar and press [Return]. This takes you to Scott Stevenson's site. It's a great resource on Mac OS X programming using Cocoa, incidentally.

5 Type **uk.yahoo.com** and press [Return] to navigate to YahooUK. After navigating to it, enter **index.html** after the trailing slash. Your browser navigates to the same page.

another via headers. After the protocol comes the server's name. The server name specifies the computer name of the resource's location. It specifies the apartment complex, for example.

After the resource's server name, comes the path to the actual resource's location. Note that the path can simply be a / when the resource is in the website's root folder.

```
http://www.myserver.com/mypath/
```

Finally, after the path comes the actual resource.

```
http://www.myserver.com/mypath/mypage.html
```

4

In the last task I introduced URLs. URLs are what you use to navigate the Web. They are also the way users navigate both to and from your site. URLs can be either external or internal. An external URL points to another website, while an internal URL points to another resource on your site. An absolute URL shows the entire path to a resource. You use absolute URLs to point to external resources. A relative URL is for navigating from one section of a site to another. For example, in our apartment complex example in the previous task, moving from one apartment complex to another would require an absolute URL. Navigating within the same apartment complex allows the use of relative URLs.

You use the anchor tag **<a>** to reference other locations. Those locations can be other locations in the same document or different documents. The marking up anchors task illustrates the use of the anchor tag for linking to other locations in the same document. This task illustrates the use of the anchor tag for navigating to other documents. You use the anchor tag's href attribute to specify to other documents. This task illustrates using href to point to external sites using absolute URLs. The next task illustrates internal links using relative URLs.

Table 3.1 Tag covered in this task	
Tag	**Function**
<a></a>	Specifies an anchor. A link to another document or another location in a document.

Cross reference

See **tasks_html/task_html_links_ absolute/links.html** for completed example.

Using hyperlinks – absolute URLs

Task steps

1 Open the template and save it with a different name.

2 Find two or three sites you wish to link to and jot down the Web address. Also, note the title that your browser displays for the pages and jot that down also.

3 Between the body tags in **links.html**, create an unordered list, with the same number of items as the sites identified in Step 2. (7–18)

4 Enter the Web page titles as the list elements. (10, 14, 16)

5 Now, at the beginning of each title type the **<a>** opening tag and for the href attribute type the URL. (8, 13, 15)

6 At the end of each title, type the closing **</a>** tag. (12, 14, 17)

7 Save and open in your browser.

3

Using hyperlinks – absolute URLs (cont.)

```
1 <!DOCTYPE HTML PUBLIC "-//W3C//DTD HTML
2 4.01 Transitional//EN"
3 "http://www.w3.org/TR/html4/loose.dtd">
4 <html>
5 <body>
6 <img src="./internet.png"/>
7 <ul>
8 <li><a
9 href="http://www.cyclingnews.com">
10 www.cyclingnews.com - the first WWW
11 cycling results and news
12 service</a></li>
13 <li><a href="http://www.youtube.com">
14 YouTube - Broadcast Yourself</a></li>
15 <li><a href="http://www.chrishoy.com/
16 chris_hoy_biography.html">Chris Hoy |
17 Olympic Champion Cyclist</a></li>
18 </ul>
19 </body>
20 </html>
```

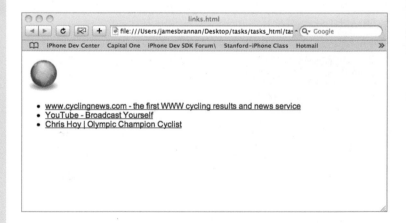

You use relative URLs to link to documents within your website. In this example you explore relative URLs. If you followed the absolute URL to the left corner of the master bedroom:

```
127 Garden Grove Apartments/Apt
#27/Master Bedroom/left corner
```

then, to get to the kitchen, you wouldn't want to go back outside the apartment complex and navigate back to the kitchen:

```
127 Garden Grove Apartments/Apt
#27/kitchen
```

Instead, you would simply want to go back to the apartment's main entrance and navigate to the kitchen:

```
../kitchen
```

Relative URLs allow simpler navigation within the same website.

Important

You need to know a little about navigating computer file paths using the command line to successfully understand relative URLs. If you use Windows, type cmd in Run to go to the commandline prompt. For example, on Windows XP, from the Start Menu choose Run. In the Run window's open dialogue box, type cmd and press [Return]. This takes you to the command prompt. To navigate a level up type cd followed by a space and two periods (**cd ..**), to navigate a level down type **cd ./** and the directory's name.

On OS X, go to Utilities and open **Terminal.app**. A bona fide UNIX command terminal is opened (you did know OS X is a UNIX variant, right?). If you want to know your current directory, type pwd. To navigate up a directory type **cd ..**, to navigate down a directory type **cd ./** followed by the directory name.

Using hyperlinks – relative URLs

Task steps

1. Save the template twice, assigning the filenames **main.html** and **sub.html**.

2. Create a folder named **asubfolder** in the same folder as the two newly created HTML pages.

3. Create an HTML page in the newly created folder. Name the file **subtwo.html**.

3. Open **main.html** and type some text. Create a link around some text. In the href, have it point to a **sub.html**. (11)

4. Create another link in **main.html** and have it point to the **subtwo.html** page in the **asubfolder** subfolder. (8, 9)

5. Save **main.html** and open **sub.html**.

6. Type some text and create a hyperlink to **main.html**. (22, 23)

7. Save and open **subtwo.html**.

3

Using hyperlinks – relative URLs (cont.)

Cross reference

See **tasks_html/task_html_links_relative/main.html** for completed example.

8 Save **subtwo.html** and open **main.html** in your browser. Navigate through the added links on the three pages.

The link in **main.html** to **sub.html** simply references the file, as they are in the same folder. The link from **main.html** to **subtwo.html** includes a . to indicate the current directory, a forward slash, the subdirectory's name and the file. The link from **subtwo.html** back to **main.html** includes a .. which navigates back to the next level up. Finally, in **sub.html**, note that you can combine .. and . into a complete path, even if they are nonsensical, like the example.

```
1 <!DOCTYPE HTML PUBLIC "-//W3C//DTD HTML
2 4.01 Transitional//EN"
3 "http://www.w3.org/TR/html4/loose.dtd">
4 <html>
5 <body>
6 <img src="./gaim.png"/>
7 <h1>About Me</h1>
8 I love cycling, see <a href="./
9 asubfolder/subtwo.html">hello</a>. I
10 also love programming and writing. See
11 my <a href="sub.html">online resume</a>
12 for my programming experience.
13 </body>
14 </html>

15 <!DOCTYPE HTML PUBLIC "-//W3C//DTD HTML
16 4.01 Transitional//EN"
17 "http://www.w3.org/TR/html4/loose.dtd">
18 <html>
19 <body>
20 <img src="./klipper.png"/>
21 <h1>Resume - James A. Brannan</h1>
22 <a href="./asubfolder/../asubfolder/
23 .././main.html">back to bio the hard
24 way...</a>
25 </body>
```

```
26 </html>
27 <!DOCTYPE HTML PUBLIC "-//W3C//DTD HTML
28 4.01 Transitional//EN"
29 "http://www.w3.org/TR/html4/loose.dtd">
30 <html>
31 <body>
32 <img src="Ym.png"/>
33 <h1>HELLO</h1>
34 <a href="../main.html">Back to Bio.</a>
35 </body>
36 </html>
```

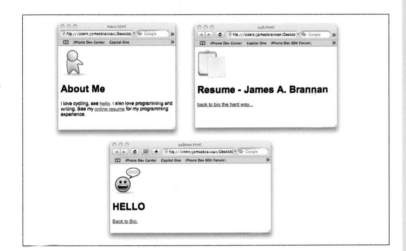

Important

If you open a.html in **tasks_html/task_html_links _relative/asubfolder/a.html** you will notice that the image tag's source is **Ym.png** *not* **ym.png**. Remember that, although in Windows URLs are not case sensitive, on Linux and OSAX they are. It is imperative you use the correct case.

3

For your information

If you wish to do so, you can make internal links fully qualified URLs. But it is much easier to use relative URLs for internal links.

Adding targets to hyperlinks

Task steps

1. Open the template and save with a different name.

2. Add three hyperlinks to an external site. (13, 19, 25)

3. In the top link, add the target attribute and assign it **_blank**. (13)

4. In another link add a target with **_self** for its value. (19)

5. In the third link, add a target with **_top** for its value. (25)

6. Save, open in your browser and observe the different behaviour of the three links.

An anchor can have a target attribute. The target attribute specifies where to open the resource linked to by the anchor element.

Table 3.2 Attributes covered in this tasks	
Attributes of an anchor element (\<a>\</a> tags)	
_blank	Open the resource in a new window or new tab.
_parent	Open the resource in the parent frame.
_self	Open the resource in the same frame.
_top	Open the resource in the same window.

Target is most useful when using framesets, but nobody uses frames these days. This book doesn't even cover frames, they have fallen so out of use. However, there is still one quick and easy use for target: when linking to a resource, you can specify that it should open in a new window or tab. For example, if you linked to another site, normally when the user clicks on the link they would leave your site when the browser loads the new site's page. When using the **_blank** attribute, the browser remains on your site, but opens a new window to display the resource.

Cross reference

Refer to **tasks_html/task_html_targets/target_blank.html** for completed example.

After completing this task, when you click on the first link, it opens in a new browser. Unless you use frames, this is by far the most useful target attribute you can use. This allows you to link to external sites and when users click on the link they don't navigate away from your site. Instead a new window opens. If you have ever been to a gambling site, or some other site offering anything 'free' – you have probably seen more examples of the **_blank** target than you care too.

```
 1 <!DOCTYPE HTML PUBLIC "-//W3C//DTD HTML
 2 4.01 Transitional//EN"
 3 "http://www.w3.org/TR/html4/loose.dtd">
 4 <html>
 5 <body>
 6 <img src="./ktip.png"/>
 7 <p>
 8 You can spend hours reading ---snip---
 9 every day. <cite>Brilliant Mac OSX
10 Leopard</cite> is a book that
11 accomplishes this, I use it.
12 </p>
13 Target=_blank: <a
14 href="http://www.pearsoned.co.uk/
15 Bookshop/detail.asp?
16 item=100000000256904" target="_blank">
17 Brilliant Mac OSX Leopard</a>
18 <br/>
19 Target=_self: <a
20 href="http://www.pearsoned.co.uk/
21 Bookshop/detail.asp?
22 item=100000000256904" target="_self">
23 Brilliant Mac OSX Leopard</a>
24 <br/>
25 Target=_top: <a
26 href="http://www.pearsoned.co.uk/
27 Bookshop/detail.asp?
28 item=100000000256904" target="_top">
29 Brilliant Mac OSX Leopard</a>
30 </body>
31 </html>
```

Adding targets to hyperlinks (cont.)

3

Adding targets to hyperlinks (cont.)

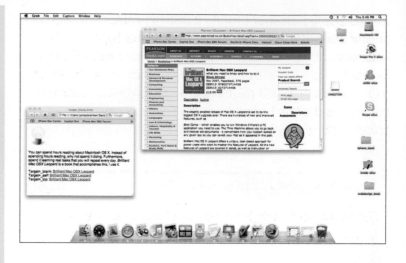

In Web slang, anchor does not refer to the anchor element. An anchor element is usually just called a link, or hyperlink. The coloquial 'anchor' definition refers to a specific type of anchor element, where the link refers to another location in the same page. For example, you might have a long page with a table of contents at the top. Each item in the table of contents can be linked to its appropriate location in the page.

> ### Cross reference
>
> See **tasks_html/task_html_anchors/anchorsexample.html** for completed example.

To get the full effect, you should resize your browser window so only the first paragraph is visible. When you click on the link, the visible text should jump to the anchor you defined. When you click on the hyperlink to the second page, it should load in the page and navigate directly to the anchor on the second page.

```
1 <!DOCTYPE HTML PUBLIC "-//W3C//DTD HTML
2 4.01 Transitional//EN"
3 "http://www.w3.org/TR/html4/loose.dtd">
4 <html>
5 <head>
6 <title>Anchor Example</title>
7 </head>
8 <body>
9 <img src="./xmag.png"/>
10 <p>You use anchors to link from one
11 location on a page to another. They are
12 most useful for long text pages that
13 users must
14 <a href="#scroll_def">scroll</a> as
15 they read the page.
16 </p>
17 <p>Anchors can also <a href=".
18 /anchorsexampleb.html#scroll_def">link
19 to</a> an anchor on another page.
20 <br/><br/><br/><br/><br/><br/><br/><br/>
21 <br/><br/>
```

Creating anchors

Task steps

1 Open the template and save it using a different name.

2 Type a simple paragraph in the document, then type ten **
** tags and enter some simple text. (20, 21)

3 In the inital paragraph, choose a word and add a link around it. But, instead of specifying another document, type the [#] key followed by a simple name. For example, **#scroll_def**. (14)

4 In the text below the **
** tags choose a word and place a link around it. Do not add an href attribute, but instead add a name attribute. For the name attribute's value, type the same name (minus the #), for example, **scroll_def**. (24)

5 Create another simple html page with about 10–15 **
** tags. After the **
** tags, add an anchor to the page. (44)

3

Creating anchors (cont.)

6 Back in the original page, create a hyperlink leading to the new page then, only at the end of the URL, add # and the anchor name you created in the other page. (17, 18)

7 Save your work and open it in your browser.

```
22 <img src="kfilereplace.png"/>
23 <dl>
24 <dt><a name="scroll_def">scroll</a></dt>
25 <dd>
26 Webopedia defines scroll as:
27 <blockquote citation="http://www.
28 webopedia.com/TERM/s/scroll.html">
29 To view consecutive lines of ---snip---
30 up one row, so that the top line
31 disappears.
33 </dd>
34 </dl>
35 </body>
36 </html>

37 <!DOCTYPE HTML PUBLIC "-//W3C//DTD HTML
38 4.01 Transitional//EN"
39 "http://www.w3.org/TR/html4/loose.dtd">
40 <html>
41 <body>
42 <br/><br/>--snip--<br/>
43 <img src="kfilereplace.png"/>
44 <a name="scroll_def">scroll</a>
45 All the way at the bottom.
46 </body>
47 </html>
```

Go to any website and you will usually see a 'contact me' link somewhere on the main page. When you click it, your default email program usually activates and presents you with a dialogue box to complete the email and send it. On Windows, Outlook is probably activated. On Mac, Mail is activated and a New Message dialogue box is presented.

Mail links begin with a **mailto:** rather than an **http://** at the beginning. This tells a browser that the link's protocol is email. The basic form of a mailto link is as follows.

```
<a href="mailto:me@myaddress.com">
Contact Me.</a>
```

If you want, you can even pre-fill some of the email's fields. You can specify an email's subject and even its message. You can also specify email addresses for the cc and bcc fields. And of course you can specify multiple recipients for any of the recipient fields.

> **Cross reference**
>
> See **tasks_html/task_html_email_link/mailto.html** for completed example.

Once this task is complete click on the first page's link and a dialogue box to compose an email message should appear. The subject line and recipient should be pre-filled. The second page's link should open a dialogue box with all the fields pre-filled. There should be more than one recipient.

```
1 <!DOCTYPE HTML PUBLIC "-//W3C//DTD HTML
2 4.01 Transitional//EN"
3 "http://www.w3.org/TR/html4/loose.dtd">
4 <html>
5 <body>
6 <img src="./mail.png"/>
7 <p>
8 Yes, I'm interested in iNtervalTrack!
9 <br/>
10 <a href="mailto:jamesbrannan@xxxx.net">
11 Please send me more info.</a>
```

Linking to an email address

Task steps

1. Open the template and save using a different file name.

2. Add a paragraph with some text. (7)

3. Add a link only for the href use mailto:emailaddress. Try using your actual email address. (10)

4. Copy the newly created page and save with a different name.

5. Edit the email address and add a subject. Note the **%20** for spaces, this is important. (25)

6. Add a **cc** and a **bcc**. Note the **&** between subject, **cc**, and **bcc**. Also, note that the values for these fields do not have a single or double quote. (27, 28)

7. Add another **cc** value by placing a semicolon and a second email address. You can send emails, cc and bcc to as many addresses as desired by using semicolons between addresses. (28)

8. Add a body value by typing: **&body**. (29)

3

Linking to an email address (cont.)

9 Save and open in your browser. Move your mouse over the link, and notice the lower left corner of the browser's status bar.

10 Click on the link, and your system's mail program should open with an email ready to send, with the To, cc, bcc, Subject and Body fields pre-filled.

For your information

Unless typing an extremely short body message, you wouldn't normally want to populate the body. It is just too cumbersome to type the message in-line.

```
12 </p>
13 </body>
14 </html>

15 <!DOCTYPE HTML PUBLIC "-//W3C//DTD HTML
16 4.01 Transitional//EN"
17 "http://www.w3.org/TR/html4/loose.dtd">
18 <html>
19 <body>
20 <img src="./mail.png"/>
21 <p>
22 Yes, I'm interested in iNtervalTrack!
23 <br/>
24 <a href="mailto:jamesbrannan@xxxx.net?
25 subject=I%20am%20interested%20in%20iNter
26 valTrack.
27 &cc=jbxxx@nowhere.com;jbrannan@xxxxx.biz
28 &bcc=james.a.brannan@xxxx.com
29 &body=I%20am%20definitly%20interested.">
30 Please send me more info.</a>
31 </p>
32 </body>
33 </html>
```

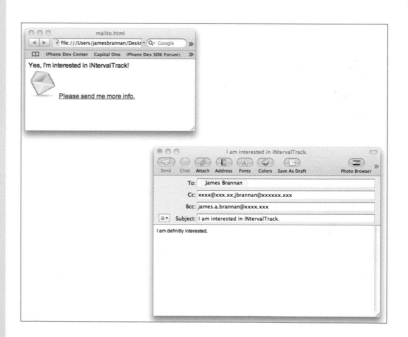

Cross reference

In Chapter 6, I show you how to design a form that a user submits via email.

Jargon buster

Plug-in – Additions you can install in your browser that allow playing multimedia content not otherwise supported by a browser. For instance, Adobe Flash is a plug-in you must install separately from your browser.

'Google it' – In Web vernacular, 'googling it' is looking up something online using Google.

Important

For the mailto to work, you must have a system mail client. If you use Explorer and Outlook, chances are this just works. The same is true for Safari and Mail on Macs. If it doesn't work, you should consult your system's documentation to set up your mail client.

3

Adding images to your Web page

Introduction

Two or three years ago, it was important that a book like this started a chapter on images with a lengthy discussion about optimising images for the Internet. Now, not so much. In the day of YouTube, and high-speed Internet access in the interior of Brazil, image optimisation is not so crucial. In less than five years, the average person has gone from using a 56K dial-up connection to an always on cable modem or ISDN line. Do you remember the days when you would sit and literally wait for an image to load? Seems like a distant memory, doesn't it? Do you remember 640 x 480 or 800 x 600 screen resolution? Well, today 1024 x 768 is really the lowest screen resolution you need to worry about. And almost all computer monitors display more colours than you could ever possibly use in your images.

Actually, there are a couple things you should know about Web images. Also, if you are uploading photos from your digital camera, then optimisation is important. So this chapter does begin with a brief discussion on image optimisation.

These days, there isn't really all that much you need to know when optimising images for the Web. Remember the following five points and you'll do fine.

1. For photographs, use the JPEG format.
2. For artwork, use the PNG format.
3. Try to avoid the GIF format and use PNG instead.
4. Read your image software's Help! And, even more important, do not try to optimise the image too much.

5. Keep your image's dimensions reasonable. Remember, your camera saves images as high resolution TIFF or JPEG files. They are huge!

The three primary image formats on the Web today are the Joint Photographic Experts Group format (JPEG), the Graphics Interchange Format (GIF) and Portable Network Graphics format (PNG). When saving photographs, use JPEG. For various reasons, the JPEG format is good for photographs. Unless creating an animated GIF, don't use GIF format. Instead use the PNG format. The PNG format is a more modern image format that has rich colour support, advanced compression schemes, 24-bit colour, adaptive transparency and several other features that make it a better choice than GIF.

Okay, so I know I just got finished writing that image optimisation isn't so crucial these days. In general that's true, but there is one complicating factor that causes me to still briefly discuss image optimisation: digital cameras. Digital cameras have made taking photos, uploading them to a computer, and sharing them on the Internet easier than ever before. But there's just one problem with images from digital cameras. Typically, digital cameras share images as large, high-resolution, TIFFs or JPEGs. These images are too large for displaying on the Internet. You must reduce the image's file size and dimensions.

But this chapter isn't just about image optimisation. In this chapter, you also learn how to add images to your Web page. You use the **`<img/>`** tag to insert images to a Web page. This element has several attributes. In this chapter I cover the src attribute, the height and width attribute and, the alt attribute.

```
<img src="/path/to/my/image/myimage.png"
width="100" height-"200" alt="A photo of
me."/>
```

I largely ignore the deprecated align attribute. But I do briefly discuss it, as it is still in use, even though it is deprecated.

Important   !

Prior to Internet Explorer 7, some PNG features such as adaptive transparency were not fully supported.

This topic really isn't as crucial as it used to be. Use PNG for artwork and JPEG for photographs. But if you want to upload your photos from your digital camera and add them to your web page, then this task is important. Digital cameras save large, high-resolution JPEG or TIFF files. You should optimise these images before adding them to your Web page.

You probably don't have Adobe Photoshop. But if you have a Mac, you should have Preview. Double click on the image and it should open in Preview. After loading the image, choose Tools, Adjust Size …, and a dialogue box allowing you to reduce the image's size appears. If you are using Windows, there is a good chance your camera came with image editing software that has a size reduction feature. And if your camera didn't come with software, then there are ample shareware and open source software resources available for basic image editing on the web. The key feature is that it allows you to reduce the image dimensions. I don't recommend tinkering with colour optimisation, lower-resolutions (unless changing from high to medium resolution for a JPEG) and other image file size reduction optimisations unless your website is for cable modem subscribers in some remote village somewhere – and even they probably have ISDN, monitors that display thousands of colours, and 1024 × 768 display resolution.

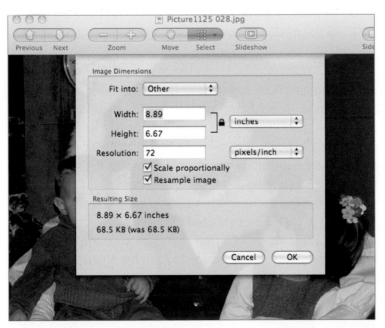

Task steps

1 Navigate to your images folder from your digital camera and double-click on a photograph. I'm assuming your computer opens it in either the default program for that file type or some type of 'preview' program.

2 For example, when I double-click on an image it opens in Apple Preview.

3 Whoa Nelly! My photograph's dimensions are 1600 × 1200 pixels, and size is 815kb. The photograph is so large, I can't even see the whole photograph on my screen.

4 So, I go to my image software's image-size option and reduce the image to 640 × 480 and save it as a jpeg. Now the image is only 41.1 kb and will display nicely in a Web page.

Adding images to a Web page

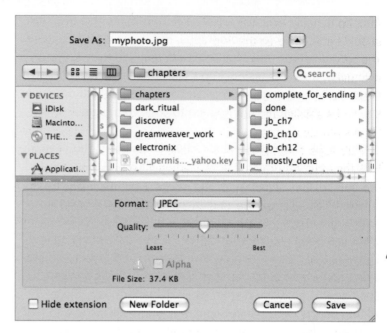

For your information

If saving a JPEG, try changing the image's quality from *high* to *medium*. This reduces the image's file size with no loss in viewing quality.

Important

If an image is saved without the correct .jpg, .gif, or .png extension then your computer will not recognise the file format!

If you aren't at least slightly familiar with the `<img/>` tag by this chapter, then you haven't been paying attention in Chapters 2 and 3. Just to add a little spice to the tasks, I added simple images to the examples in those chapter's tasks. I did that using the image element. The image element uses the `<img/>` tag to insert images into Web pages. Note, what you're really doing is providing your browser with a URL that points to the image's file. The browser then retrieves the image from the location specified in the src attribute and renders the image in the specified location on the Web page.

Image elements have several attributes, I cover the alt, src and height and width attributes in this task. The alt attribute provides a short image description. The src attribute specifies the image's location. Browsers use this attribute to retrieve the image. The height and width attribute specifies the image's height and width to be displayed on the page. If the height and width do not match the image's actual height and width, then the image is enlarged or reduced to match the given space. But note, the actual image file size in bytes remains the same, your browser simply scales the image to fit in the allotted size specified by the attributes.

After completing this task and viewing the results your browser should have displayed the first image as it was meant to be seen. The second image should be stretched and displayed larger then it actually is. You should avoid doing this – images displayed at a larger size than saved almost always look awful. The third image should be smaller and not appear distorted. You can almost always reduce an image without it appearing awful, provided the image's aspect ratio remains unchanged. The fourth image should look the most distorted of all. It illustrates two dangers of not using an image's actual width and height. First, the image looks terrible when enlarged. Second, images have what's called an aspect ratio. The **freebsd.png** has an aspect ratio of 1:1. But when you assign it a 20% height and a 100% width, you are assigning it an aspect ration of 1:5. This is not the image's aspect ratio, and so it appears distorted.

```
1 <!DOCTYPE HTML PUBLIC "-//W3C//DTD HTML
2 4.01 Transitional//EN"
3 "http://www.w3.org/TR/html4/loose.dtd">
4 <html>
5 <body>
6 <p>
7 Actual Size: <img src="./freebsd.png"/
8 height="72" width="72" alt="FreeBSD
9 Actual Size"/><br/>
10 Bigger: <img src="./freebsd.png"/
11 height="200" width="200" alt="FreeBSD
12 Bigger"/><br/>
13 Smaller: <img src="./freebsd.png"/
14 height="22" width="22" alt="FreeBSD
15 Smaller" /><br/>
16 Percentage:<img src="./freebsd.png"/
17 height="40%" width="100%" alt="FreeBSD
18 Percentage" /><br/>
19 </p>
20 </body>
21 </html>
```

Adding images to a Web page (cont.)

1   Obtain an image to use in this example. Preferably a smaller one. You can use the BSD devil image used in this example if you have downloaded the completed examples. In the following instructions, I assume you use this image.

2   Add four **<img/>** tags to your page and make all four reference the **freebsd.png** image file. (7, 10, 13, 16)

3   In the first image element, assign it the image's actual size of 72 pixels high and 72 pixels wide. (8)

4   Assign the second image element a size of 200 pixels high by 200 pixels wide. (11)

5   Assign the third image element a size of 22 pixels high by 22 pixels wide. (14)

6   Assign the fourth image element a size of 20% high by 100% wide. (17)

7   If you didn't add alt attributes to each image while creating them, add alt attributes to each image element.

8   Save and view in your browser.

4

Adding images to a Web page (cont.)

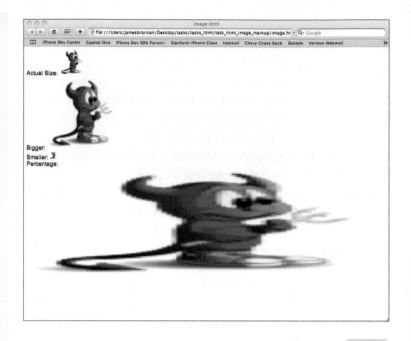

Cross reference

See **tasks_html/task_html_image_markup/image.html** for completed example.

For your information

Another attribute you can add is a title: when a user moves their mouse over the image a Tooltip with the title's text is displayed. Tooltips are also referred to as ScreenTips or hover boxes, depending on the system.

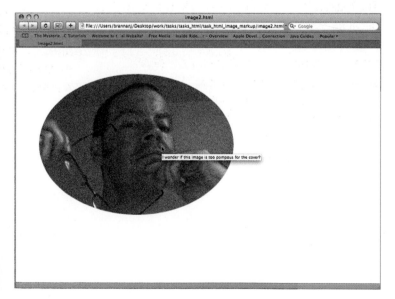

How to display a custom icon in a browser (a favicon)

Navigate to **theocacao.html**. After the page loads, notice the little icon before the URL in your browser's address bar. Bookmark the site, and the same icon appears in your bookmark list. Pretty cool. These are called favicons – favorites icons – in Web vernacular.

The reason favicons are not a task in this book is because you can't see the results unless your page is on a Web server. Creating an icon and then assigning it a relative path for a locally served page (using the `file://` protocol) just doesn't work. On my computer, it dislays in FireFox's address bar, but not in the Bookmarks list when bookmarked. The icon doesn't display at all in Explorer or Safari.

```
<head>
<meta http-equiv="Content-Type"
content="text/html;
charset=UTF-8">
<link rel="shortcut icon"
href="./favicon.ico"
type="image/x-icon"/>
<title>James's Super-Cool
WebSite</title>
</head>
```

Creating a favicon is easy. Find a small image that is 16 x 16 pixels (remember, icons are small). There are many open-source/free images on the Web you can use. For example, Crystal Project and Vista Inspirate, from **www.kdelook.org,** both have 16 × 16 icons. After obtaining the image, you save the image as a `.ico` file. Many image editing programs can save an image as an ico, but you can always go to **www.favicon.cc**'s favicon creation utility and create an icon online and download it.

4

Creating image links

1. Save template.html with a different name.

2. Add six images to the page. The finished example has six images you can use.

3. Add an anchor element around all six images. Make each link to a different site.

4. Save and display in your browser.

A common practice on the Web is using images for hyperlinks. It's easy, instead of wrapping text in **<a></a>** tags, wrap the **<img/>** tag in them. There is one slight problem, Internet Explorer and Firefox place a blue border around the image. This makes sense, the image is a hyperlink – your browser wants to notify the reader of that fact. But often, aesthetically, the border appears out of place. Removing the border is pretty easy. If you don't mind using deprecated attributes you can specify that an image has no border.

```
<img src="./image.png" border="0"
height="20" width="20" alt="A image with
no border."/>
```

But you really should use CSS instead. If you are using Safari, notice it does not add a border to image links unless you specify the image has a border.

Cross reference

In the 'Formatting hyperlinks – image links' task in Chapter 10 (see p. 184), you specify an image with no border using CSS.

Cross reference

Refer to **tasks_html/task_html_image_links/ imagelink.html** for completed example.

The results are straightforward: after completing the task you should see six images, each with a blue border indicating that each is a hyperlink.

```
 1 <!DOCTYPE HTML PUBLIC "-//W3C//DTD HTML
 2 4.01 Transitional//EN"
 3 "http://www.w3.org/TR/html4/loose.dtd">
 4 <html>
 5 <body>
 6 <a href="http://fedoraproject.org"><img
 7 src="../images/fedora.png" height="32"
 8 width="32"/></a>Fedora Linux<br/><br/>
 9 <a href="http://www.redhat.com"><img
10 src="../images/redhat.png" height="32"
11 width="32"/></a>Redhat Linux<br/><br/>
12 <a href="http://www.freebsd.org"><img
13 src="../images/freebsd.png" height="32"
14 width="32"/></a>Free BSD<br/><br/>
15 <a href="http://www.openbsd.org"><img
16 src="../images/openbsd.png" height="32"
17 width="32"/></a>Open BSD<br/><br/>
18 <a href="http://www.opensuse.org"><img
19 src="../images/suse.png" height="32"
20 width="32"/></a>SUSE Linux<br/><br/>
21 <a href="http://www.ubuntu.com"><img
22 src="../images/ubuntu.png" height="32"
23 width="32"/></a>Ubuntu Linux
24 </body>
25 </html>
```

4

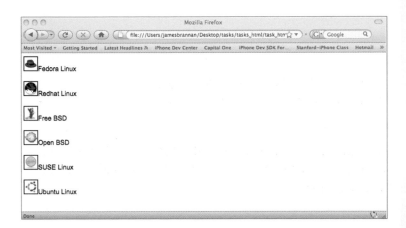

Creating image links – thumbnails

1. Open and save the template with a different name. Repeat, and name one page fullsize.html and the other thumbnail.html.

2. Open thumbnail.html and add the `freebsd_thumb.png` to the page, make it an imagelink pointing to fullsize.html. In the hyperlink, be sure to add a target attribute and have it point to `_blank`. (6, 7)

3. Save thumbnail.html and open `fullsize.html`. Add the image freebsd.png to the page. (22)

4. Save and open `thumbnail.html` in your browser.

A common practice is displaying a small image and then, when the user clicks it, the browser loads a full-size image into the browser. For example, navigate to www.google.com, select images, type in a search term, and click the Search Images button. What returns is a page of thumbnail images. When you click on one of them, a frameset loads in your browser. The top frame shows the image's thumbnail while the bottom loads the original page the image comes from. The thumbnail in the top frame is a link. Click on it, and your browser loads the original full-size image.

Cross reference

See **tasks_html/task_html_image_thumbnails/ thumbnail.htm**l for completed example.

After completing the test and viewing its results in your browser you should see the smaller image as an image link. When you click on the thumbnail, a new browser window pops open, or a new tab is displayed, with the full-size image.

Important

In the previous task you made an image smaller by making its dimensions smaller (height and width). When you do this using the image element's height and width attributes, you don't make the image's size in bytes any smaller. The browser just scales the image; downloading a 500K image takes the same amount of time regardless of its height and width. Thumbnails, in contrast, allow you to display smaller images and if the user is really interested in seeing the full-size 500K image of your cute puppy dog, they can click on the thumbnail to download it.

```
 1 <!DOCTYPE HTML PUBLIC "-//W3C//DTD HTML
 2 4.01 Transitional//EN"
 3 "http://www.w3.org/TR/html4/loose.dtd">
 4 <html>
 5 <body>
 6 <a href="./fullsize.html"
 7 target="_blank"><img
 8 src="freebsd_thumb.png" height="22"
 9 width="22"/></a><p>Mac OS X uses a
10 FreeBSD version as its base operating
11 system? The user-friendly Mac is <a
12 href="http://www.apple.com/macosx/techno
13 logy/unix.html">UNIX at its
14 core</a>!</p>
15 </body>
16 </html>

17 <!DOCTYPE HTML PUBLIC "-//W3C//DTD HTML
18 4.01 Transitional//EN"
19 "http://www.w3.org/TR/html4/loose.dtd">
20 <html>
21 <body>
22 <img src="freebsd.png" height="128"
23 width="128"/></a></body>
24 </html>
```

Creating an image map

Image maps contain an image with one or more clickable areas called hotspots. A hotspot is a location on an image that, when clicked, causes a function to execute. In a Web page, that function is usually navigating to another resource via a hyperlink. Each clickable area is a hyperlink to another resource. That resource can be anything normally handled by hyperlinks.

Creating an image map involves three steps. First, determine the image's dimensions in pixels. For example, the image used in this task – clock.png – is 128 x 128 pixels. Second, sketch the image on paper and draw the areas to turn into hotspots. Determine the dimension of each hotspot. And third, add the information to the image in the Web page.

1. This example assumes you have downloaded this book's examples. Navigate to the **task_html_image_maps** folder and get the **clock.png** graphic. It's 128 × 128 pixels.

2. Save the template with a different name.

3. Sketch the clock on a piece of paper.

4. On the paper, divide the graphic into four quadrants. These are the four regions you will turn into hotspots.

5. On the paper, figure out the coordinates moving counter clockwise. From (0,0) to (64,64) – or 9 o'clock to 12 o'clock – is region one. From (0,64) to (64,128) – or 9 o'clock to 6 o'clock – is region two. From (64,64) to (128,128) – or 6 o'clock to 3 o'clock – is region three. Finally, from (64,0) to (128,64) – or 3 o'clock to 12 o'clock – is region four.

6. Now you're ready to turn the image into an image map. If you haven't already, open template.html and save it under a different name.

Table 4.2 Tag covered in this task	
Tag	**Function**
<map></map>	Specifies an image map.

Important

An image's top left corner is the (0,0) coordinates. The Y axis is positive moving downward. The X axis is positive moving right.

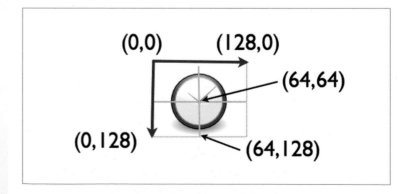

Cross reference

See **tasks_html/task_html_image_map/example_imagemap.html** for completed example.

Creating an image map (cont.)

Upon completing this task and loading the results in your browser the first thing you should notice if you're using Firefox or Explorer is a big blue border around the image. Remember, once you learn CSS removing that border is easy. You could use the deprecated border attribute if you really wanted to, although I don't recommend it. Move your cursor to different areas on the image and your browser's status bar should display the URL the hotspot is linked to. Try clicking on the different hotspots; your browser should open a new window - or tab - navigating to each area's respective link.

```
1  <!DOCTYPE html PUBLIC "-//W3C//DTD HTML
2  4.01 Strict//EN"
3  "http://www.w3.org/TR/html4/strict.dtd">
4  <html>
5  <head>
6  <meta http-equiv="Content-Type"
7  content="text/html; charset=UTF-8">
8  <title>Image Map Example</title>
9  </head>
10 <body>
11 <map name="time">
12 <area alt="9 o'clock to 12 o'clock"
13 shape="rect" coords="0,0,64,64"
14 href="http://uk.yahoo.com"/
15 target="_blank" />
16 <area alt="9 o'clock to 6 o'clock"
17 shape="rect" coords="0,64,64,128"
18 href="http://www.google.com"/
19 target="_blank" />
20 <area alt="6 o'clock to 3 o'clock"
21 shape="rect" coords="64,64,128,128"
22 href="http://www.youtube.com"/
23 target="_blank" />
24 <area alt="3 o'clock to 12 o'clock"
```

7 Add the image element. (29)

8 Just above the image tag, type the **<map></map>** tags. Assign the map a name using its name attribute. (11, 28)

9 Add the first **<area></area>** tags. Assign the values we determined in step four. Make the alt attribute's value '6 o'clock to 9 o'clock', the coordinates attribute '0,64,64,128' and the href attribute **http://uk.yahoo.com** and target attribute **_blank**. (12)

10 Repeat for the other three areas, with the appropriate values determined in step four. Assign each area a different URL. (16, 20, 24)

11 Return to the image tag added in step six. Add a usemap attribute and assign it the map's name, but prepend a # sign. (30)

12 Save your work, open it in your browser and click on all four hotspots to view the results.

Creating an image map (cont.)

```
25 shape="rect" coords="64,0,128,64"
26 href="http://www.metacafe.com"/
27 target="_blank" />
28 </map>
29 <img src="../images/clock.png"
30 usemap="#time" /></body>
31 </html>
```

For your information

A hotspot can be shapes other than a rectangle. Valid shapes are point, rectangle, circle and polygon. Circles take three values in the coord attribute: the centre point and radius. A polygon can take any number of points that join into a shape. For example, returning to the clock, you could define an circle of (64,64,20). This area would make a circular hotspot from the clock's centre outwards 20 pixels.

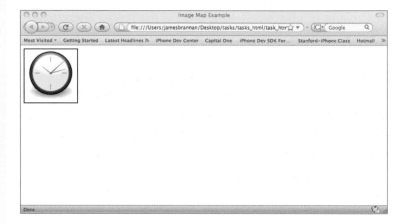

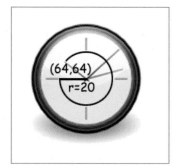

Jargon buster

Aspect ratio – An image's proportion expressed as width divided by height. For instance, a 100 pixel x 100 pixel image has a 1:1 aspect ratio. A 300 pixel x 100 pixel image has 3:1 aspect ratio.

HTML tables

Introduction

You use HTML tables to present tabular data on a Web page. You can also use tables for page layout. Tables allow data to be arranged into rows and columns of data cells. You can put just about anything in a table's cells, including images, paragraphs and even other tables. This flexibility makes tables useful for page layout and presenting tabular data. In this chapter you learn how to add tables to your HTML documents.

Cross reference

The task, 'Creating a liquid layout using a table', in Chapter 13 covers using tables for page layout.

You define a table using the **<table></table>** tags. The **<tr></tr>** tags divide a table into rows. The **<td></td>** tags further divide rows into data cells. Each row and column can also have a header cell. Header cells use the **<th></th>** tags. You can also separate a table into its header, footer and body using the **<thead></thead>**, **<tfoot></tfoot>**, and **<tbody></tbody>** tags. And you can assign the table a caption using the **<caption></caption>** tags.

What you'll do

Create table rows and data cells

Add padding and spacing to table cells

Add headings to tables

Add a caption to tables

Add frame attributes to tables

Specify column spans and row spans

Specify a table's header, body and footer

Add table dividing lines using rules

Figure 5.1 Table tags

Tag	Function
<table></table>	Specifies a table.
<tr></tr>	Specifies a table row.
<td></td>	Specifies table data cell.
<th></th>	Specifies a table header cell
<thead></thead>	Specifies table header rows.
<tfoot></tfoot>	Specifies table footer rows.
<tbody></tbody>	Specifies table body rows.
<caption></caption>	Specifies a table caption.

The table element has several important attributes. The border, cellpadding, cellspacing, frame, rules and width attributes all enable formatting of the way in which browsers display a table. In this chapter you learn how to use these attributes.

For your information

Tables also have an align and bgcolour attribute, but they are deprecated and are not used in this chapter.

Table 5.2 Table attributes covered in this chapter

Attribute	Function
<table border="n"…	Specifies table border thickness in pixels.
<table cellpadding="n"…	Specifies padding in table cell.
<table cellspacing="n"	Specifies cellspacing between cells.
<table frame="value"	Specifies where to place lines around table. Valid values are: void, above, below, hsides, lhs, rhs, vsides, box, and border.
<table rules="value"	Specifies where to place dividing lines in a table. Valid values are: none, groups, rows, cols, and all.
<table width="n" … or width="n%"	Specifies table width in pixels (absolute) or percentage.

Tables are composed of rows. Each row has one or more data cells. The **<tr></tr>** tags specify a row in a table. Table rows have an align attribute. This attribute specifies the alignment of elements in a row's data cells. Valid align values are: right, left, center, justify and char. Table rows also have a valign attribute that specifies an element's vertical alignment in a row's data cells. Valid valign values are top, middle and bottom.

```
<tr align="center" valign="top"/>
```

Table rows are comprised of one or more data cells. The **<td></td>** tags specify a data cell in a row. Like a row, data cells also have an align attribute. So you can specify the align in a table row to align all the cells at once, or you can use the align attribute in each cell. The cell's align attribute overrides a table row's align attribute for that cell. You can also specify a valign attribute to override a table row's valign attribute.

Table 5.3 Table tags covered in this task	
Tag	**Function**
<tr></tr>	Specifies a row in a table.
<td></td>	Specifies a table data cell in a table.

Cross reference

See **tasks_html/task_html_table_cells/ tablerow_cellsimple.html** for completed example.

Creating table rows and data cells

Task steps

1 Save the template with a new name.

2 Add a table element with a one pixel border. (8)

3 Add four sets of **<tr></tr>** tags. (9, 12, 17, 20)

4 In each row element, add three **<td></td>** sets. (9, 24)

5 Make the first table row have a centre alignment. (9)

6 Add data to the three data cells in the first row. (9–11)

7 In the second row's first data cell add data followed by a **
** tag, followed by more data, followed by another **
** tag, followed by more data. (12, 13)

8 Make the second data cell have a top vertical alignment and the third cell have a bottom vertical alignment. Add some data to the cell. (14, 15)

9 In the third row, make the first cell have a right alignment. Add some data to the cell. (17)

10 Assign the second cell a centre alignment and add data. (18)

5

Creating table rows and data cells (cont.)

You should notice different cell's data positioned differently. You added **
** tags and extra data to make the cells different in size. Think about it, cells with the same width and height, no matter how you align them, are going to appear the same in the browser. So you made the cells different sizes in order to see the results of varying the alignment and vertical alignment.

11 Assign the third cell a left alignment and add data. (19)

12 Assign the fourth row's first cell a right alignment. (20)

13 To the fourth row, first cell, add some data, followed by a **
** tag, followed by some more data. (20)

14 In the second cell, assign it a centre alignment and a bottom vertical alignment. Add some data. (22)

15 Assign the third cell a left alignment and a top vertical alignment and add some data. (24)

16 Save and display in your browser.

```
1 <!DOCTYPE HTML PUBLIC "-//W3C//DTD HTML
2 4.01 Transitional//EN"
3 "http://www.w3.org/TR/html4/loose.dtd">
4 <html>
5 <body>
6 <img src="./calc.png"/>
7 <h4>Calculating Costs</h4>
8 <table border="1">
9 <tr align="center"><td>&pound;33</td>
10 <td>&pound;200</td>
11 <td>&pound;300</td></tr>
12 <tr><td>&pound;400
13 xxxxx<br/>xxxxx<br/>xxxxx</td>
14 <td valign="top">&pound;500 xxxxx</td>
15 <td valign="bottom">&pound;600 xxxxx
16 </td></tr>
17 <tr><td align="right">&pound;300</td>
18 <td align="center">&pound;22</td>
19 <td align="left">&pound;100</td></tr>
20 <tr><td align="right">&pound;300<br/>
21 xxxxxxx</td>
22 <td align="center" valign="bottom">
23 &pound;22</td>
24 <td align="left" valign="top">&pound;
25 100</td></tr>
26 </table>
27 </body>
28 </html>
```

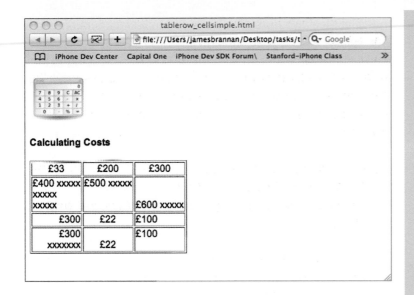

Adding padding and spacing to table cells

Task steps

1. Open the template and save with a different name.

2. Create three simple tables with two rows and two columns. (6, 12, 19)

3. Set the second table's cellpadding to 10. (12)

4. Set the third table's cellspacing to 10. (19)

5. Save and view in your browser.

Cross reference

See **tasks_html/ task_html_table_various/ task_html_padding_ spacing.html** for completed example.

In the last task, you assigned cells different alignment. You can also specify a cell's spacing and padding. Padding is the space between the cell's content and the cell's border. Spacing is the space between adjacent cell's borders. Cell padding and spacing can be given either pixel values or percentages.

```
<table cellpadding="5" cellspacing=
"10%" />
```

Percentages are the space's or padding's percentage of the table's total height or total width. Unlike alignment, cellpadding and cellspacing are set in the **<table>** tag and can only be applied to the entire table. Individual cells cannot have different padding and spacing when using the cellpadding and cellspacing HTML attributes.

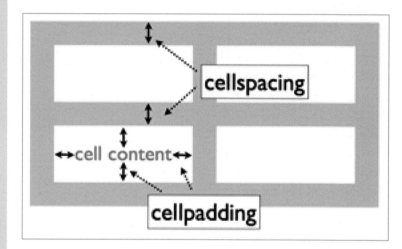

Table 5.4 The cellpadding and cellspacing attributes

Table attributes, cellpadding and cellspacing.	
cellpadding="n" (pixels) or "n%" (percentage)	Specifies pixel space between cell content and cell wall.
cellspacing="n" (pixels) or "n%" (percentage)	Specifies pixel space between cells.

After completing the task and opening it in your broswer, you should see the first table compact, with no spacing or padding. The second table should have about 10 pixels of white space between the text and the cell's borders. The third table should have 10 pixels of space between each table data cell border.

```
 1 <!DOCTYPE HTML PUBLIC "-//W3C//DTD HTML
 2 4.01 Transitional//EN"
 3 "http://www.w3.org/TR/html4/loose.dtd">
 4 <html>
 5 <body>
 6 <table border="1"><tr><td>&pound;233
 7 </td><td>&pound;354</td></tr>
 8 <tr><td>&pound;343</td><td>&pound;443
 9 </td></tr>
10 </table>
11 <br>
12 <table border="1" cellpadding="10">
13 <tr><td>&pound;151</td><td>&pound;
14 315</td></tr>
15 <tr><td>&pound;665</td><td>&pound;
16 867</td></tr>
17 </table>
18 <br>
19 <table border="1" cellspacing="10">
20 <tr><td>&pound;151</td><td>&pound;
21 315</td></tr>
22 <tr><td>&pound;665</td><td>&pound;
23 867</td></tr>
24 </table>
25 </body>
26 </html>
```

Adding padding and spacing to table cells (cont.)

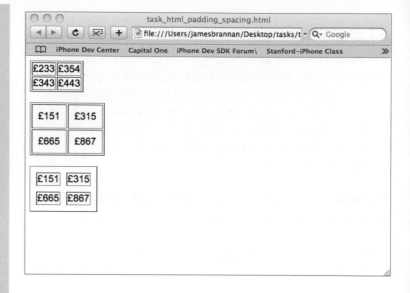

You can assign headings to rows and columns using the `<th></th>` tags. The text in table headers is often emboldened. To specify a heading for a table's columns, replace the first row's table data cells with table header cells.

```
<tr><th>heading one</th><th>heading
two</th></tr>
<tr><td>value one</td><td>value
two</td></tr>
```

To specify a heading for a particular row, replace the first table data cell with a table header cell.

```
<tr><th>the header</th><td>the
value</td></tr>
```

You can set a table header's alignment and vertical alignment using the align and valign attributes, the same as a data cell.

<table>
<tr><td colspan="2">Table 5.5 Tags covered in this task</td></tr>
<tr><td>Tag</td><td>Function</td></tr>
<tr><td><th></th></td><td>Specifies a table heading cell in a table.</td></tr>
</table>

Cross reference

See **tasks_html/task_html_table_headings/ tableheadings.html** for completed example.

After completing this task and viewing it in your browser you should see a row containing bold text. This row is the table's column headers. You should also see a column of bold text in the first column. This column is the table's row headers.

Adding headings to tables

Task steps

1. Open the template and save with a different name.

2. Create a table with three rows and three columns. Enter some data in each. (12, 15, 17)

3. Insert a table row at the top of the table, making a total of four rows. (9)

4. Add four `<th></th>` tags in the top row and add heading text for each. (9, 10, 11)

5. In each of the remaining three rows, before each row's `<td></td>` tags, add a set of `<th></th>` tags. Enter an appropriate heading for each row in the headings. (12, 15, 17)

6. Save and view in your browser.

5

Adding headings to tables (cont.)

```
1  <!DOCTYPE HTML PUBLIC "-//W3C//DTD HTML
2  4.01 Transitional//EN"
3  "http://www.w3.org/TR/html4/loose.dtd">
4  <html>
5  <body>
6  <img src="./calc.png"/><h2>Calculating
7  Cost</h2>
8  <table border="1">
9  <tr><th> </th><th>Shipping
10 Cost</th><th>Processing Cost</th>
11 <th>Marketing Cost</th></tr>
12 <tr><th>2005</th><td>&pound;33</td><td>&
13 pound;200</td>
14 <td>&pound;300</td></tr>
15 <tr><th>2006</th><td>&pound;400</td><td>
16 &pound;500</td>
17 <td>&pound;600</td></tr><tr><th>2007
18 </th><td> </td>
19 <td>&pound;22</td><td>&pound;100</td>
20 </tr>
21 </table>
22 </body>
23 </html>
```

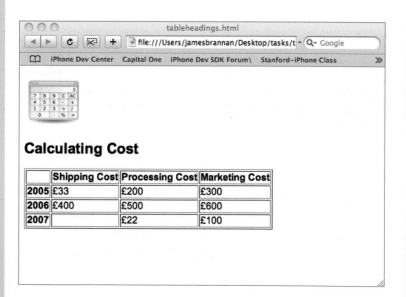

	Shipping Cost	Processing Cost	Marketing Cost
2005	£33	£200	£300
2006	£400	£500	£600
2007		£22	£100

A table can have a caption at its top. You add a caption to a table by placing **<caption></caption>** tags immediately after the **<table>** tag.

```
<table><caption>This is my
table.</caption> ... </table>
```

You should only have one caption per table and the **<caption>** tag must go immediately after the **<table>** tag. The caption is then centred just above the table.

Adding a caption to a table

Table 5.6 Tags covered in this task	
Tag	**Function**
<caption></caption>	Specifies a caption for a table.

Cross reference

See **tasks_html/task_html_table_caption/tablecaption. html** for completed example.

After completing this task you should see the text you entered in the table's caption centred, just above the table. Note that, in the example, I added **** tags to add a footnote. Adding formatting to a caption is legal, although you are better off waiting until you learn CSS and use it instead for formatting.

```
1 <!DOCTYPE HTML PUBLIC "-//W3C//DTD HTML
2 4.01 Transitional//EN"
3 "http://www.w3.org/TR/html4/loose.dtd">
4 <html>
5 <body>
6 <img src="./calc.png"/><h2>Calculating
7 Cost</h2>
8 <table border="1">
9 <caption><b>The Cost of Selling
10 Books<sup>*</sup></b></caption>
```

Task steps

1 Save the previous task's page with a new name.

2 Just below the opening **<table>** tag, but above the first **<tr>** tag, add **<caption></caption>** opening and closing tags. (9)

3 Enter an appropriate table caption between the tags.

4 Save and display in your browser.

5

```
11 <tr><th> </th><th>Shipping
12 Cost</th><th>Processing Cost</th>
13 <th>Marketing Cost</th></tr>
14 <tr><th>2005</th><td>&pound;33</td><td>&
15 pound;200</td>
16 <td>&pound;300</td></tr>
17 <tr><th>2006</th><td>&pound;400</td><td>
18 &pound;500</td>
19 <td>&pound;600</td></tr><tr><th>2007
20 </th><td> </td>
21 <td>&pound;22</td><td>&pound;100</td>
22 </tr>
23 </table>
24 <sup>*</sup><i>Cost does not include
25 returns.</i>
26 </body>
27 </html>
```

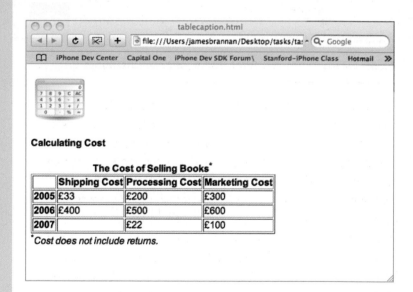

In the early days of HTML, the only formatting you had for a table was its border. You couldn't specify that only the right border or top border be displayed. Now this can be done using the frame attribute. You use frame in conjunction with the table's border. The frame attribute instructs browsers which sides of an outside border should be visible.

Table 5.7 Frame attribute values	
<table frame="*value*"...	
frame="void"	Specifies no frame.
frame="above"	Specifies frame line above table only.
frame="below"	Specifies frame line below table only.
frame="hsides"	Specifies frame lines above and below table.
frame="vsides"	Specifies frame lines on vertical sides
frame="lhs"	Specifies frame line on left table side.
frame="rhs"	Specifies frame line on right table side.
frame="box"	Specifies frame lines on all sides.
frame="border"	Specifies frame lines on all sides.

Possible values for the frame attribute are: border, box, void, above, below, lhs, rhs, hsides and vsides. Border and box place four lines around the table, while void specifies that no outer box should be drawn. For example, if you set border to one and frame to void, then lines would appear dividing the cells into columns and rows, but no outer border would be rendered. Above places a single line above the table while below places a single line below. The lhs value places a single vertical line on the table's left side while rhs places a single vertical line on the table's right. The hsides value places horizontal lines above and below the table. The vsides value places vertical lines on both the right and left table sides.

Adding frame attributes to tables

5

Cross reference

See **tasks_html/task_html_table_various/task_html_ frames.html** for completed example.

Adding frame attributes to tables (cont.)

Task steps

1. Open the template and save with a new name.

2. Create a simple table with two rows and two cells in each row. Add data to both cells. (8)

3. In the table's opening tag, add a frame attribute and set its value to border. (8)

4. Save and view in your browser.

5. Change border to box, save and view in your browser.

6. Repeat step five for the above, below, hsides, vsides, lhs and rhs values.

7. Add a border attribute to the table, assign it a value of one, and then set the frame attribute to void.

8. Save and view in your browser.

This task's results are straightforward. Every time you save and view the page, you should see a different border. Note that, in the completed example, a separate table is included for each frame attribute value. For brevity, the HTML for all nine tables is not shown here.

```
1 <!DOCTYPE HTML PUBLIC "-//W3C//DTD HTML
2 4.01 Transitional//EN"
3 "http://www.w3.org/TR/html4/loose.dtd">
4 <html>
5 <head><title>The Frame Attribute for
6 Tables</title></head>
7 <body>
8 <table frame="border">
9 <caption>Border</caption>
10 <tr><td>&pound;300</td><td>&pound;
11 200</td></tr>
12 <tr><td>&pound;50</td> <td>&pound;
13 30</td>
14 </tr>
15 </table>
16 <br>
17 </body>
18 </html>
```

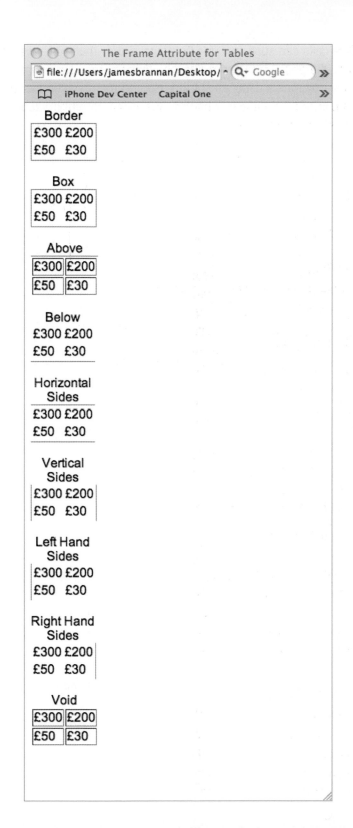

5

Specifying column spans and row spans

Table cells can span multiple columns and/or multiple rows. The columnspan (colspan) attribute tells the browser how many columns a data cell should use and the rowspan the number of rows. These two attributes are important if you want visually appealing tables.

colspan of 2 columns			
rowspan of 3 rows			
	colspan of 2 columns, rowspan of 2 rows		

Cross reference

See **tasks_html/task_html_table_various/task_html_ colspan_rowspan.html** for completed example.

After completing the task the first column should be blank and take up two rows. The second column on the first row should be taking up two columns – it's a column heading for the next row's column headings. Note that when you specify a colspan of more then one, you must omit a **<td></td>** for every column spanned in the row. When spanning rows, you omit a **<td></td>** for each row that is being spanned.

Task steps

1 Save the template under a new name.

2 Add a table with four rows. (6)

3 In the first row, add a table header with a rowspan of two. (10)

4 Add another table header to the first row, but with a colspan of two. (11)

5 Add two table headers to the second row. (14)

6 Add two more table rows. Add three cells to the first row and add one to the last row. (15)

7 Make the last row's cell have a colspan of three. (17)

8 Save and view in your browser.

```
1 <!DOCTYPE HTML PUBLIC "-//W3C//DTD HTML
2 4.01 Transitional//EN"
3 "http://www.w3.org/TR/html4/loose.dtd">
4 <html>
5 <body>
6 <table frame="box" rules="all" width=
7 "75%">
```

```
 8 <caption>Cost of doing business.
 9 </caption>
10 <tr><th rowspan="2"> </th><th
11 colspan="2">Costs</th></tr>
12 <tr><!— note omitted th here because
13 prev. row is rowspan=2 —>
14 <th>USA</th><th>UK</th></tr>
15 <tr><td>Material</td><td>&pound;455</td>
16 <td>&pound;987</td></tr>
17 <tr><td colspan="3">Total = 
18 &pound;1442</td></tr>
19 </table>
20 </body>
21 </html>
```

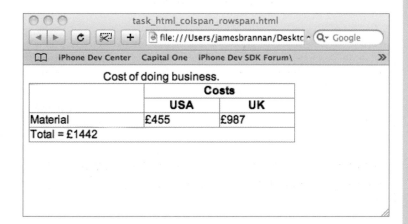

Specifying a table's header, body and footer

You can specify a table's header, body and footer using the **<thead></thead>** tags, **<tbody></tbody>** tags and **<tfoot></tfoot>** tags. The meanings of the three tags are as you might imagine: **<thead></thead>** specifies the header, **<tbody></tbody>** specifies the table's body and **<tfoot></tfoot>** specifies the the table's footer.

Task steps

1 Open one of the previous tables or create a new one.

2 Add the **<tfoot></tfoot>** tags between the opening **<table>** tag and the table's first **<tr>** tag. (14)

3 In the table footer, add a table row. In the table row add a table cell with a colspan of three. Add some text to the cell. (14)

4 After the table footer add **<thead></thead>** tags. Add a table row and insert a table data cell with a colspan of three. (20)

5 Save and display in your browser.

Table 5.8 Table related tags covered in this task

Tag	Function
<thead></thead>	Specifies table header.
<tbody></tbody>	Specifies table body.
<tfoot></tfoot>	Specifies table footer.

Cross reference

See **tasks_html/task_html_table_various/task_html_grouping.html** for completed example.

```
1 <!DOCTYPE HTML PUBLIC "-//W3C//DTD HTML
2 4.01 Transitional//EN"
3 "http://www.w3.org/TR/html4/loose.dtd">
4 <html><head><title>Tables: Footers,
5 Table Body, and Column
6 Groups</title></head>
7 <body>
8 <p>Sorry I'm so ugly, but the author
9 doesn't want to waste your time by
10 showing you deprecated HTML formatting
11 tags when you can use CSS.</p>
12 <table rules="cols" frame="border"
13 width="50%">
14 <tfoot><tr><td colspan="3"><small>
15 Illustrating a table
16 footer.</small></td></tr></tfoot>
17 <caption>Column Rules, Footer, Body, and
18 Column Grouping</caption>
```

**Specifying a
table's header,
body and footer
(cont.)**

5

```
19 <colgroup span="2"/>
20 <thead><tr><td colspan="3">A table
21 header.</td></tr></thead>
22 <tbody>
23 <tr><td>&pound;300</td><td>&pound;
24 200</td><td>&pound;200</td></tr>
25 <tr><td>&pound;50</td><td>&pound;30</td>
26 <td>&pound;200</td></tr>
27 <tr><td>&pound;300</td><td>&pound;
28 200</td><td>&pound;200</td></tr>
29 </tbody>
30 </table>
31 </body>
32 </html>
```

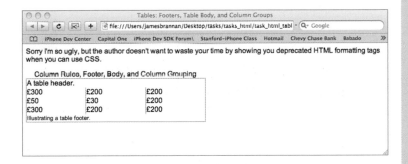

Adding table dividing lines using rules

Task steps

1. Open the HTML document from the previous task and save with a different name.

2. In the table's opening tag, add a rules attribute and assign its value as cols. (6)

3. Save and view in your browser.

4. Repeat, as desired, changing the value to 'all', rows and none.

5. After reviewing the rows, cols and none values, add a new row above the first row of the table and a new row as a last row.

6. Add three **<th></th>** tags to the first row and add some data. (20)

7. Add one **<td></td>** tag set to the last row and assign it a colspan of three. (33)

8. Wrap the first row in **<thead></thead>** tags. (19)

9. Wrap the last row in **<tfoot></tfoot>** tags. (32)

10. Wrap the other rows in **<tbody></tbody>** tags. (24)

Often you might wish to display borders between only some table rows or columns. HTML tables have a rules property that allows you to do just that. If you only wish to show lines between rows, you assign the value rows to the rules attribute. To show only lines between columns, you assign the value cols. If you don't want any lines, you specify none as the value. If you want lines between columns and rows, you specify all for the rules attribute. You can also specify rules dividing a table's major groupings (thead, tfoot and tbody elements) by assigning rules to the value groups.

Table 5.9 Table rules attribute

<table rules="*value*"...

rules="none"	Specifies no rules.
rules="groups"	Specifies only add rules between </thead><tbody>, </tbody><tfoot> tags.
rules="rows"	Specifies rules between all rows.
rules="cols"	Specifies rules beteween all columns.
rules="both"	Specifies rules between columns and rows.

Cross reference

See **tasks_html/task_html_table_various/task_html_rules.html** for completed example.

When you completed this task's first part you specified cols as the rules attribute's value and should have seen lines between the columns only. Then, when you specified rows, you should have seen lines between the rows. You should have also seen no rules when you specified none, and rules between both columns and rows when you specified all. In the final Task steps, you should have seen rules dividing the table's header, body and footer.

```
1 <!DOCTYPE HTML PUBLIC "-//W3C//DTD HTML
2 4.01 Transitional//EN"
3 "http://www.w3.org/TR/html4/loose.dtd">
4 <html>
5 <body>
6 <table rules="cols" frame="border">
7 <caption>Column Rules</caption>
8 <tr><td>&pound;300</td><td>&pound;
9 200</td><td>&pound;200</td></tr>
10 <tr><td>&pound;50</td><td>&pound;30</td>
11 <td>&pound;200</td></tr>
12 <tr><td>&pound;300</td><td>&pound;
13 200</td><td>&pound;200</td></tr>
14 </table>
15 <br>
16 ---snip---
17 <table rules="groups" frame="border">
18 <caption>Groups</caption>
19 <thead>
20 <tr><td>Heading One</td><td>Heading
21 Two</td><td>Heading Three</td>
22 </tr>
23 </thead>
24 <tbody>
25 <tr><td>&pound;300</td><td>&pound;
26 200</td><td>&pound;200</td></tr>
27 <tr><td>&pound;50</td><td>&pound;30</td>
28 <td>&pound;200</td></tr>
29 <tr><td>&pound;300</td><td>&pound;
30 200</td><td>&pound;200</td></tr>
31 </tbody>
32 <tfoot>
33 <tr><td colspan="3">This is a footer.
34 </td></tr>
35 </tfoot>
36 </table>
37 </body>
38 </html>
```

Adding table dividing lines using rules (cont.)

11 Change the rules attribute's value to groups. (17)

12 Save and view in your browser.

5

Adding table dividing lines using rules (cont.)

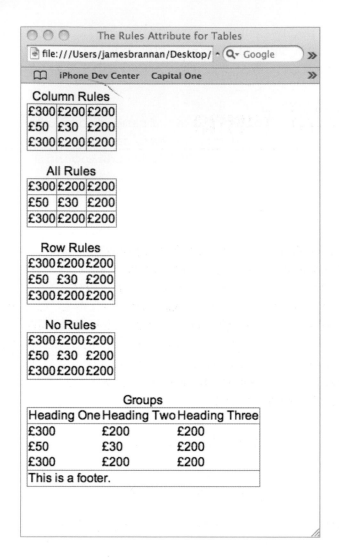

Jargon buster

Tabular data – Data that typically can be represented in a spreadsheet.

HTML forms

Introduction

Forms capture user input from HTML pages. Forms are composed of check boxes, radio buttons, menus, text boxes, text areas and buttons. Forms are probably familiar to you if you have ever submitted information over the Internet. First you complete the form's fields. Once completed, you click the submit button and submit the form. Your browser then sends the form's data as name/value pairs to a remote server. The server receives the form's data, which it processes and optionally returns a result.

What you'll do

Build a simple form

Add a check box

Add radio buttons

Add file fields

Add a text area

Add select elements (lists and menus)

Add a fieldset and legend

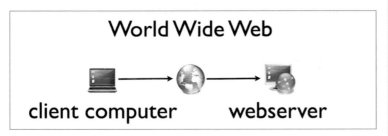

The **`<form></form>`** tags define a form. The **`<form>`** opening tag contains an action attribute. In the action attribute, you place the URL to the server script that processes the form. A server script is a computer program dedicated to processing submitted form data. Common server scripting languages include Java, PHP, ASP, .NET, C and Perl. Server form processing is beyond the scope of this book; however, there are ample resources both online and in print about server form processing.

```
<form name="myform" method="post"
action="./mypath/my_script.php">
```

The **\<form\>** tag also contains a name and method attribute. The method attribute specifies whether the form is sent using the Post or Get protocol. Like form processing, a complete explanation of the Post and Get protocols is beyond the scope of this book. Just know that the Post protocol places a form's data in what's called an HTTP header and sends it to a server.

```
POST ./mypath/my_script.php HTTP/1.0
Accept: www/source
Accept: text/html
---snip---
Content-type: application/x-www-form-
urlencoded
field1=value1
&field2=value2
```

The Get protocol places a form's data directly in the URL and submits them to a server.

```
./mypath/my_script.php?field1=value1&fie
ld2=value2
```

You place the various data entry fields between the **\<form\>** and **\</form\>** tags. Elements include input elements, labels, textarea elements and select elements. Input elements can have a type of check box, file, text, password, submit or reset.

```
<input type="text" name="myTextBox" />
```

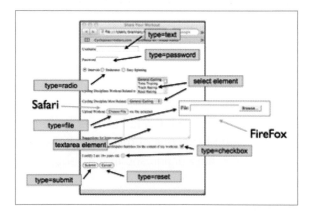

You add a form to an HTML page using the
`<form></form>` tags. Two common form fields are text
fields and password fields. These two form fields are both
input elements, where text fields have their type indicated as
text and password fields as password. Password fields mask
the letters as you type so nobody can observe your password
when you are typing. You can specify the width of either field
using the size attribute, and you can also pre-fill either field
with a default value by specifying a value attribute.

```
<input type="password" name="passOne"
size="20" value="Default Value"/>
```

You can add a label to any form field using the
`<label></label>` tags. You tie a label to its field using the
'label for' attribute.

```
<label for="textOne">TextOne: .
</label><input type="text"
name="textOne"/>
```

Most forms have a submit and reset button. The submit button
submits the form. The reset/cancel button resets all the form's
fields to blank or their default value. Submit buttons are input
elements of type submit. Reset buttons are input elements of type
reset. You assign both button's text label using the name attribute.

```
<input type="submit" name="Submit"/>
<input type="reset" name="Cancel"/>
```

Building a simple form

Task steps

1. Open the template and save with a different name.

2. Add a form element. (12)

3. Make the form element's method post and its action the mailto: protocol. (12, 13)

4. Create an input element and assign its type as text. Create a label for the element.

5. Create another input element and assign its type as text. Assign it a label. (16, 17)

6. Make an input of type submit, and an input of type reset. Assign submit and cancel as the button's respective values. (24, 25)

7. Save and display in your browser.

8. Fill out the form and click submit.

6

Cross reference

See **tasks_html_form_w_
inputs/simple_form.html**
for the completed example.

Building a simple form (cont.)

Table 6.1 Form elements specified in this task	
Tag	**Function**
<form></form>	Specifies a form for user data input.
<input type="text" ...	Specifies a text box.
<input type="password" ...	Specifies a text box where typed text is hidden.
<input type="submit" ...	Specifies a submit button.
<input type="reset" ...	Specifies a cancel/reset button.

Upon completing the exercise and loading it in your browser, and then clicking submit, your email program should have opened with the form data in the email body. The name and value of each field are placed on their own line in the email. Note that you can set the subject and recipients just as you did in the email hyperlink task in Chapter 3 (see pp. 55–57).

```
1  <!DOCTYPE HTML PUBLIC "-//W3C//DTD HTML
2  4.01 Transitional//EN"
3  "http://www.w3.org/TR/html4/loose.dtd">
4  <html>
5  <body>
6  <img src="evolution-contacts.png"/>
7  <h2>Welcome to the Lonely-Hearts Dating
8  Site.</h2>
9  <p>Please fill out contact information
10 so a representative can contact
11 you.</p>
12 <form method="post"
13 action="mailto:jamesbrannan@earthlink.
14 net?subject=Interest%20In%20Site"
15 enctype="text/plain">
16 <label for="name">Name:</label>
17 <input type="text" name="name"size=
18 "20" />
19 <br/>
20 <label for="phone">Phone Number:</label>
21 <input type="text" name="phone"
22 size="20" />
```

```
23 <br/>
24 <input type="submit" value="Submit" />
25 <input type="reset" value="Cancel"/>
26 </form>
27 </body>
28 </html>
```

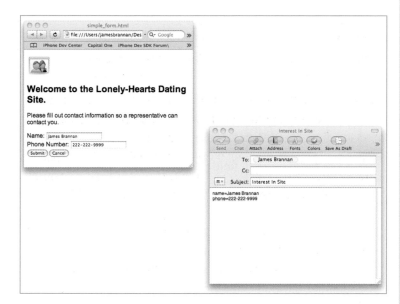

For your information

In 1995 I worked for a company that processed large amounts of data. We were trying to convince the data entry personnel in our company to change from DOS applications to a Web-based one. We created HTML forms to replace the DOS forms, but we didn't think about our form's tab order. It just so happened they relied heavily on the tab key to move between form fields. So, when using our forms, users had problems because the field order in our forms was nonstandard, and so clicking the tab key took them to fields they didn't expect. Speed and accuracy suffered until we specified tab order.

Building a simple form (cont.)

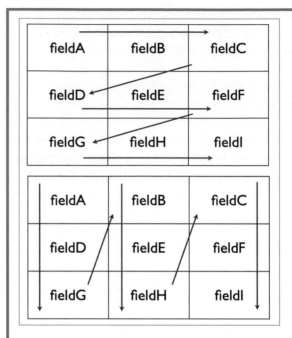

The default tab order is the order in which elements appear in the form. However, in some situations, you might need to alter the tab order. You specify the tab order using the tabindex attribute. You can use the tabindex attribute with the **<input>**, **<a>**, **<textarea>**, **<select>** and **<button>** tags; and if you wish to exclude an element from the tabindex, you assign that element's tabindex value to zero.

```
<form>
First Field:<input type="text"
name="field1" tabindex="1" />
Second Field:<input type="text"
name="field2" tabindex="3" />
Third Field:<input type="text"
name="field3" tabindex="2" />
</form>
```

You use check boxes in two situations. When providing users with a yes or no type question a check box is the most appropriate field element to use.

```
<input type="checkbox"
name="mailinglist" value="true"/>
```

When providing users with a choice, where they can select one or more choices from several choices, a check box is often appropriate (you can also use a select element). For example, you might ask users what flavour ice-cream they like, giving them the options: chocolate, vanilla and strawberry. They might check none, chocolate only or any combination of the three flavours.

```
<input type="checkbox" name="flavours"
value="chocolate"/>
<input type="checkbox" name="flavours"
value="vanilla"/>
<input type="checkbox" name="flavours"
value="strawberry"/>
```

Suppose you select vanilla and chocolate. The vanilla and chocolate check boxes would be submitted. The other check boxes would not.

Check boxes are on or off. When checked, the check box is on and has a value when submitted. When unchecked, the check box is off and is not sent as part of the form submission when submitted. In other words, when unchecked, the check box doesn't get sent to the server. This is important when you decide to learn how to process forms using a programming language. If you try to process a nonexisting check box, you end up with a null-pointer exception. You don't need to worry about this now, just make a mental note to remember this for future reference.

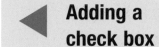

Adding a
check box

6

Adding a
check box (cont.)

Task steps

1. Save the template with a different name.

2. Create a form and add three input elements of type check box. Assign all three the same name, but different values. (13, 16, 11)

3. Choose one input element and make it checked. (14)

4. Create two more input elements of type check box. Assign them the same name, but different ones from the preceding three check boxes. (19, 22)

5. Add a submit button. (25)

6. Make certain the form's action is the mailto: protocol. (7)

7. Save and view in your browser. Check one other check box – so two in total are checked – and click submit. Be sure not to check a check box in the second two check boxes.

Table 6.2 Form element specified in this task	
Tag	Function
<input type="checkbox" ...	Specifies a check box.

You create a check box using the input element and assigning its type as "checkbox". You assign its value by setting its value attribute. When checked, the check box value is the value in the attribute. For instance:

```
<input type="checkbox" name="signup"
value="yes"/>
```

is sent to the server as the name/value pair,

```
signup=yes
```

when submitted. You can specify a check box is checked by default by specifying the attribute checked equal to checked.

```
<input type="checkbox" value="signup"
value="yes" checked="checked"/>
```

Cross reference

See **tasks_html/task_form_checkbox/checkbox.html** for completed example.

After completing this task and loading the results into your browser you should see a simple form with three check boxes. The middle check box should be checked. After clicking submit, your email browser should have appeared with a pre-filled form. The email illustrates an important point. Check boxes that are unchecked do not exist when submitted to the server. The second check box set has no value (assuming you followed the instructions and didn't check one). The first check box group has two values, one for the default checked box and one for the box you checked (again, assuming you followed the instructions).

```
 1 <!DOCTYPE HTML PUBLIC "-//W3C//DTD HTML
 2 4.01 Transitional//EN"
 3 "http://www.w3.org/TR/html4/loose.dtd">
 4 <html>
 5 <body>
 6 <form name="input"
 7 action="mailto:james@earthlink.net?subje
 8 ct=checkbox%20example" method="post">
 9 <img src="./evolution-contacts.png"/>
10 <h2>Acceptable Dating Age Ranges</h2>
11 <br/>18-30:<input type="checkbox"
12 name="age" value="18" />
13 <br />31-60:<input type="checkbox" name=
14 "age" value="31" checked="checked" />
15 <br />   60+:<input
16 type="checkbox" name="age" value="60" />
17 <br /><br />
18 <h2>Acceptable Weight Ranges</h2>
19 100 lb or less: <input type="checkbox"
20 name="weight" value="100"/>
21 <br/>
22 101 lb or more:<input type="checkbox"
23 name="weight" value="101"/>
24 <br/><br/>
25 <input type="submit" value="Submit" />
26 </form>
27 </body>
28 </html>
```

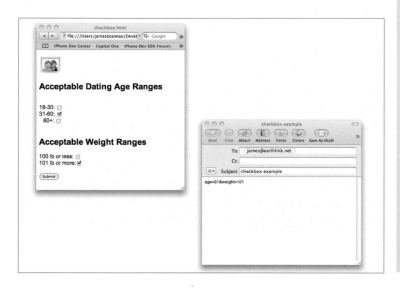

Adding radio buttons

Task steps

1. Save the template with a different name.
2. Create a form element. (6)
3. Add three input elements of type radio. Assign them all the same name but different values. (11, 14, 17)
4. Make one input element checked. (15)
5. Add a submit button. (20)
6. Save and view in browser. Submit the form.

A radio button is an input of type radio. You use radio buttons to select one of two or more values from a group of related choices. For instance, you might be asked to choose your favourite flavoured ice cream from the choices: vanilla, chocolate and strawberry. However, unlike a check-box, a radio button only allows you to choose one of the three.

```
<input type="radio" name="flavour"
value="vanilla"
checked="checked"/>
<input type="radio" name="flavour"
value="chocolate"/>
<input type="radio" name="flavour"
value="strawberry"/>
```

You create a mutually exclusive radio button group by setting all the radio button names the same. Browsers know that radio buttons with the same name are mutually exclusive. When clicking one of the radio buttons, the checked radio button is unchecked and the clicked one is checked. When submitting the form, only one name/value pair is submitted.

Table 6.3 Form element specified in this task	
Tag	**Function**
<input type="radio" ...	Specifies a radio button.

Cross reference

See **tasks_html/task_form_radio_button/radio.html** for completed example.

The results of this task are straightforward. You should see three radio buttons that only allow you to choose one. When you submit the form you get one value for the three elements. This is in contrast to check-boxes that allow you to choose multiple values for the same field.

```
1 <!DOCTYPE HTML PUBLIC "-//W3C//DTD HTML
2 4.01 Transitional//EN"
3 "http://www.w3.org/TR/html4/loose.dtd">
4 <html>
5 <body>
6 <form name="input"
7 action="mailto:jamesbrannan@earthlink.
8 net?subject=radio" method="post">
9 <img src="./evolution-contacts.png"/>
10 <h2>What is your age range?</h2>
11 18-30:<input type="radio" name="age"
12 value="18" />
13 <br />
14 31-60: <input type="radio" name="age"
15 value="31" checked="checked" />
16 <br />   60+:
17 <input type="radio" name="age"
18 value="60" />
19 <br /><br /><input type="submit"
20 value="Submit" />
21 </form>
22 </body>
23 </html>
```

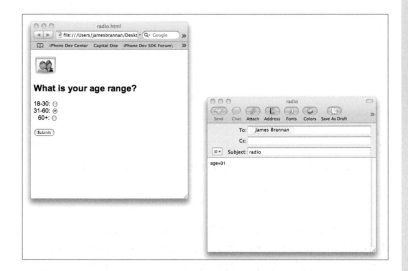

Adding file fields

File fields are inputs of type file. This field lets users choose a file from their computer and upload it when the form is submitted. Forms that submit files must have an encoding type of multipart/form-data.

```
<form name="input" action="nothing.php"
method="post" enctype="multipart/form-
data">
```

Task steps

1. Save the template with a different name.

2. Add a form. (9)

3. Add an input element and assign file as its type. (13)

4. Add a submit button. (17)

5. Save and view in your browser. Be sure to click the Browse/Upload button and load a file.

Cross reference

See **tasks_html/task_form_file_field/simple_form.html** for completed example.

Table 6.4 Form element specified in this task

Tag	Function
<input type="file" …	Specifies a file form field.

You can't use the mailto: protocol in this task, so you can't really see this task's results. However, you can choose a file, and see the file's name. Note the differences between Safari and Firefox in the two figures in this task.

```
1 <!DOCTYPE HTML PUBLIC "-//W3C//DTD HTML
2 4.01 Transitional//EN"
3 "http://www.w3.org/TR/html4/loose.dtd">
4 <html>
5 <body>
6 <img src="evolution-contacts.png"/>
7 <h2>Show your face to the world.</h2>
8 <p>Please upload your picture...</p>
9 <form name="input" action="nothing.php"
10 method="post" enctype="multipart/form-
11 data">
12 <label for="name">File:</label>
13 <input type="file" name="name"
14 size="20" />
15 <br/>
16 <br/>
17 <input type="submit" value="Submit"/>
18 <input type="reset" value="Cancel"/>
19 </form>
20 </body>
21 </html>
```

Adding a text area

Task steps

1. Save template with a different name.

2. Add a form. (8)

3. Add a text area element, remember to assign a row and column size. (10)

4. Save and view in your browser.

An input element of type text only allows a limited number of characters. Besides, even if you could enter a paragraph's worth of text in a text field, you wouldn't want to. Instead you use a text area. Text areas allow entering large amounts of data. You specify a text area using the `<textarea></textarea>` tags. Text areas have a name, cols, rows, wrap, read-only and disabled attribute. The cols attribute specifies how many columns wide to make the field, while the rows attribute specifies how many rows in height to make it. The wrap attribute tells the browser if it should wrap text in the field. The read-only attribute specifies that the field is read only. The disabled attribute makes the field disabled.

Table 6.5 Form element specified in this task	
Tag	**Function**
<textarea></textarea>	Specifies a text area in a form.

Cross reference

See **tasks_html/task_form_textarea/simple_form.html** for completed example.

The results of this task are straightforward. You should see a text area element with the specified number of columns and rows.

```
1 <!DOCTYPE HTML PUBLIC "-//W3C//DTD HTML
2 4.01 Transitional//EN"
3 "http://www.w3.org/TR/html4/loose.dtd">
4 <html>
5 <body>
6 <img src="evolution-contacts.png"/>
7 <h4>Tell us more about yourself...</h4>
8 <form name="input" action="nothing.php"
9 method="get">
10 <textarea rows="10" cols="20">
11 </textarea>
12 <br/>
```

```
13 <input type="submit" value="Submit" />
14 <input type="reset" value="Cancel"/>
15 </form>
16 </body>
17 </html>
```

Adding select elements (lists and menus)

Task steps

1. Open the template and save with a different name.

2. Add a select element, make it a multiple selection list. (10)

3. Give the element a size of four. (10)

4. Create a few options in the list. Be sure to assign each a value and text. (13–17)

5. Make one option selected. (13)

6. Add a couple **
** tags after the select element and add another select element. (19, 22)

7. Add several options to the select element. (23–25)

8. This time, don't specify a size.

9. Add a couple **
** tags after the second select element and add a third select element. (28, 31)

10. In the third select element add four option elements. Group the first two option elements in an optgroup element. (32)

The select element allows you to choose one or more values from a list of values. You add select elements to a form using the **<select></select>** tags. Within a select element there are one or more option elements. Option elements specify the names that appear in the select element. The option element's text is what appears in the select element as a choice. The option element's value is the value the select element takes when the option is selected.

```
<select>
<option value="1">Choice One</option>
<option value="2">Choice Two</option>
<option value="3">Choice Three</option>
</select>
```

The select element has a name, size and multiple attribute. The name attribute is the name submitted to the server for the select element. The size attribute is the number of options that should be visible in a browser. A value of one creates a drop-down list (also called menu). A value of two or more creates a list. The size element's default value is one when unspecified. The multiple attribute is true or false and specifies whether you can choose one option or multiple options.

Select elements place no limits on how many options are added. However, sometimes you might wish to make it easier for users by grouping similar choices into categories. You use the **<optgroup></optgroup>** tags for this grouping.

```
<select>
<optgroup label="Numbers">
<option value="1">Choice One</option>
<option value="2">Choice Two</option>
</optgroup>
<optgroup label="Letters">
</optgroup>
<option value="a">Choice A</option>
<option value="b">Choice B</option>
</select>
```

Table 6.6 Form elements specified in this task	
Tag	**Function**
<select></select>	Specifies a menu/drop-down list.
<option></option>	Specifies an option in select element.
<optgroup></optgroup>	Specifies a group of options.

Cross reference

See **html_tasks/task_form_lists_menus/forms.html** for completed example.

11 Group the second two option elements in an optgroup element. Assign both optgroups a label. (40)

12 Save and view in your browser.

Upon completing this task and viewing the results in your browser you should see three different select element variants. The first select box is a list that allows multiple selections. The second is a traditional drop-down box. The third is a traditional drop-down box, but the choices are grouped in two groupings. Notice the difference between how Safari and Firefox render select elements.

```
1 <!DOCTYPE HTML PUBLIC "-//W3C//DTD HTML
2 4.01 Transitional//EN"
3 "http://www.w3.org/TR/html4/loose.dtd">
4 <html>
5 <body>
6 <img src="./evolution-contacts.png"/>
7 <form>
8 <label for="hair">What hair colors do
9 you like? </label>
10 <select multiple="multiple" size="4"
11 name="hair">
12 <option value="black">Brunette</option>
13 <option selected="selected"
14 value="blond">Blond</option>
15 <option value="red">Redhead</option>
16 ---snip---
17 <option value="other">All</option>
18 </select>
```

Adding select elements (lists and menus) (cont.)

```
19 <br/><br/>
20 <label for="weight">What is your
21 salary? </label>
22 <select name="salary">
23 <option selected value="na">Private
24 </option>
25 <option value="25k">25K-50K</option>
26 ---snip---
27 </select>
28 <br/><br/>
29 <label for="weight">What is your
30 height? </label>
31 <select name="height">
32         <optgroup label="Short">
33         <option selected
34         value="short1">0ft-1ft</option>
35         <option value="short2">1ft-
36         2ft</option>
37         <option value="short3">2ft-
38         3ft</option>
39         </optgroup>
40         <optgroup label="Normal">
41         <option selected
42         value="normal1">3ft-4ft</option>
43         <option value="normal2">4ft-
44         5ft</option>
45         <option value="normal3">5ft-
46         6ft</option>
47         </optgroup>
48         </select>
49 <br/><br/>
50 <input type="submit" value="Submit"/>
51 <input type="reset" value="Cancel"/>
52 </form>
53 </body>
54 </html
```

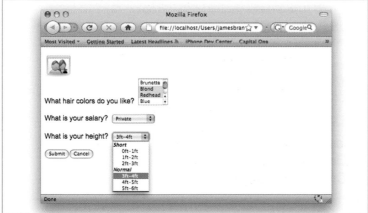

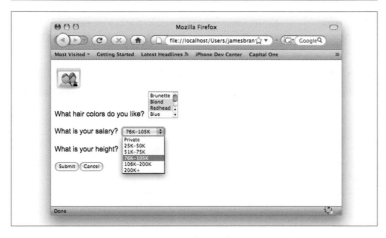

Adding a fieldset and legend

Sometimes you might want to group form fields that are for similar items. Grouping like fields helps users understand the form better. Better understood forms result in more submissions and greater data accuracy. You group fields using the fieldset element. The fieldset element renders a box around form elements within its **<fieldset>** opening and **</fieldset>** closing tags. You can also label a fieldset element by assigning a legend.

```
<fieldset>
<legend>Dairy Products</legend>
Ice Cream <input type="checkbox"/><br/>
Cream <input type="checkbox"/><br/>
Cream Cheese <input type="checkbox"/>
</fieldset>
```

Task steps

1. Save your template with a different name.

2. Add a form to the page. (6)

3. Add three radio buttons to the form. (13, 16, 19)

4. Before the first radio button, add the **<fieldset>** tag. (10)

5. After the last radio button, add the **</fieldset>** closing tag. (21)

6. Immediately following the **<fieldset>** tag, add a legend. (11)

7. Save and view in your browser.

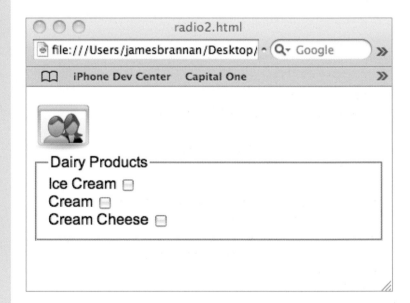

Table 6.7 Form elements specified in this task	
Tag	**Function**
<fieldset></fieldset>	Species that a box be drawn around the elements within its tags.
<legend></legend>	Specifies a fieldset caption.

Cross reference

See **tasks_html/task_forms_fieldsets/radio.html** for completed example.

The task's results are straightforward. You should see three radio buttons. Around the radio buttons you should see a labelled box. The text for the label should match what you entered for the legend.

```
1 <!DOCTYPE HTML PUBLIC "-//W3C//DTD HTML
2 4.01 Transitional//EN"
3 "http://www.w3.org/TR/html4/loose.dtd">
4 <html>
5 <body>
6 <form name="input" action="nowhere.psp"
7 method="get">
8 <img src="./evolution-contacts.png"/>
9 <h2>What is your age range?</h2>
10 <fieldset>
11 <legend>Age Range</legend>
12 18-30
13 <input type="radio" name="age"
14 value="18" />
15 31-60
16 <input type="radio" name="age"
17 value="31" checked="checked" />
18 60+
19 <input type="radio" name="age"
20 value="60" />
21 </fieldset>
22 <br /><br />
23 <input type="submit" value="Submit" />
24 </form>
25 </body>
26 </html>
```

Adding a fieldset and legend (cont.)

Introducing Cascading Style Sheets (CSS)

7

Introduction

Cascading Style Sheets (CSS) are what you use to apply style to your HTML documents. A CSS document is a text document that contains one or more rules which tell browsers how to format the elements on an HTML page. A rule consists of a selector that specifies the element to which to apply a style and a declaration that declares which style to apply. A declaration consists of a property and a value. There are many CSS properties you can set, including properties for positioning and sizing elements, properties for setting an element's font and colour, and numerous others.

You simply cannot create professional websites these days without using a CSS stylesheet. Stylesheets move HTML pages into the realm of graphic arts. Gone are the days when a programmer, such as the author, could throw together a couple images and text mixed with some HTML tags, and call it a professional website. Consider a website (Theocacao, for example, p.118) with and without a CSS stylesheet applied. The difference is striking. CSS makes HTML Web pages as professional as printed magazine layout and design.

What you'll do

Understand 'ids' and class names

Understand the 'div' element

Understand the 'span' element

Understand CSS rules

Specify CSS styles

Add CSS comments

With a stylesheet applied…

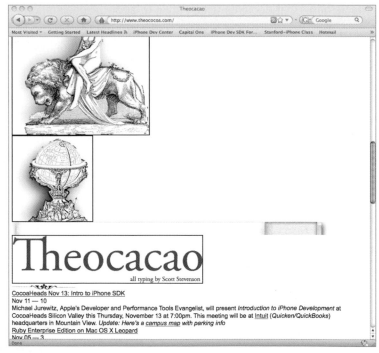

and without a stylesheet.

This is the first of several disclaimers I make in the remaining chapters. By profession I am a Web developer not a web designer. That means I know HTML, CSS; I can write programs that dynamically generate HTML, and I can write programs that process form submissions. But, unlike the good old days of the 1990s, being a developer today doesn't make one a Web designer. Treat this book as an introductory text on HTML and CSS syntax, not a book on designing with CSS. Once you have finished with this book, however, you can move on to books on CSS design. Moreover, as you will have already learned CSS syntax from this book, understanding the style books will prove easier. When you're finished with this book, go to the bookshop, buy a latte or tea, and peruse a stack of CSS style books; it's great fun.

7

Understanding ids and class names

Before understanding CSS you must understand the HTML id attribute and class attribute. Every HTML element can have an id and class attribute. The id attribute assigns an element a unique name, while a class assigns the element a class name.

Before understanding CSS you must understand the HTML id attribute and class attribute. Every HTML element can have an id and class attribute. The id attribute assigns an element a unique name, while a class assigns the element a class name.

```
<p id="ralph"
class="important_paragraphs"></p>
```

Task steps

1. Navigate to **www.freecsstemplates.org** and download any of the free CSS templates. If you don't want to do that then, from this book's sample site, navigate to **tasks/tasks_css/pastries** and open the style.css file.

2. Open index.html in your browser, review, then close.

3. Open index.html in your text editor.

4. Notice that all HTML div elements have an id or class assignment.

5. Also notice many other elements also have an id or class assignment.

If you are familiar with object-oriented programming then understanding an HTML class is easy. But for those who are not familiar with object-oriented programming, a class is a way to group similar elements. For instance, picture a website based on this book, with important information summarised in a table. Each page has its own table, but you want each table formatted similarly. You use a class.

```
<table class="callout"> --- table info
here --- </table>
```

However, suppose you wanted one of the tables to use its own formatting. You would assign the particular table an id.

```
<table class="callout" id="specialTable">
--- table info here---</table>
```

Table 7.1 The id and class attributes

Attribute	Function
id	Specifies a unique id for an element.
class	Specifies a group membership for an element.

Cross reference

See **tasks/tasks_css/pastries/index.html** for the template used in this task.

```
Source of index.html

<!DOCTYPE html PUBLIC "-//W3C//DTD XHTML 1.0 Strict//EN"
"http://www.w3.org/TR/xhtml1/DTD/xhtml1-strict.dtd">
<!--
Design by Free CSS Templates
http://www.freecsstemplates.org
Released for free under a Creative Commons Attribution 2.5 License

Name        : Pastries
Description: A two-column, fixed-width design with dark color scheme.
Version     : 1.0
Released    : 20080617

-->
<html xmlns="http://www.w3.org/1999/xhtml">
<head>
<meta http-equiv="content-type" content="text/html; charset=utf-8" />
<title>Pastries by Free CSS Templates</title>
<meta name="keywords" content="" />
<meta name="description" content="" />
<link href="style.css" rel="stylesheet" type="text/css" media="screen" />
</head>
<body>
<div id="header">
        <div id="logo">
                <h1><a href="#">Pastries </a></h1>
                <p>  by  <a href="http://www.freecsstemplates.org/">Free
CSS Templates</a></p>
        </div>
        <div id="search">
                <form method="get" action="">
                        <fieldset>
                        <input id="search-text" type="text" name="s" value="Search"
size="15" />

                        <input type="submit" id="search-submit" value="Search" />
                        </fieldset>
                </form>
        </div>
        <!-- end #search -->
</div>
<!-- end #header -->
```

Cross reference

In this chapter's task, 'Understanding CSS rules', you look at this template's CSS rules.

7

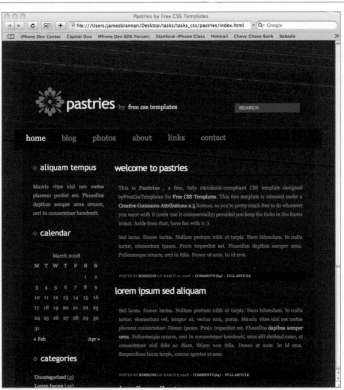

Understanding the div element

The div element is a block-level element that defines logical sections in an HTML document. CSS enables these logical sections to be formatted independently. Think of **`<div></div>`** tags as the basic building blocks in your HTML page. You position and format the blocks to achieve the desired page appearance.

You should always define a top-level division for your page.

```
<body><div id="outermost"></div></body>
```

You then add nested **`<div></div>`** tags as needed to achieve the desired layout.

Task steps

1. Save template.html using a different name.

2. Add one **`<div></div>`** tag set in the body element and assign an id to the div element. (26)

3. Add two **`<div></div>`** tag sets to the previously added div element. Assign both an id. (27,33)

4. In the first of the two nested div elements, add two more **`<div></div>`** tag sets. Assign both the same class name. (28, 30)

5. Add content to both elements.

6. In the second of the two outer div elements, add two **`<div></div>`** tag sets and assign both the same class name used in step 4. (34, 44)

7. Add content to both elements.

8. Save and view in your browser.

For your information

In this task you use several CSS formatting properties not yet covered. Don't worry if you don't understand the formatting, just try to understand the purpose of the div element.

Table 7.2 HTML element covered in this task

Tag	Function
<div></div>	Specifies a section in an html document.

Cross reference

See **tasks/tasks_css/task_div_span/div.html** for completed example.

Once the task is complete load it into your browser. Unless you cut and paste the formatting from the completed example code, you're not going to see much other than the text you typed into the nested div elements. This is because div elements group other elements into sections. Unless you apply a CSS style to the div, such as a border or background colour, you won't see the div element rendered by the browser.

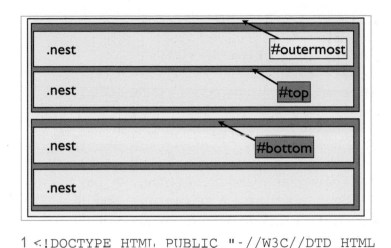

```
1  <!DOCTYPE HTML PUBLIC "-//W3C//DTD HTML
2  4.01 Transitional//EN"
3  "http://www.w3.org/TR/html4/loose.dtd">
4  <html>
5  <head>
6  <title>Div</title>
7  <style type="text/css">
8  body {background-color:black;}
9  div#outermost {border-
10 style:dotted;border-color:lime;border-
11 width:3px;margin:5px;}
12 div#top {border-style:solid;border-
13 color:orange;border-
14 width:2px;background-
15 color:lime;margin:5px;}
16 div#bottom {border-style:solid;border-
17 color:lime;border-width:2px;background-
18 color:orange;margin:5px;}
19 div.nest {border-style:dotted;
20 background-color:whitesmoke; border-
21 width:2px;margin:5px;}
22 img {float:left;}
23 </style>
24 </head>
25 <body>
26 <div id="outermost">
27 <div id="top">
28 <div class="nest"><h2>nested
29 div</h2></div>
30 <div class="nest"><h2>nested
```

```
31 div</h2></div>
32 </div>
33 <div id="bottom">
34 <div class="nest"><img
35 src="./services.png"/><h2>nested
36 div</h2><p>A paragraph about nothing.
37 A paragraph about nothing. A paragraph
38 about nothing. A paragraph about
39 nothing. A paragraph about nothing.
40 A paragraph about nothing. A paragraph
41 about nothing. A paragraph about
42 nothing. A paragraph about nothing.
43 </p></div>
44 <div class="nest"><h2>nested
45 div</h2></div>
46 </div>
47 </div>
48 </body>
49 </html>
```

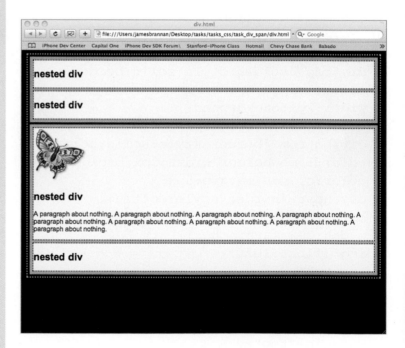

Cross reference

In Chapter 13 you use the div element extensively to lay out HTML pages using CSS.

Important

The div element is a block-level element. The purpose of the element is to divide the HTML page into logical sections, not other block-level elements. You can't nest the div element in a paragraph or blockquote, for instance. Instead, these elements should be nested in the div element. Think of the div element as the building blocks for a page.

Understanding the div element (cont.)

7

Understanding the span element

Task steps

1. Save template.html using a different name.

2. Add a paragraph to the page. (20)

3. Select some text and place `<span></span>` tags around the text. Assign the span element an id. (18)

4. Select some text and place `<span></span>` tags around the text. Assign it a class name. (20)

5. Repeat step three twice more, but assign the span elements different ids. (22, 27)

6. Save and view in your browser.

7. From the completed example, copy from the opening `<style>` tag to the closing `</style>` and paste into the `<head></head>` tags in your document. (6–14)

8. Change your span element ids and class name to match those in the cut and pasted code. The ids are h, b and c. The class name is a.

9. Save and view in your browser.

The span element is an in-line-level element and groups in-line content. It allows you to specify CSS formatting for arbitrary text and other in-line elements. You can wrap any in-line content in a span and then apply CSS formatting to it.

Table 7.3 HTML element covered in this task	
Task	**Function**
`<span></span>`	Specifies a section in an html document.

Cross reference

See **tasks/tasks_css/task_div_span/span.html** for completed example.

After completing this task you won't see anything, because span elements by themselves don't do anything other than group in-line content, for applying a style to. Notice, in the completed example, however, I added CSS formatting.

You should see that the text inside each span is formatted differently from the surrounding text.

```
1 <!DOCTYPE HTML PUBLIC "-//W3C//DTD HTML
2 4.01 Transitional//EN"
3 "http://www.w3.org/TR/html4/loose.dtd">
4 <html>
5 <head>
6 <style type="text/css">
7 span#h {color:red;font-family:cursive;}
8 span.a{font-size:xx-
9 large;color:green;border-style:solid;}
10 span#b {font-size:x-large;color:red;}
11 span#c {font-size:xx-
12 large;color:green;background-
13 color:aqua;}
14 </style>
15 </head>
16 <body>
```

```
17 <div id="body_div">
18 <span id="h"><h2>A Paragraph About
19 Nothing</h2></span>
20 <p><span class="a">This is some
21 content.</span>The paragraph is <span
22 id="b">a</span><span
23 class="a">b</span>out nothing. This is
24 some content. The paragraph is about
25 nothing. This is some content.
26 The paragraph is about nothing. <span
27 id="c">This is some content. The
28 paragraph is about nothing.</span> The
29 paragraph is about nothing. The
30 paragraph is about nothing.
31 This is some content. The paragraph is
32 about nothing. The paragraph is about
33 nothing. This is some content.
34 The paragraph is about nothing. The
35 paragraph is about nothing. This is
36 some content. The paragraph is about
37 nothing.
38 </p>
39 </div>
40 </body>
41 </html>
```

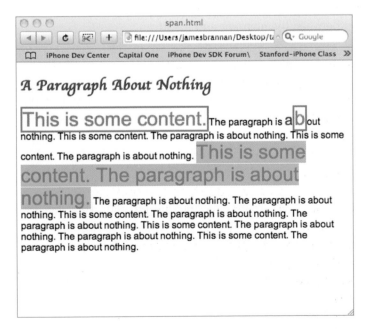

Understanding
CSS rules

A CSS rule consists of two parts, the selector and the declaration.

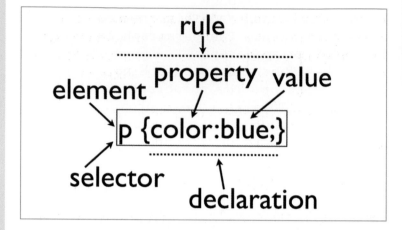

The selector determines the element(s) affected by the rule. The declaration specifies the action taken. When specifying a selector, you can narrow the affected element to only elements of a specific class or a specific id. When specifying elements of a specific class you use a period between the element and the class name.

```
element.classname
```

When specifying an element with a specific id you place a hash sign between the element and the id.

```
element#id
```

When the browser reads the selector, it knows to only apply the declaration to the elements specified by the selector. For instance,

```
p {color:red;}
```

tells the browser, 'make all paragraph text red'. The selector,

```
p#a1 {color:green;}
```

tells the browser, 'make paragraph a1's text green'. The selector,

```
p.important {color:orange;}
```

tells the browser, 'make all important paragraphs have orange text'.

The declaration is the actual style to apply to the selector. A declaration consists of an opening curly brace, the property, a colon, the property's value and a closing curly brace. You can optionally include a semicolon if desired (I always do).

```
element#id {property:value}
```

or

```
element#id {property:value;}
```

If specifying multiple declarations for one selector, you include a semicolon between the declarations.

```
element#id {property1:value1;property2:
value2;property3:value3}
```

You can also specify the same declaration for multiple elements. To do this, place a comma between the elements.

```
element, element {property:value;}
```

Important

In this book almost all the tasks set CSS properties using the HTML style element. This is merely a convenience, so you can see the style and HTML in the same code. In the real world you should almost always use an external stylesheet.

Understanding CSS rules (cont.)

Task steps

1 Navigate to **www.freecsstemplates.org** and download any of the free CSS templates. If you don't want to do that, then from this book's sample site, navigate to **tasks/tasks_css/pastries** and open the style.css file.

2 Open index.html in your browser, review, then close.

3 Open and review the stylesheet, style.css, in your text editor.

7

Understanding CSS rules (cont.)

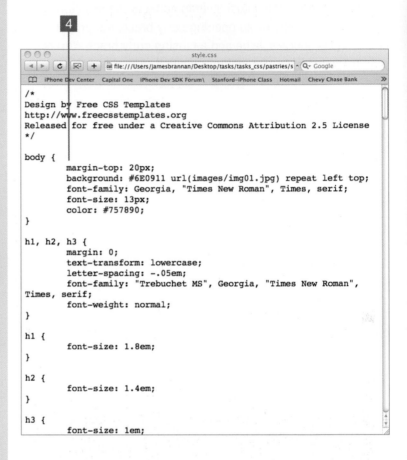

4 Note the body element's rule. The text **body** is the rule and there are five declarations, each separated by a semicolon.

5 Notice that many rules specify multiple selectors for the same declarations.

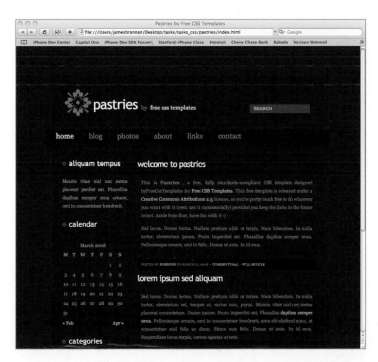

```
                                        style.css
◄ ► C ⌗ + 🔖 file:///Users/jamesbrannan/Desktop/tasks/tasks_css/pastries/style.css    ⌃ Q▾ Google
   iPhone Dev Center   Capital One   iPhone Dev SDK Forum\   Stanford-iPhone Class   Hotmail   Chevy Chase Bank   Babado   Verizon Webmail   »

#sidebar {
        float: left;
        width: 220px;
        margin-left: 25px;
        color: #7893AE;
}

#sidebar ul {
        margin: 0;
        padding: 0;
        list-style: none;
}

#sidebar li {
}

#sidebar li ul {
        padding: 10px 0 15px 15px;
}

#sidebar li li {
        padding-left: 10px;
}

#sidebar h2 {
        padding-bottom: 10px;
        padding-left: 20px;
        margin: 5px 22px;
        font-size: 1.5em;
        border-bottom: 2px solid #000000;
        background: url(images/img06.jpg) no-repeat left 35%;
        color: #FFFFFF;
}
```

6 Notice some selectors begin
with a hash and only include
the id, not the element

7

Understanding
CSS rules (cont.)

Timesaver tip

On finishing this book, you will be armed with enough knowledge to create an HTML page and format it using CSS. But rather than starting from scratch, you might want to consider using a template as a starting point. A template is a completed HTML page with a CSS stylesheet. You then replace the template's content with your own. Or, if you prefer, you can use the template as a starting point and modify the template to better suit your desired page style.

One website you can obtain free CSS templates is **freeCSStemplates.org**. This site has over 300 templates you can download for free. The **freeCSStemplates.org** site is just one of many sites you can find free CSS templates; enter 'free CSS templates' into any search engine and you'll find many other sites.

You can specify CSS styles three different ways. First, you can include an external stylesheet in your HTML page.

```
<head>
<link href="mystylesheet.css"
rel="stylesheet" type="text/css"/>
</head>
```

Second, you can include a style element in your HTML page's header, and place the CSS formatting within the **<style></style>** tags.

```
<head>
<style>
p {border-style:solid;}
</style>
</head>
```

Third, you can include the style inline, directly in the tag as an attribute.

```
<p style="border-style:dotted;">
```

The order of precedence goes from styles set in an external stylesheet, to styles set in a style element, to styles set in an actual HTML tag. For instance, if you set an element's colour in an external stylesheet to blue,

```
p {color:blue;}
```

but then set the same element's colour to red in the page's style element,

```
<head><style>
p{color:red;}</style></head>
```

the value from the style element would override the style set in the external stylesheet, and the colour would be red. If you then set the colour to purple in the tag,

```
<p style="color:purple;">
```

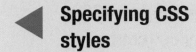

Specifying CSS styles

7

Specifying CSS styles (cont.)

Task steps

1 Save template.html using a different name.

2 Create an external stylesheet; be certain to give the file a .css extension. (1–2)

3 In the html page, add four **\<p>\</p>** tag sets. Assign three paragraphs a different id. I use ids **a**, **b** and **c**. Add some text to each paragraph. (17, 19, 21, 23)

4 Open the stylesheet and assign paragraph elements the colour green. (2)

5 Save and close the stylesheet.

6 Include the stylesheet in the HTML page. (8)

7 Add **\<style>\</style>** tags to the HTML page's head element. (10)

8 Assign paragraph **a** the colour lime and paragraph **b** orange. (11, 12)

9 Add a style attribute to paragraph **c** and assign it the colour blue. (21)

10 Save and view in your browser.

the in-line style would override the style set in the style element, and the colour would be purple.

> **Cross reference**
>
> See **tasks/tasks_css/task_specify/specify.html** and **tasks/tasks_css/task_specify/specify.css** for completed examples.

After completing this task load it into your browser. Paragraph **a** should have lime text, paragraph **b** orange text, paragraph **c** blue text, and the anonymous paragraph green text. Although you set paragraph **a**'s text colour to blue in the external stylesheet, the lime colour set in the HTML page's style element overrode the external stylesheet. The same is true for paragraph **b**, only the style attribute in the actual paragraph element overrode the external stylesheet.

```
1 body {background-color:lightgray;}
2 p{color:green;}

3 <!DOCTYPE HTML PUBLIC "-//W3C//DTD HTML
4 4.01 Transitional//EN"
5 "http://www.w3.org/TR/html4/loose.dtd">
6 <html>
7 <head>
8 <link href="./specify.css"
9 rel="stylesheet" type="text/css">
10 <style type="text/css">
12 p#a {color:lime;}
13 p#b {color:orange;}
14 </style>
15 <title>StyleSheets</title>
16 </head>
17 <body>
18 <p id="a">This is first paragraph. It
19 should be lime.</p>
20 <p id="b">This is second paragraph. It
21 should be orange.</p>
22 <p id="c" style="color:blue;">This is
23 third paragraph. It should be blue.</p>
```

```
24 <p>This is a fourth paragraph. It
25 should be green.
26 </body>
27 </html>
```

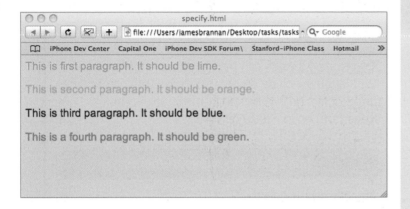

Specifying CSS styles (cont.)

For your information

Most CSS properties take a measurement unit as a value. For instance, you might want to set a paragraph's font size.

```
p {font-size: value}
```

The property's value can be a length or a percentage. Valid lengths include points (pt), picas (pc), centimetres (cm), inches (in), millimetres (mm), pixels (px), em space (em) and x space (ex).

Table 7.4 CSS measurements

Absolute measurements

points	pt	Measurement defined in points, 72 points per inch.
picas	pc	Measurement defined in picas, 6 picas per inch.
centimetres	cm	Measurement defined as centimetres.
inches	in	Measurement defined as inches.
millimetres	mm	Measurement defined as millimetres.

Relative measurements

pixels	px	Measurement defined by a point on monitor, between 72 and 90 pixels per inch, depending on monitor.
em space	em	Measurement defined by current font. One em space (1em) equals the user's current browser font size letter M.
x space	ex	Measurement defined by font's x-height. X-height is usually equal to a font's lowercase x.
percentage	%	Measurement defined as percentage relative to another element, usually an enclosing parent element.

You should reserve using absolute values for printing. Use relative values for display.

CSS comments, like HTML comments, explain your code. You add CSS comments by using a forward slash followed by a star, the comment and then another star followed by another forward slash.

```
/* this is a css comment */
```

Cross reference

See **tasks/tasks_css/task_div_span/ div_withcomments.html** for completed example.

After completing this task the results should be straightforward – you should see the exact same page as the previous task. The comments are not rendered by the browser. However, if you look at the source, you will see the comments in the source.

```
1 <!DOCTYPE HTML PUBLIC "-//W3C//DTD HTML
2 4.01 Transitional//EN"
3 "http://www.w3.org/TR/html4/loose.dtd">
4 <html>
5 <style type="text/css">
6 /* *********
7 * James A. Brannan
8 * Disclaimer: This is a
9 comment example
10 * ********** /
11 body {background-color:black;} /* I want
12 the background black */
13 div#outermost {border-
14 style:dotted;border-color:lime;border-
15 width:3px;margin:5px;}
16 div#top {border-style:solid;border-
17 color:orange;border-width:2px;
18 background-color:lime;margin:5px;}
19 div#bottom {border-style:solid;border-
20 color:lime;border-width:2px;background-
21 color:orange; /* margin:4000px; */
22 margin:5px;}
23 div.nest {border-style:dotted;
```

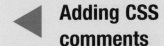

Adding CSS comments

Task steps

1 Open the previously saved task with a style element.

2 Add a couple of comments.

3 Save and view in your browser.

7

Adding CSS comments (cont.)

```
24 background-color:whitesmoke; border-
25 width:2px;margin:5px;}
26 </style>
27 <title>CSS Comments</title>
28 <head>
29 <body> ---snip--- </body>
30 </html>
```

Jargon buster

Template – A pattern. In this book HTML or CSS documents are used as your starting point so you're not required to recreate common HTML or CSS code each time you create a new document.

Object-oriented programming – A programming style where constructs are treated as objects.

GNU – An organisation started in 1984 to promote a free operating system similar to UNIX. The GNU software was eventually combined with Linux. GNU now exists for a much broader purpose of promoting open-source software. GNU wrote both the LGPL and GPL licensing schemes and is active in ensuring others follow the licences.

For your information

Just because you see something on the Web, it doesn't mean you can use it. That photo, font or video might belong to somebody, who put hard effort into creating it, and probably wouldn't appreciate someone else stealing it. But there are legal ways to obtain content on the Web if you pay attention to licensing schemes. Notice, for instance, that this book includes fonts from the Vista-Inspire and Crystal Project icon collections. Did I steal them? No. The Crystal Project is licensed under the GNU Lesser General Public License (LGPL). This licence states that I have freedom to use and modify the licensed work in both open-source and commercial projects. The Vista-Inspirate icons are licensed under the GNU General Public License (GPL). This licence is a little more restrictive. I'm free to use and modify the licensed work in both open-source and commercial projects, but any derivative works, or modifications to the originals must be made available freely to requesters. Sometimes the licensing is tricky. For instance, had I used the icons as the book's illustrations, it could be argued that the book should be GPL. But I didn't use the icons for the book, I used them for the book's sample code. The sample code and the icons used are freely provided via the book's completed examples. The LGPL and GPL are included in the website as well.

The CSS templates used from **freecsstemplates.org** are licenced under the Creative Commons Attribution 2.5 licence. This licence allows you to share, adapt and generally reuse the licensed work, provided you provide attribution to the original author. At **freecsstemplates.org**, for instance, the creator requests that you leave the link to his site intact.

Adding CSS comments (cont.)

Finally, notice that some of the book's examples show the quintesential stock-photos of 'happy people doing happy things'. You can buy these images online or in your local retail store. I bought them from a German company called Hemera in the mid 1990s as part of the Photo Objects 50,000 Premium Image Collection. I'm free to use these images in commercial and personal projects, provided I don't make the original image freely available for download. I can use them on a Web page, provided I use a lesser-quality derivative of the original image. But that's okay, the original images are high-quality TIFFs and the file sizes are huge.

You must pay attention to licensing schemes. When doing searches for icons and clipart, I find **www.kdelook.org** a good place to start. For images, I start with my Photo Objects collection. But, as you probably don't have that collection, as an alternative I'd suggest flickr at **www.flickr.com**. When searching, you can choose advanced search. Then select the Only search within Creative Commons-licensed content check box. When deciding upon a CC licensed image, still read the author's restrictions, you may have to attribute the photographer.

Formatting fonts and text using CSS

Introduction

Fonts are fundamental to all written communication. Fonts convey emotion, style and help your writing convey implicit meaning. For instance, if you are chatting in a chat-room or emailing someone and you type USING ALL CAPS, a common Web convention is that you are yelling.

A font's meaning can be subtle. A choice as simple as using Comic Sans rather than Arial can convey an entirely different mood.

Welcome to My Site (Comic Sans)

The Comic Sans font conveys a loose and informal site while Arial seems more formal.

Welcome to My Site (Arial)

The Lucida Blackletter font conveys something out of *Bram Stoker's Dracula*. It is neither loose and informal, nor formal. It's spooky.

Welcome to My Site (Lucida Blackletter)

All three font choices give users entirely different expectation of a site's content. I would expect a goth rock band to use Lucida Blackletter, but not an online banking firm. A goth band that used Arial for its site would seem rather boring; and I definitely would not bank on an online banking site that used Comic Sans. Different fonts are appropriate, depending upon the impression you want to give. Choose your site's fonts carefully.

What you'll do

Set an element's font-family

Set an element's font-style

Set an element's font-weight and size

Setting an element's font using the font declaration

Decorate text and change case

Align text

But before getting too creative, and choosing an exotic font (such as Lucida Blackletter), note that you should choose fonts commonly found on most operating systems. If your page specifies a font that isn't installed on a user's operating system, then the browser displays your page using the user's default font set in their browser. The hours you spent agonising over a font was wasted time; users will probably view your site in Times, Courier or some equally boring font.

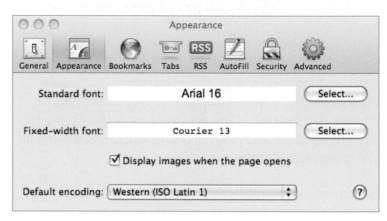

Table 8.1 CSS font properties covered in this chapter	
font-family	Specifies the font family, where the font family can be either a specific family name or a generic font family.
font-style	Specifies the font style, where the style can be normal, italic or oblique.
font-weight	Specifies a font's weight.
font-size	Specifies a font's size.
font	Property that allows you to set the font-family, font-style, font-weight and font-size in one statement.

CSS also provides several properties that replace the deprecated HTML text formatting tags and attributes such as the paragraph element's align attribute and the **<u></u>** tags that underline text. This formatting is important to the formatting of a page and adds extra formatting choices. In this chapter you learn how to use CSS to underline, overline, strikethrough, change case and make your text blink. You learn to align your text and to add spacing to your text. These properties, combined with CSS font properties, are how you should format your HTML text.

8

Setting an element's font-family

Important !

The font-family property is only one aspect of an element's font. You must also set its weight, size and style. You do this in the next three tasks; this task focuses solely on the font's family.

You declare a font's family by using the font-family property. A font-family is a family of similarly designed fonts. For instance, Arial, Helvetica and Times New Roman are all font-family examples. You can also use a generic font-family name. The generic font-family names are: serif, sans-serif, cursive, fantasy and monospace. The generic font-families are common to all browsers on all computers and so they are the safest bet if you want to be certain that all users have your specified font.

When declaring a font's family, you can list more than one font. This is important because if a user's system doesn't have the font-family needed, it looks for the next font-family in the list. When using font-family, good practice is to end the list with one of the five generic font-family values. That way a browser is provided with multiple options. For instance, if Arial isn't found, use Tahoma. If Tahoma isn't found, than use serif:

```
p {font-family: arial, tahoma, serif;}
```

Because serif is one of the generic font families, it is guaranteed to be there.

Elements inherit font-family from their parent, and can override their parent's font. The best way to specify fonts is by assigning the body a font-family – that way your pages will all share the same base font. Then, for paragraphs, headings and other text where you want the font to be different, you can override the body element's font.

Table 8.2 Generic font families and example member font families	
Name	**Example members**
Generic font-family	Font families belonging to a generic family
Cursive	Comic Sans MS, Apple Chancery, URW Chancery, Monotype Corsiva, Bradley Hand ITC
Fantasy	Impact, Papyrus, Marker Felt, Felix Titling
Monospace	Courier, Courier New, Lucida Console, Monaco, Free Mono
Sans-serif	Microsoft Sans Serif, Arial, Helvetica, Veranda, Liberation Sans
Serif	Palatino Linotype, Georgia, Times New Roman, Baskerville, American Typewriter

8

Cross reference

See **tasks_css/task_css_fonts_multiple_tasks/ font_family.html** for completed example.

Setting an element's font-family (cont.)

Task steps

1. Open template.html and save with a different name.

2. Add **<q></q>** tags. (12)

3. Add three short paragraphs, wrapping each paragraph with **<p></p>** tags. Emphasise a few words using the **<em></em>** tags. (15, 17, 20)

4. In the heading add an opening and closing **<style>** tag. (17)

5. Make the quotation element's font-family cursive. (7)

6. Make the emphasised element's font-family Arial Black.

7. Assign one of the paragraphs an id, for example id="disclaimer". (22)

8. Make the same paragraph's font-family serif. (9)

9. Save and view in your browser.

The results of this task are straightforward. The two paragraphs without ids have whatever font your browser lists as its standard font. For instance, my browser's standard font is Times 12. The paragraph with the id should be serif. Because serif is one of the generic font-families, you are certain to see this text rendered using this font-family. The quotation is cursive, also a generic font-family. If your computer has Arial, the emphasised text's font should be Arial, otherwise sans-serif. If your computer has neither font, this paragraph should also be in your browser's standard font.

```
1  <!DOCTYPE HTML PUBLIC "-//W3C//DTD HTML
2  4.01 Transitional//EN"
3  "http://www.w3.org/TR/html4/loose.dtd">
4  <html>
5  <head>
6  <title>Font-Family Example</title>
7  <style type="text/css">q{font-
8  family:cursive;}
9  p#disclaimer{font-family:serif;}</style>
10 </head>
11 <body>
12 <p><q>Which iNtervalTrack version should
13 I buy?</q></p>
14 <p>It depends upon your operating
15 system. Buy the Mac edition for <em
16 style="font-family:'arial black'">OS
17 X</em>, the Linux version for <em
18 style="font-family:'arial
18 black'">Linux</em>, and the Windows
20 version for <em style="font-
21 family:'arial black'">Windows</em>.</p>
22 <p id="disclaimer">Note that only
23 Windows XP, Ubuntu Linux, and Mac OSX
24 Leopard on an Intel, have been
25 tested</p>
26 </body>
27 </html>
```

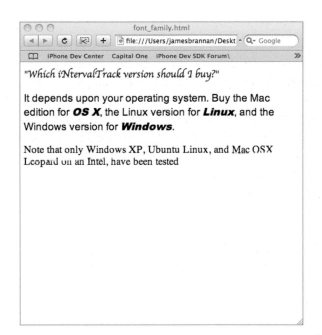

Important !

When using font-family, if the font's name has white space in it, you must enclose the font-family value in single or double quotations.

```
p{font-family:
  "DejaVu Sans";}
```

For your information

Web-safe fonts

Just because you can use a font, doesn't mean you should. Take, for example, the font called Barbaric. It's a clever barbed wire themed font by Aeryn. It's free and you can download it from several sites. Suppose you were working on a tattoo parlour's website and you simply had to have that font. So you downloaded it, installed it in your system fonts, and created your site using the font. For example, consider the following HTML page.

```
<!DOCTYPE HTML PUBLIC "-//W3C//DTD
HTML 4.01 Transitional//EN"
"http://www.w3.org/TR/html4/loose.
dtd">
<html><head><title>Font</title>
</head>
<body>
<p style="font-family: Barbaric;
font-size: 5em;">Tattoos are
cool.</p>
</body>
</html>
```

8

Setting an element's font-family (cont.)

Load this page in your browser and it looks great.

But, what do your site's visitors see? Chances are, they will see their browser's default font and not Barbaric, because they don't have the font installed in their system's font folder.

I bet you don't have Barbaric installed. If you're using a Mac, start the Font Book application. If using Windows, go to the fonts sub-folder in your Windows directory. The fonts you see listed are the fonts you have. Your browser uses those fonts. If the font family your CSS specifies is not there, your browser resorts to its default font.

You could instruct users to download and install the Barbaric font for best viewing results, but what's the chances of a casual surfer doing that? Instead, your best bet is to stick to the five generic font-family values, or a few common fonts such as Courier, Times New Roman or Arial. If you simply must use an uncommon font, then only use it for headings and titles by making them a png image with a transparent background. You can even add drop-shadows and other special effects. See a book on graphic Web design or Adobe Photoshop for more information.

A font can have one of three styles. The font's style can be normal, italic or oblique. Most fonts have a bold and italic style. All fonts have a normal style, although a normal style is nothing more than a font's default style if the font-style declaration is omitted. Normal sets the font to normal. Italic sets the font to italic and oblique sets the font to oblique. Note that italic and oblique have a subtle difference. Italic italicises the font and is an actual font. For example, Arial italics is a system font. When a browser loads this font it says, 'Okay, I need to load the Arial italics font', not, 'Okay, I have an Arial font that I must italicise'. In contrast, oblique is not an actual font. Oblique simply slants the font selected. Although similar to italicising, there can sometimes be slight visual differences between the two property values.

Setting an element's font-style

Cross reference

Remember, there are many HTML tags that change text's appearance. See 'Marking up other text elements' in Chapter 2. In many situations these tags are more appropriate than specifying a font.

8

Table 8.3 CSS font-style values	
Style	**Value**
font-style:normal	Specifies font's normal style.
font-style:italic	Specifies font's italics style.
font-style:oblique	Instructs browser to slant font's normal style font.

Cross reference

See **tasks_css/task_css_fonts_multiple_tasks/ font_style.html** for completed example.

Setting an element's font-style (cont.)

Task steps

1. Open the HTML page from the previous task.

2. Make the quotation element's font-style oblique. (8, 9)

3. Add a font-family and font-style declaration for the paragraph element. (10)

4. Make the paragraph with an id have an italic font-style. (12)

5. In one of the paragraphs without an id, add a font-style normal in the paragraph's opening tag. (19)

6. Save and display in your browser.

After completing the task and reloading the page in your browser, you should see that the italics worked as expected for the paragraph with the id, but not for the other paragraphs. What happened? The syle for the quotation overrode the parent paragraph's style. The paragraph with the style attribute in its opening tag also overrode its style set in the `<style></style>` tags. Note that the quotation's oblique style didn't seem to do anything (at least it didn't on my Safari browser). Think about it, the oblique value tells the browser to try to slant the text, the text is already slanted, as it's cursive.

```
1  <!DOCTYPE HTML PUBLIC "-//W3C//DTD HTML
2  4.01 Transitional//EN"
3  "http://www.w3.org/TR/html4/loose.dtd">
4  <html>
5  <head>
6  <title>Font Style</title>
7  <style type="text/css">
8  q{font-family:cursive; font-style:
9  oblique;}
10 p{font-family:arial,sans-serif;font-
11 style: normal;}
12 p#disclaimer{font-family:serif;font-
13 style:italic;}
14 </style>
15 </head>
16 <body>
17 <p><q>Which iNtervalTrack version should
18 I buy?</q></p>
19 <p style="font-style: normal;">It
20 depends upon your operating system. Buy
21 the Mac edition for <em style="font-
22 family:'arial black'">OS X</em>, the
23 Linux version for <em style="font-
24 family:'arial black'">Linux</em>, and
25 the Windows version for <em style="font-
26 family:'arial black'">Windows</em>.</p>
27 <p id="disclaimer">Note that only
28 Windows XP, Ubuntu Linux, and Mac OSX
29 Leopard on an Intel, have been
30 tested</p>
31 </body>
32 </html>
```

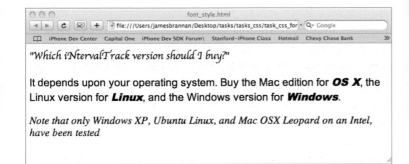

"Which iNtervalTrack version should I buy?"

It depends upon your operating system. Buy the Mac edition for **OS X**, the Linux version for **Linux**, and the Windows version for **Windows**.

Note that only Windows XP, Ubuntu Linux, and Mac OSX Leopard on an Intel, have been tested

For your information

There are three other font properties not covered in this chapter. The font-size-adjust property allows adjusting a font's size, while font-stretch allows stretching or condensing a font. The font-variant property allows setting a font's variant, but there are only two variants: normal and small-caps. For more information on these three properties go to one of the websites referenced in Chapter 1.

8

Setting an element's font-weight and size

Task steps

1. Open the page from the previous task.

2. Change the **<em></em>** tags to **<span></span>** tags. (21, 24, 28)

3. Make the quotation's font-size 150% of its parent, the paragraph element. (9)

4. Assign the paragraph element a bold font-weight. (11)

5. Assign the paragraph with an id a lighter font-weight and a small font-size. (13, 14)

6. Assign an oblique font-style to the first span element. Give it an xx-large font-size. (22)

7. Assign the second span element a normal font-weight. Remove the second span's font-family so that it uses its paragraph parent's Arial font-family. (24)

8. Remove the style attribute from the third span so that it has no formatting. Of course, it inherits its parent paragraph's style. (24)

You can set a font's weight and size. You declare a font's weight using the font-weight property. Valid values are: normal, bold, bolder, lighter and 100, 200, 300, 400, 500, 600, 700, 800 and 900, or a percentage. A font's default weight is normal.

```
p{font-weight:bolder;} p.big1{font-
weight:900} p.big2{font-weight:500%;}
```

A font's weight is inherited. For instance, setting a division element's font-weight to bold causes a paragraph element occurring in the division to also have bold text. The values bolder and lighter are relative to the element's parent font. The declaration is instructing your browser to 'set the font bolder than the parent's value'. Specifying a percentage value sets the font relative to its parent.

You declare a font's size using the font-size property. Valid values are: xx-small, x-small, small, medium, large, x-large, larger, smaller, a percentage or a length. The first five values (xx-small through x-large) are absolute values, as is setting an actual length. The larger, smaller and percentage are relative to its parent's font-size. The relative length units are em, ex and px.

```
p{font-size:16px;} h1{font-size:2em;}
```

Table 8.4 CSS Properties covered in this task	
Property	**Function**
font-weight	Specifies a font's weight.
font-size	Specifies a font's size.

Cross reference

See **tasks_css/task_css_fonts_multiple_tasks/ font_weight.html** for completed example.

When loading the finished task in your browser, you should see the quotation 50% larger than its parent paragraph. The paragraph should be bold, the first span xx-large, the second span normal text (overriding its parent's bold font-weight) and the third span should have inherited the bold font-weight from its parent. The paragraph with an id should be small and light. As an aside, remember the oblique having no effect in the last task? Note that in this task it does. The text in the first span should be slanted.

9 Save and open in your browser.

```
1 <!DOCTYPE HTML PUBLIC "-//W3C//DTD HTML
2 4.01 Transitional//EN"
3 "http://www.w3.org/TR/html4/loose.dtd">
4 <html>
5 <head>
6 <title>Font Weight and Size</title>
7 <style type="text/css">
8 q{font-family:cursive; font-
9 weight:normal;font-size:150%;}
10 p{font-family:arial,sans-serif;font-
11 style:normal; font-weight: bold;}
12 p#disclaimer{font-family:serif;font-
13 style:italic;font-weight:lighter; font-
14 size:small;}
15 </style>
16 </head>
17 <body>
18 <p><q>Which iNtervalTrack version should
19 I buy?</q></p>
20 <p>It depends upon your operating
21 system. Buy the Mac edition for <span
22 style="font-family:arial;font-size:xx-
23 large;font-style:oblique;">OS X</span>,
24 the Linux version for <span
25 style="font-
26 weight:normal;">Linux</span>, and the
27 Windows version for
28 <span>Windows</span>.</p>
29 <p id="disclaimer">Note that only
30 Windows XP, Ubuntu Linux, and Mac OSX
31 Leopard on an Intel, have been
32 tested</p>
33 </body>
34 </html>
```

8

Setting an element's font-weight and size (cont.)

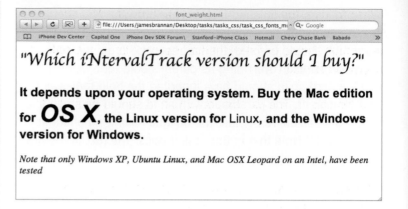

You can specify CSS lengths and widths using several different measurement units. Relative units are: em, ex, and px. The fixed units are: mm, cm, pt, pc, and in. The following table lists the units. In this book, I use the em and px units. The other units are more applicable when printing your document.

For your information

em	The letter "m" height.
ex	The letter "x" height.
px	pixel
mm	millimetre
cm	centimetre
pt	point
pc	pica
in	inch

You don't have to set all the CSS properties for a font using separate declarations. CSS provides a convenient font declaration. Using this declaration, you can set all the font properties at once.

```
p{font: normal bold 12pt Times,serif;}
```

Cross reference

See **tasks_css/task_css_font/task_css_font_property/ font_prop.html** for completed example.

After completing the task, the results are straightforward, although reinforce an important CSS concept. When you specify a style directly in an HTML element's opening tag, it overrides styles already specified for that element type.

```
1 <!DOCTYPE HTML PUBLIC "-//W3C//DTD HTML
2 4.01 Transitional//EN"
3 "http://www.w3.org/TR/html4/loose.dtd">
4 <html>
5 <head>
6 <title>Font Tag All In One
7 Example</title>
8 <style type="text/css">
9 p {font:oblique normal normal xx-large
10 sans-serif;}
11 </style>
12 </head>
13 <body>
14 <p style="font:normal normal small
15 arial">Why am I learning HTML and CSS?
16 Doesn't iWeb do it all for me?</p>
17 <p>Well, yes, you could use iWeb if you
18 want your website to conform to iWeb's
19 predefined templates. In fact, I have a
20 confession. For my shareware product's
21 website...I'm using iWeb. But note, I'm
22 also using iWeb's HTML Snippet
23 functionality extensively. So I still
24 must know HTML. And if you are
25 creative, well forget about applying
```

Setting an element's font using the font declaration

Task Steps

1. Open template.html and save using a different name.

2. Add a paragraph and enter some text in it. (17)

3. Add **<style></style>** tags, to the header element, and then add the font's style as one statement. (8–11)

4. Add another paragraph and assign it an in-line font style. This style overrides the style specified in the header. (14)

5. Save and view in your browser.

8

Setting an element's font using the font declaration (cont.)

```
26 your own style to iWeb.</p>
27 <img src="screen.jpg" width="525"
28 height="404" alt="screen"/>
29 </body>
30 </html>
```

In Chapter 2 you learned several HTML tags for text formatting. But most of the useful HTML formatting tags for text formatting, for instance: the underline element (`<u></u>`), are deprecated. Instead you should use CSS for this type of text formatting. CSS has properties for underlining, crossing out text, making text upper-case or lower-case, making every word begin with a capital letter and even making text blink.

Table 8.5 Text decorations and case properties

Property	Function
text-decoration:underline	Specifies text underlined.
text-decoration:overline	Specifies text has line above text.
text-decoration:line-through	Specifies text has a line through it.
text-decoration:blink	Specifies the text blinks.
text-decoration:none	Specifies no text decoration.
text-transform:uppercase	Specifies text is upper-case.
text-transform:lowercase	Specifies text is lower-case.
text-transform:capitalize	Specifies first letter of every word capitalised.
text-transform:none	Specifies no text transformation.

Upon completing the task and viewing it in a browser, the results are straightforward. The first paragraph is underlined and upper-case, the second is overlined and lower-case, the third is crossed out and every word's initial letter is capitalised and the fourth line blinks.

```
 1 <!DOCTYPE html PUBLIC "-//W3C//DTD HTML
 2 4.01 Transitional//EN"
 3 "http://www.w3.org/TR/html4/loose.dtd">
 4 <html>
 5 <head>
 6 <title>Decoration and Case
 7 Change</title>
 8 </head>
 9 <body>
10 <p style="text-decoration:
```

Decorating text and changing case

Task steps

1. Save template.html using a different name.

2. Add four paragraphs and add content to each. (10, 15, 19, 23)

3. Underline the first paragraph and make it upper-case. (10)

4. Overline the second paragraph and make it lower-case. (15)

5. Strike-out the third paragraph and make every word begin with a capital letter. (19)

6. Make the fourth paragraph blink. (23)

7. Save and view in your browser.

8

Decorating text and changing case (cont.)

```
11  underline;text-
12  transform:uppercase;">This is an
13  underlined paragraph that is also
14  uppercase.</p>
15  <p style="text-decoration:
16  overline;text-transform:lowercase;">THIS
17  IS AN OVERLINE PARAGRAPH THAT IS
18  LOWERCASE.</p>
19  <p style="text-decoration: line-
20  through;text-transform:capitalise;">This
21  is a line-through paragraph where every
22  word's first letter is captialised.</p>
23  <p style="text-decoration: blink;">This
24  is a blinking paragraph, hey what
25  the...I'm not blinking in
26  Safari...someone call Steve Jobs!</p>
27  </body>
28  </html>
```

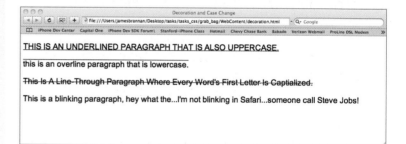

Cross reference

See **tasks/task_css/task_decoration/decoration.html** for completed example.

Sometimes you might wish to left align, right align, centre or justify your paragraphs. The paragraph element has an alignment attribute; however, the attribute is deprecated. Instead you should use the CSS properties to align a paragraph's text.

Table 8.6 Aligning text	
Property	**Function**
text-align:left	Specifies text is left aligned.
text-align:right	Specifies text is right aligned.
text-align:center	Specifies text is centred.
text-align:justify	Specifies text is justified.

Upon completing this task you should see four paragraphs, each one aligned differently. The first should be left justified, the second right justified, the third centred and the fourth justified.

```
1  <!DOCTYPE html PUBLIC "-//W3C//DTD HTML
2  4.01 Transitional//EN"
3  "http://www.w3.org/TR/html4/loose.dtd">
4  <html>
5  <head>
6  <style type="text/css"> div {border-
7  style:solid;margin:5px;}</style>
8  <title>Text alignment</title>
9  </head>
10 <body>
11 <div>
12 <p style="text-align:left;">This is a
13 left justified paragraph. There isn't
14 much to it, it's a typical paragraph.
15 This is just wording to make the
16 paragraph wrap and
17 show the behaviour of the paragraph's
18 alignment.</p>
19 </div>
20 <div>
21 <p style="text-align:right;">This is a
```

Aligning text

Task steps

1 Save template.html using a different name.

2 Add four paragraphs and add enough text to each so they are multi-line. (12, 21, 29, 37)

3 Left justify the first paragraph. (12)

4 Right justify the second paragraph. (21)

5 Centre the third paragraph. (29)

6 Justify the fourth paragraph. (37)

7 Save and view in your browser.

8

Aligning text (cont.)

```
22 right justified paragraph. There isn't
23 much to it, it's a typical paragraph.
24 This is just wording to make the
25 paragraph wrap and show the behaviour
26 of the paragraph's alignment.</p>
27 </div>
28 <div>
29 <p style="text-align:center;">This is a
30 centered paragraph. There isn't much to
31 it, it's a typical paragraph. This is
32 just wording to make the paragraph wrap
33 and show the behaviour of the
34 paragraph's alignment.</p>
35 </div>
36 <div>
37 <p style="text-align:justify;">This is a
38 justified paragraph. There isn't much to
39 it, it's a typical paragraph. This is
40 just wording to make the paragraph wrap
41 and show the behaviour of the
42 paragraph's alignment.</p>
43 </div>
44 </body>
45 </html>
```

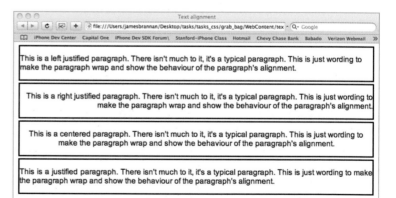

Cross reference

See **tasks/tasks_css/task_csstext_align/textalign.html**
for the completed example.

Sometimes you might wish to add spacing between words or between letters. The CSS word-spacing and letter-spacing properties allow this behaviour to be specified.

Table 8.7 CSS word-spacing and letter-spacing properties	
Property	**Function**
word-spacing	Specifies space added between words.
letter-spacing	Specifies space added between letters.

Upon completing this task and viewing it in your browser the results are straightforward. The paragraph you assigned a 12-px word spacing should have 12px between words. The paragraph you assigned 5px letter spacing should have five pixels between letters.

```
1  <!DOCTYPE html PUBLIC "-//W3C//DTD HTML
2  4.01 Transitional//EN"
3  "http://www.w3.org/TR/html4/loose.dtd">
4  <html>
5  <head>
6  <title>WordSpacing</title>
7  <style>
8  body{background-color:whitesmoke;}
9  </style>
10 </head>
11 <body>
12 <h2>Sometimes you might want extra word
13 spacing or letter spacing.</h2>
14 <p style="word-spacing:12px;">This text
15 has extra word spacing.</p>
16 <p style="letter-spacing:5px;">This text
17 has extra letter spacing.</p>
18 </body>
19 </html>
```

Task steps

1. Save template.html using a different name.
2. Add two paragraphs with content. (14, 16)
3. Assign one paragraph a 12px word-spacing. (14)
4. Assign the other paragraph 5px letter-spacing. (16)
5. Save and display in your browser.

8

Formatting text using word and letter spacing (cont.)

Sometimes you might want extra word spacing or letter spacing.

This text has extra word spacing.

This text has extra letter spacing.

Cross reference

See **tasks/tasks_css/task_word_letter_spacing/word_ letter_spacing.html** for completed example.

For your information

You can also specify a paragraph's wrapping behaviour using the CSS white-space property. Valid values are normal, pre and nowrap.

```
p {white-space: nowrap;}
```

Specifying pre causes the text to preserve all a paragraph's white space. This property's behaviour is the same as the html **<pre>** tag. Specifying nowrap causes the text to not wrap. So if you have a really long text line, you force users to scroll horizontally to read the line.

Using CSS to assign colour

Introduction

Choosing the right colours is as important as choosing the correct fonts. The right colours can make your site feel spooky, professional or even whimsical. Colours, like fonts, help your site convey different feels depending upon your choices. But choosing colours seemingly at random can make your website's pages appear unrelated to one another and unprofessional. Colour is important; ignore it and your site suffers.

Before continuing, a note on style and taste. As this book starts discussing design more, the best advice I can give is do as I say, not necessarily as I do. I'm a programming nerd. On my legs, I have tattoos of a bicycle, a coral snake, a tribal pattern and a naked lady. On my back I have a shark tattoo and my daughter's name. I think bicycles without brakes are

9

What you'll do

Understand Web colours – choosing a palette

Specify a colour four different ways

Set background colours

Set foreground colours

brilliant. I'm 40 years old and still listen to techno music. I shave my legs but my face often goes unshaven. Understand? What is sensible to me might not appear very sensible to you. But rest assured, I won't waste your time – you will learn to format HTML using CSS. This is not a book on design however.

I do, however, include one design task, but it's a safe one – it uses a tool to make a design choice for me. The next section, 'Understanding Web colours – choosing a palette', illustrates how to generate a pleasing colour combination for your website using on-line tools. Based on my colour choices in this and subsequent chapters, I thought it the least I could do. But then again, maybe you too like techno, tattoos and bikes without brakes. And maybe you think Rock Racing's website (**www.rockracing.com**) is an example of brilliant Web design. You have to admit, Rock Racing's website is stunning, if not brilliant.

Colours are specified using RGB, hexadecimal or name values. Much like optimising images, a few years ago a book like this would have opened with a discussion admonishing you to choose web-safe colours. It used to be that you could only count on users having 256 colours. Actually, it was worse than that. You could only rely on Netscape and Internet Explorer consistently displaying 216 different colours. If you wanted your site's colours to look the same across browsers, you limited yourself to those Web-safe colours.

On-line, some people still persist with the myth that you must choose Web-safe colours. It is a myth. You can count on users having thousands, if not millions, of colours; and if you don't believe me, just go to **www.thecounter.com** and look up colour depth statistics. No less then 74 per cent of all Web users have 32-bit colour. Less than 1 per cent have 256 colours. Sixteen bits provide 65,536 colour choices while 32 bits provide 16,777,216 colour choices – plenty of colours to choose from. Media hype aside, even Brazilian favelas have high-speed Internet access and monitors that can display thousands of colours.

Although ample colour choice is available, there are two important design considerations when choosing your site's colours. First, just because you can use thousands of colours doesn't mean you should. Some colours look good together and some don't. Second, many users' monitors aren't calibrated correctly and so might not display subtle colour differences correctly. You might waste hours choosing a subtle, artistic, colour combination that doesn't display well for the majority of your site's users. You should aim for contrast rather than subtle colour differences.

But contrast does not mean your site must be garish, although if you're like me, it does. Which is why I rely on tools that generate colour palettes for me. I don't know about you but, for me, producing a colour palette is a daunting task without a tool.

Completing this task's steps are straightforward: enter a base colour and get back a palette complementing that colour. True, this task advocates removing some of your creativity, for which I

Understanding Web colours – choosing a palette

Task steps

1. Open your Web browser.
2. Navigate to the Color Schemer Online color palette tool (**www.colorschemer.com/ online.html**).
3. Enter #B22222 (firebrick) as the hexadecimal value and click the Set HEX button.
4. A set of complementary colours is displayed.

Understanding Web colours – choosing a palette (cont.)

apologise. If you have good taste, then do it yourself – you don't need a tool. But if you're artistically challenged, like me, then use a palette. Whatever you do, though, don't pick colours at random. Rainbows are for a sky after a thunderstorm, not your website.

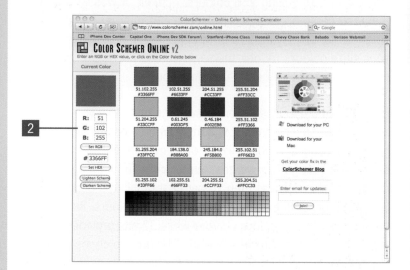

2

Timesaver tip

Adobe Air is the latest in Web technologies. Adobe Air allows you to use interactive Web applications on your desktop without using a browser. The Kuler Desktop application is an Adobe Air application. I didn't use it in this chapter's task because it requires you to download software. But don't worry, Kuler Desktop is made by Adobe Labs and is safe to download. You can find the application at **labs.adobe.com/technologies/kuler**. Somewhere on the page you should see a "Get the Kuler Desktop" link. Click it and download Kuler to your Desktop. If you don't yet have Adobe Air installed, it will install that too. Again, don't worry, Adobe Air is from the same source that brought you the Adobe Flash media player, and I'm sure you have that installed.

Once installed, you can browse countless colour schemes on your desktop. When you find one you like, right click on the swatch, select Copy Theme Values, and then paste the results in a text editor. You should see each colour's hexadecimal value. For more information on Kuler, go to **kuler.adobe.com**, but note that the on-line tool only allows you to save selections as an Adobe Swatch Exchange file (.ase). To view the hexadecimal values easily, you should download the desktop application.

9

Important !

When using a tool such as Kuler Desktop, don't forget that subtle colour differences often do not render well on some monitors. Go for more rather than less colour contrast.

Specifying a colour four different ways

Task steps

1 Save template.html using a different name.

2 In the body add three different `<h1></h1>` tags. Type some text in each. (3, 5, 7)

3 Add the style attribute to each element's tag in this example.

4 In the first `<h1>` tag add the colour firebrick by specifying its name. (4)

5 Add the colour to the second `<h1>` tag by specifying its RGB value. (5)

6 Add the colour to the third `<h1>` tag by specifying its hexadecimal value. (7)

7 Save and view in your browser.

You specify an element's colour one of four different ways. If you pick one of the 216 Web-safe colours, you can usually specify the colour's name.

```
h1{color: cornflowerblue;}
```

You can also specify a colour using its hexadecimal value. The value is case-sensitive, so be careful to use the correct case.

```
h1{color: #6495ED}
```

Or you can specify a colour's RGB value. RGB stands for red, green, blue, and the number signifies the percentage of red, green and blue in a colour. There are two ways to specify colour using RGB. You can specify the percentage of red, green and blue.

```
h1 {color: rgb(39%,58%,93%);}
```

Or you can specify the RGB colour values directly.

```
h1 {color: rgb(100,149,237);}
```

Almost nobody specifies a colour using its RGB percentage. However, the name, hexadecimal value or RGB value are all commonly used.

Table 9.1 The name, RGB and hexadecimal value of a few select colours			
Asparagus	asparagus	rgb(123,160,91)	#7BA05B
Alice Blue	aliceblue	rgb(240,248,255)	#f0f8ff
Blanched Almond	blanchedalmond	rgb(255,235,205)	#ffebcd
Turquoise	turquoise	rgb(64,224,208)	#40e0d0

The results of this task are straightforward. You should see three headings, the text of each should be firebrick red.

```
 1 <html>
 2 <body>
 3 <h1
 4 style="color:firebrick;">firebrick</h1>
 5 <h1 style="color:rgb(178,34,34);">rgb
 6 value: rgb(178,34,34)</h1>
 7 <h1 style="color:#B22222;">hexadecimal
 8 value: #B22222</h1>
 9 </body>
10 </html>
```

9

Cross reference

See **tasks/tasks_css/task_css_color_3way/ color3way.html**

Setting background colour

Task steps

1. Open template.html and save with a new name.

2. Add some text in a paragraph element. Assign the paragraph an id. (13)

3. Create another paragraph. Place **`<div></div>`** tags around it. (19, 20)

4. Add a style element to the header. (19)

5. Assign the body element a beige background colour. (5)

6. Assign the paragraph with the id a whitesmoke background colour. (6)

7. Add the style attribute to the **`<div>`** opening tag and assign it a cyan background colour. (19)

8. Save your work and open in your browser.

Any block-level element may have a background colour. CSS makes background colours possible through the background-colour declaration. An element whose background is declared, when displayed in a Web browser has the specified colour as its background colour.

Table 9.2 Property covered in this task	
Property	**Function**
background-colour	Specifies an element's background colour.

An element's background colour might appear to be inherited, but it's not. Think about it, elements with no background colour specified have a transparent background. You are seeing the back element's background (assuming it had a background colour specified).

Cross reference

See **tasks_css/task_css_background_color/ mailto_background_color.html** for completed example.

Upon completing the task and displaying it in a browser, you should immediately notice how ugly the page is! The body's background should be tan while the paragraph is whitesmoke. The div element's background should be cyan.

```
 1 <html>
 2 <head>
 3 <title>Background Color</title>
 4 <style>
 5 body {background-color: beige;} p#pitch
 6 {background-color: whitesmoke;}
 7 </style>
 8 </head>
 9 <body>
10 <img src="wonder3cc.png" height="200"
11 width="200"/>
12 <h2>Express Your Interest</h2>
```

```
13 <p id="pitch">iNtervalTrack is a
14 multimedia bicycle computer for your
15 Mac, Windows, or even Linux computer.
16 It's easy ---snip--- more information,
17 email me and I'll send you more
18 information.</p>
19 <div style="background-color:cyan;">
20 <p>
21 <img src="mozilla-thunderbird.png"/><a
22 href="mailto:jamesbrannan@xxxxxx.net">
23 Please send me more information.</a>
24 </p></div></body>
25 </html>
```

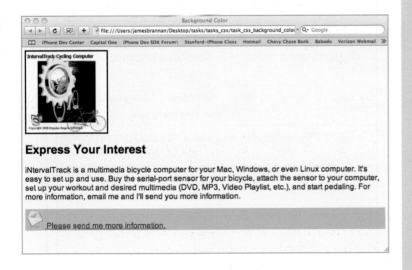

Setting background colour (cont.)

Setting background images

You can specify any block-level element for a background image using the CSS background-image property.

```
body {background-image:
url(./myimage.png);}
```

Table 9.3 Background image CSS properties	
Property	**Function**
background-image: url(path)	Specifies a background image for element.
background-repeat: repeat	Specifies a background image is tiled.
background-repeat: repeat-y	Specifies a background image is tiled vertically.
background-repeat: repeat-x	Specifies a background image is tiled horizontally.
background-repeat: no-repeat	Specifies a background image does not repeat.
background-attachment: fixed	Specifies a background image not scroll with a page (a fixed background).
background-attachment: scroll	Specifies a background image scrolls with the page.
background-position:	Specifies a background image position on page.

You can have a background image tiled horizontally across your page.

```
<style>
body {background-color:
blanchedalmond; background-image:
url(./cyclist27b.tiff); background-
repeat: repeat-x;}
</style>
```

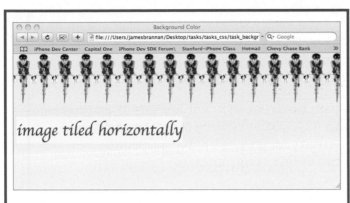

image tiled horizontally

Or you can have a background image tile vertically down
your page.

```
<style>
body {background-color:
blanchedalmond; background-image:
url(./cyclist27b.tiff); background-
repeat: rcpeat-y;}
</style>
```

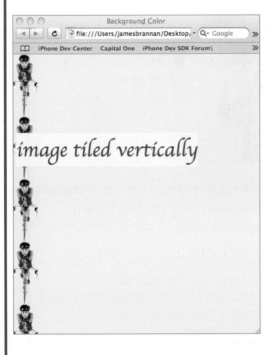

image tiled vertically

Or if you want, you can choose an image and centre it on your page.

```
<style>
body {background-color:
blanchedalmond; background-image:
url(./cyclist27.tiff); background-
repeat:no-repeat; background-
position: top center;}
</style>
```

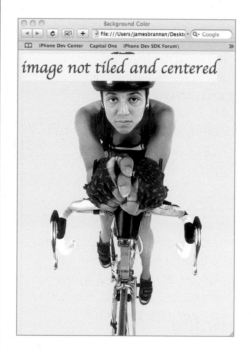

Incidentally, note that the way I made the caption stand out in these screen captures is by creating a span element and making its background colour whitesmoke.

```
<span style="font-size:40px; font-
family:cursive; color:firebrick;
background-color: whitesmoke;">image
not tiled and centered</span>
```

Assigning a colour (foreground colour) to an element is easy when using CSS. You declare the element's colour.

```
body {background-color: black; color:
lime;}
```

The colour property applies to text in elements. This includes formatting HTML tags such as **<em>**, **<strong>** and **<sup>**.

```
strong {color: red;}
em {color: #E3372E;}
```

Any element can have a colour declared; however, setting the colour for an element without text content (such as a horizontal rule) has no effect. Just remember this rule of thumb: no text – no colour, yes text – yes colour.

<table>
<tr><td colspan="2">Table 9.4 Property covered in this task</td></tr>
<tr><td>Property</td><td>Function</td></tr>
<tr><td>color</td><td>Specifies an element's text colour.</td></tr>
</table>

In this task, you learn foreground colour by making a page's body background black and body colour lime. You override the lime colour for one paragraph by setting the paragraph's colour to orange. As with the previous task, the colour choices picked might offend your sensibility; just have fun with it.

Cross reference

See **tasks_css/task_css_foreground_color/foreground. html** for completed example.

After completing the task and loading it in your browser the page should be black. The heading colour should be lime and the paragraph text orange. Notice that the heading has inherited the body's colour.

```
1 <html>
2 <header>
```

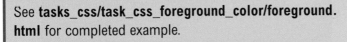

Task steps

1 Open template.html and save using a new name.

2 Declare the body element's background black and its colour lime. (5)

3 Add a heading and a paragraph. (14, 15)

4 Assign the paragraph an orange colour. (7)

5 Display and view the result in your browser.

9

Setting foreground colour (cont.)

Important

If you want your website's CSS to validate, you must limit your colour names to the 17 CSS colour names. These names are: aqua, black, blue, fuchsia, gray, green, lime, maroon, navy, olive, orange, purple, red, silver, teal, white and yellow. If you don't mind whether your page validates – nothing is going to happen if it doesn't – than you can safely use the 216 web-safe colour names. Of course, you can always play it safe and use a colour's RGB or hexadecimal value.

```
 3 <title>Foreground Color</title>
 4 <style>
 5 body {background-color: black; color:
 6 lime;}
 7 p {background-color: black; color:
 8 orange}
 9 </style>
10 </header>
11 <body>
12 <img src="./wonder3cc.png" width="200"
13 height="200"/>
14 <h2>Express Your Interest</h2>
15 <p>iNtervalTrack is a multimedia bicycle
16 computer for your Mac, Windows, or even
17 Linux computer. It's easy ---snip---
18 more information.</p>
19 </body>
20 </html>
```

Jargon buster

Hexadecimal – A base-16 numbering system used to represent binary data (zeros and ones) in a more human friendly way. Used extensively in computer science and electronics field.

Using CSS to format hyperlinks

Introduction

The formatting you applied to other elements in Chapters 8 and 9, can also be applied to hyperlinks. Moreover, you can apply these styles to hyperlinks depending upon the hyperlink's state. You already know a hyperlink's states from using the Web. Hyperlinks can be in one of five states: unvisited, moused-over, focused or active and visited. Before you click on a link, it is unvisited. As you move your mouse over the link, it is moused-over. When you actually click the link it is active. Alternatively, you could say a link has focus when it is actually clicked. After you have clicked the link, it's visited.

Using what's called a pseudo-class, CSS allows you to specify a link's appearance differently depending upon its state. A pseudo-class is so-named because there is no actual class. For example, there are no HTML hyperlink classes called active, hover, link or visited. Active, hover, link, focus and visited are all adjectives describing the hyperlink class. The terms are not bona-fide classes, hence the term pseudo-class.

In this chapter you apply CSS styles to hyperlinks depending upon the link's state. In the first task you change a link's colour using pseudo-classes. In the second task you apply several other formats to hyperlinks. And in the third task you revisit the second task to fix some problems the formatting causes to image links.

Table 10.1 Pseudo-classes for formatting hyperlinks depending upon link's state

Pseudo-class	Meaning
a:link	Refers to unvisited hyperlinks.
a:visited	Refers to visited hyperlinks.
a:active	Refers to hyperlinks selected by mouse and about to activate.
a:hover	Refers to hyperlinks a mouse pointer is currently hovering over.
a:focus	Refers to hyperlinks selected by keyboard and about to activate.

For your information

Timesaver tip

There are more pseudo-classes than the font pseudo-classes discussed in this chapter. The other pseudo-classes are first-child and lang. There are also the following pseudo-elements: first-letter, first-line, before and after. Usage is the same as using pseudo-classes with hyperlinks.

To illustrate the use of pseudo-classes and pseudo-elements, consider the first-child pseudo-class and the first-letter pseudo-element. Using the first-child pseudo-class, you specify that an element that occurs as another element's first child has a style applied to it. For instance,

```
p:first-child {color:orange;}
```

makes any paragraph that is the first child of another element the colour orange. First-letter applies a style to the first letter of some text, for instance,

```
p:first-letter {color:red;font-size:x-large;}
```

would make the first letter of any paragraph element the colour red and the size extra large.

```
<body>
<p>Test</p><p>Test Two</p>
</body>
</html>
```

Table 10.2 Other pseudo-classes and pseudo-elements	
pseudo-classes	
:first-child	Specifies a style is applied to element that is a first child of any other element.
:lang	Specifies a language for an element.
pseudo-elements	
:first-letter	Specifies a style is applied to the first letter in text.
:first-line	Specifies a style is applied to the first line in text.
:before	Specifies content inserted before an element.
:after	Specifies content inserted after an element.

10

Formatting hyperlinks – colour

Task steps

1. Open template.html and save it with a different name.

2. Add a few links to external sites. (13, 17, 20)

3. In the style element, make the link colour brown, the visited colour black, the hover colour red and the active colour orange. (5, 6, 7, 8)

4. Save your work and view in your browser. Click on a link, move your mouse over a link, and notice the link's behaviour.

You can format links to have a different appearance depending upon the link's state. You achieve this by using the link, visited, hover and active pseudo-classes.

Table 10.3 Using a pseudo-class and its effect on hyperlinks

Pseudo-class	Result
a:link {color:red;}	unvisited links are red
a:visited {color: green;}	visited links are green
a:hover {color:orange;}	moused-over links are orange
a:active {color:pink;}	while being clicked, links are pink

Cross reference

Refer to **tasks_css/task_css_hyperlinks/link_states.html** for completed example.

Upon completing the task and viewing the results in your browser, the links should be brown. However, when you move your mouse over a link, the link should turn red. When you click on it, the link should be orange. After clicking on the link, the link should turn black.

```
1 <html>
2 <head>
3 <title>Link States - CSS</title>
4 <style>
5 a:link{color: brown;}
6 a:visited{color: black;}
7 a:hover{color: red;}
8 a:active{color: orange;}
9 </style>
10 </head>
11 <body>
12 <ul>
13 <li><a href="http://www.cyclingnews.com"
14 target="_blank">www.cyclingnews.com -
```

```
15 the first WWW cycling results and news
16 service</a></li>
17 <li><a href="http://www.youtube.com"
18 target="_self">YouTube - Broadcast
19 Yourself</a></li>
20 <li><a href="http://www.chrishoy.com/
21 chris_hoy_biography.html" target="_top">
22 Chris Hoy | Olympic Champion
23 Cyclist</a></li>
24 </ul>
25 </body>
26 </html>
```

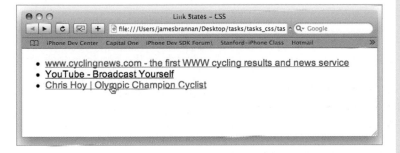

Formatting hyperlinks – lines, borders, background colour

You can format pseudo-classes just as you can format other elements using CSS. You can apply borders, background colours, font styles and various other CSS formatting to the links depending upon their state. In this task, you set a background colour, assign a border and remove the underline from a link. Note, borders are not covered until the next chapter. But using a border is so intuitive, its inclusion in this task should not cause confusion.

Task steps

1. Open the HTML page from the previous task.

2. In the style element, modify visited to have no text-decoration. (6)

3. Modify hover to have a khaki background colour, a 1-pixel solid brown border, an upper-case text-transform and a 2-pixel padding. (9)

4. Save your work and view in your browser.

> **Cross reference**
>
> Refer to **tasks_html/task_css_defining_link_states_multiple_tasks/link_states_underline.html** for completed example.

As you have visited these links already in the previous task, you will probably have to clear your browser's cache to achieve the full effect of this task. Pay particular attention to the behaviour when you move your mouse (hover) over the links. When you mouse-over the links, you browser should paint a box around the link, make the text larger and change its colour.

```
1 <html>
2 <head>
3 <title>Link States - CSS</title>
4 <style>
5 a:link{color: brown;}
6 a:visited{color: black; text-decoration:
7 none;}
8 a:hover{color: red; background-color:
9 khaki; border: 1px solid brown; text-
10 transform: uppercase; padding: 2px;}
11 a:active{color: orange;}
12 </style>
13 </head>
14 <body>
15 <ul>
16 <li><a href="http://www.cyclingnews.com"
17 target="_blank">www.cyclingnews.com -
18 the first WWW cycling results and news
```

```
19 service</a></li>
20 <li><a href="http://www.youtube.com"
21 target="_self">YouTube - Broadcast
22 Yourself</a></li>
23 <li><a href="http://www.chrishoy.com/
24 chris_hoy_biography.html" target="_top">
25 Chris Hoy | Olympic Champion
26 Cyclist</a></li>
27 </ul>
28 </body>
29 </html>
```

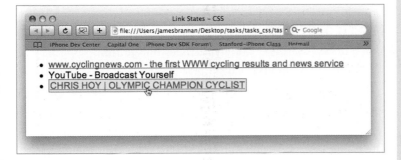

Formatting hyperlinks – image links

Task steps

1. Open the template and save with a different name.

2. Add the link formatting from the previous task to the style element of this new page.

3. Add an image link. (16)

4. Save and display in your browser.

5. In order to see the difference, add two regular links and assign them a class name, which is different from the image class name. (40, 42)

6. Modify the link in the style element. Change the link formatting to refer to only the class name of the two newly created links.

7. Save your work and display in your Web browser. (25–32)

As interesting as the last task was, there are always dangers when applying a global format to all elements in your site. The previous task's special effects work fine for text links, but what about image links? What happens to an image in a hyperlink when you specify that a hyperlink has a border and background colour? The results are not what you would expect.

In this task you see what can happen if your aren't careful and how you can fix the problem. The task is split into two parts. First, we add an image link incorrectly, then we fix the problem.

Cross reference

See **tasks_css/task_css_hyperlinks/imagelink_ imagestates_incorrect.html** and **tasks_css/task_css_ hyperlinks/imagelink_imagestates_correct.html** for completed examples.

Once this task is complete move your cursor over the image and observe the results – not what you wanted at all. The problem is that the link style was specified for all hyperlinks. Instead, what you need to do is define separate classes for text versus image links using the class attribute (alternatively, you could also use the id attribute just as effectively).

```
1  <html>
2  <head>
3  <title>Image Links The Wrong Way</title>
4  <style>
5  a:link{color: brown;}
6  a:visited{color: black; text-decoration:
7  none;}
8  a:hover{color: red; background-color:
9  khaki; border: 1px solid brown; text-
10 transform: uppercase; padding: 2px;}
11 a:active{color: orange;}
12 img {border-style: none;}
13 </style>
14 </head>
15 <body>
```

```
16 <a href="http://www.freebsd.org"><img
17 src="./freebsd.png" height="128"
18 width="128"/></a>Free BSD<br/><br/>
19 </body>
20 </html>
```

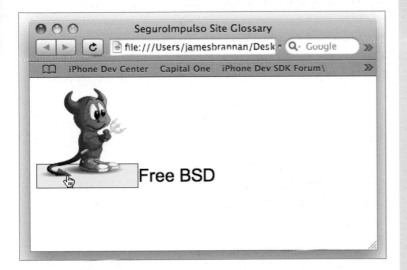

The image link should no longer have the khaki box when you
hover over the image. However, the two newly created links do.
It looks and behaves as expected.

```
21 <html>
22 <head>
23 <title>Correct Image Link</title>
24 <style type="text/css">
25 a.special:link{color: brown;}
26 a.special:visited{color: black; text-
27 decoration: none;}
28 a.special:hover{color: red; background-
29 color: khaki; border: 1px solid brown;
30 text-transform: uppercase; padding:
31 2px;}
32 a.special: active{color: orange;}
33 img {border-style: none;}
34 </style>
35 </head>
36 <body>
37 <a href="http://www.freebsd.org"><img
```

Formatting hyperlinks – image links (cont.)

```
38 src="./freebsd.png" height="128"
39 width="128"/></a>Free BSD<br/><br/>
40 <a class="special" href="http://www.
41 freebsd.org">FreeBSD </a>
42 <a class="special" href="http://www.
43 openbsd.org">OpenBSD </a>
44 </body>
45 </html>
```

Using CSS to assign padding, margins and borders

Introduction

CSS provides many properties for formatting your HTML document. In previous chapters you learned to apply fonts and colours to elements. In this chapter you learn CSS formatting properties that allow you to set an element's padding, margin and borders. You also learn CSS formatting properties for setting an element's height and width.

Understanding an element's padding, margin and borders is straightforward. An element is composed of its opening tag, closing tag, and all content in between the two tags. The box model refers to picturing all elements visually as a box that contains content and padding, and has borders and margins.

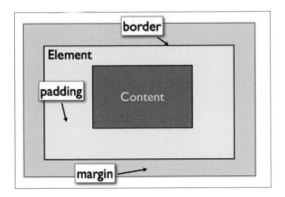

What you'll do

Set element padding

Set element margins

Set element borders

Set width and height – percentage

Set width and height – pixels

Padding is the space between a box's content and its border. A border is an invisible, or visible, line around the box. The margin is the space between a box's border and the margin of an adjacent box, or between the box's border and its parent's border minus its parent's padding.

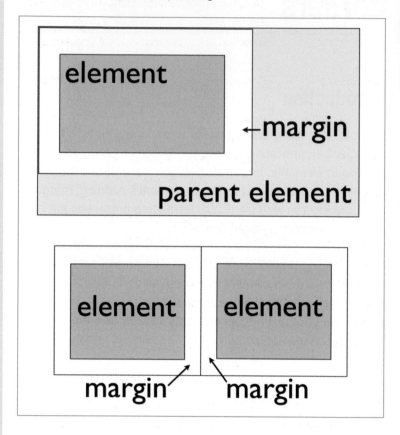

Table 11.1 CSS box properties covered in this chapter

Property	Function
padding-left	Specifies space between element's content and left border.
padding-right	Specifies space between element's content and right border.
padding-top	Specifies space between element's content and top border.
padding-bottom	Specifies space between element's content and bottom border.
padding	Specifies the space between an element's content and the element's border.
margin	
margin-left	Specifies element's space buffer to the left.
margin-right	Specifies element's space buffer to the right.
margin-top	Specifies element's space buffer to the top.
margin-bottom	Specifies element's space buffer to the bottom.
margin	Specifies element's space buffer.
border	
border-left-style	Specifies element's left border style (i.e. dashed, dotted, solid, etc.).
border-left-colour	Specifies element's left border colour.
border-left-width	Specifies element's left border width.
border-right-style	Specifies element's right border style.
border-right-colour	Specifies element's right border colour.
border-right-width	Specifies element's right border width.
border-top-style	Specifies element's top border style.
border-top-colour	Specifies element's top border colour.
border-top-width	Specifies element's to border width.
border-bottom-style	Specifies element's bottom border style.
border-bottom-colour	Specifies element's bottom border colour.
border-bottom-width	Specifies element's bottom border width.
border-style	Specifies element's border style (all borders).
border-colour	Specifies element's border colour.
border-width	Specifies element's border width.

11

Width, min-width, max-width, height, min-height and max-height are all box properties. In order to understand these properties, you need to understand block-level elements. An in-line element is an element displayed in the same line as other content. In-line elements may contain other in-line elements but not block-level elements. A block-level element is displayed on a new line. Block-level elements are intended to hold both other block-level elements and in-line elements. Only block-level elements can have a width, height, min-width, min-height, max-width or max-height specified.

Table 11.2 CSS height and width properties	
Property	**Function**
width	Specifies a block-level element's width.
min-width	Specifies a block-level element's minimum width.
max-width	Specifies a block-level element's maximum width.
height	Specifies a block-level element's height.
min-height	Specifies a block-level element's minimum height.
max-height	Specifies a block-level element's maximum height.

You can set an element's internal padding using the CSS padding property. The amount of space between an element's content and border is the element's padding. For example,

```
p {padding: 5px;}
```

assigns a 5-pixel padding between the paragraph's text and border.

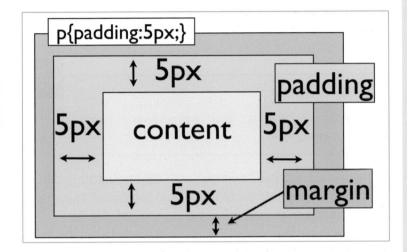

When setting padding, you can specify the top, bottom, left and right padding individually as separate declarations:

```
p{padding-top:2px;padding-
bottom:3px;padding-left:3px;padding-
right:4px;}
```

in one declaration:

```
p{padding: 2px 3px 3px 4px;}
```

or, if the values are all the same, you can set all four properties using one value:

```
p{padding:4px;}
```

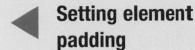

Setting element padding

Task steps

1. Save template.html with a different name.

2. Add two paragraphs. Assign both different id attribute values. (22, 24)

3. Add a style element and give the first paragraph a solid, orange, 2-pixel-wide border. (8)

4. Assign the second paragraph a solid, 2-pixel, lime border. (11)

5. Modify the first paragraph's style to have a 5-pixel padding. Set all four paddings in one statement. (10)

6. Modify the second paragraph's style to have a 2-pixel top padding, 20-pixel bottom padding, and 5-pixel right and left padding. Set all four padding properties separately. (12–15)

7. Add an image and – even though the attribute is deprecated – assign it a left alignment. (20)

8. Save and open in your browser.

11

Setting element padding (cont.)

Table 11.3 Padding properties	
Property	**Function**
padding-top	Specifies an element's top padding.
padding-bottom	Specifies an element's bottom padding.
padding-left	Specifies an element's left padding.
padding-right	Specifies an element's right padding.
padding	Specifies an element's padding.

Cross reference

See **tasks_css/task_css_padding/padding.html** for completed example.

Pretty brilliant, too bad the image uses deprecated attributes. The paragraph borders should be visible behind the image, and the text wrapping around the image on its right. But the important result you should see is the space between the right side of the image and the left side of the text, padded by 5 pixels. Actually, the results are not that brilliant. As you will see in Chapter 12, this type of formatting is simple using CSS absolute positioning. Moreover, you can achieve the results without using deprecated attributes as this example does.

```
1 <html>
2 <header>
3 <title>Padding</title>
4 <style>
5 body {background-color: black; color:
6 lime;}
7 p#pitch {color: orange; font-style:
8 italic; border-style: solid; border-
9 width :2px; border-color: orange;
10 padding: 5px 5px 5px 5px;}
11 p#easy {color: lime; line-height: 2px;
12 border-style: solid; border-width: 2px;
13 border-color: lime; padding-top: 2px;
14 padding-bottom: 20px; padding-left: 5px;
15 padding-right: 5px;}
```

```
16 </style>
17 </header>
18 <body>
19 <h2>iNtervalTrack Is Easy</h2>
20 <img id="system" src="system.png"
21 align="left"/>
22 <p id="pitch">iNtervalTrack is a
23 ---snip--- cross platform.</p>
24 <p id="easy">It's easy to set up and
25 use. ---snip--- Video Playlist, etc.),
26 and start pedalling.</p>
27 </body>
28 </html>
```

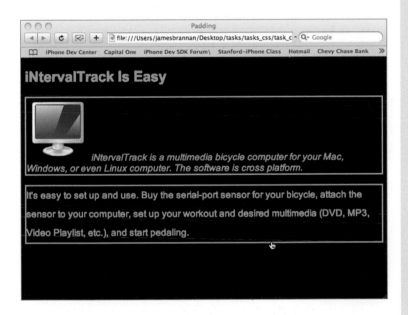

Setting element margins

Margins are the spaces between elements. A margin is the space around an element's border. It's a cushion around an element's border that no other elements may pass. For instance, if two elements had a 5-pixel margin, the space between them would be 10 pixels.

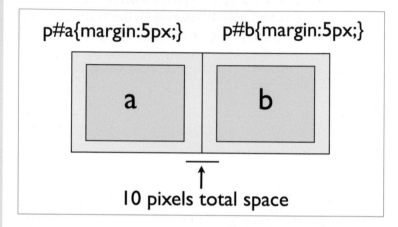

Elements have right, left, top and bottom margins. You can set the margins separately or together in one declaration. A margin's width can be a length, a percentage or auto. As with other elements, length is a fixed measurement and percentage refers to the margin's parent element. Auto lets the browser determine the best margin.

Task steps

1. Save template.html using a different name.

2. Add four paragraphs and add three images.

3. Assign each paragraph its own unique id attribute.

4. Give the images a 1-pixel, solid black border and a 2-pixel margin. (6)

5. For the first paragraph, assign all margins using the margin declaration. Make the top margin 10 pixels, the right 200, the bottom 20 and the left 13. (8)

6. Assign the second paragraph the same margin values as the first, only this time declare each margin separately. (11, 12)

7. For the third paragraph, assign a 50% right margin. (13)

8. Assign the fourth paragraph a 25% left margin. (15)

9. Assign the images a 2-pixel margin. (6)

Table 11.4 CSS margin properties	
Property	**Function**
margin-right	Specifies an element's right margin.
margin-left	Specifies an element's left margin.
margin-top	Specifies an element's top margin.
margin-bottom	Specifies an element's bottom margin.
margin	Specifies an element's margin.

Cross reference

See **tasks_css/task_css_setting_margin/margin.html** for completed example.

The results are straightforward, each paragraph has the specified margin around its border. Note the two different ways margins are rendered. When an element is contained inside another element (its parent), and there is no adjacent element also contained in the the same parent, the margin is the space the contained element is from its parent's border. The paragraphs in this task are all displayed on their own line. This is because a paragraph is a block-level element and is assigned its own new line. The images, in contrast, are in-line elements and illustrate the other way a browser renders a margin. The three images that are in a row in the last div each have four pixels between their borders. That's because each image has a 2-pixel margin. Each image has a 2-pixel top margin between it and its parent div element.

```
1 <html>
2 <head>
3 <title>Margins</title>
4 <style>
5 div {border-style: dotted; margin:5px;}
6 img {border-style: solid; border-color:
7 black; border-width: 1px; margin: 2px;}
8 p#a {border-style: dotted; margin: 10px
9 200px 20px 13px;}
10 p#b {border-style: dotted;margin-
11 top:10px; margin-right:200px; margin-
12 bottom:20px; margin-left:13px;}
13 p#c {border-style:dotted;margin-right:
14 50%;}
15 p#d {border-style:dotted;margin-
16 left:25%;}
17 </style>
18 </head>
19 <body>
20 <img src="freebsd.png" height="128"
21 width="128"/>
22 <h2>From James's warped mind...</h2>
23 <div>
24 <p id="a">Did you know that Mac OS X
25 uses ---snip--- leverage my boring day
26 job skills when I do cool multimedia
27 programming at night.</p>
```

10 Wrap each paragraph in **`<div></div>`** tags and assign the div element a dotted border. Make the bottommost div element wrap the images also. (23, 29, 33)

11 Save and display in your browser.

11

Setting element margins (cont.)

```
28 </div>
29 <div>
30 <p id="b">Mac OS X supports ---snip---
31 Linux desktop.</p>
32 </div>
33 <div>
34 <img src="ubuntu-logo.png" /><img
35 src="suse.png"/><img src="openbsd.png"/>
36 <p id="c">Of course, I'd rather ---snip-
37 -- exactly a good career move for a
38 wanna-be multimedia programmer!</p>
39 <p id="d">Where the open ---snip--- And
40 that's all I have to say about that.
41 </p>
42 </div>
43 </body>
44 </html>
```

From James's warped mind...

Did you know that Mac OS X uses a FreeBSD version as its base operating system? The user-friendly Mac is UNIX at its core! I really like OS X because I can leverage my boring day job skills when I do cool multimedia programming at night.

Mac OS X supports Bash scripting, C POSIX, and most other UNIX programming constructs. Sure, it is probably better to use Objective-C and Cocoa (and I do plan on taking them up eventually), but when will I use that at work? To me, OS X seems like a well thought-out Linux desktop.

Of course, I'd rather program for the real thing, like Ubuntu, SUSE, or OpenBSD, but when's the last time a Linux user paid for anything? Not exactly a good career move for a wanna-be multimedia programmer!

Where the open source model really thrives is at the university. Universities can share the results of their research with the larger community. Open source gives back value from Universities. FreeBsd, for example, comes from BSD, which was a product of the University of California, Berkley. So everyone benefits, the professors, the students, and industry. And that's all I have to say about that.

Elements have borders. Even if you don't specify a border, it's still there. The border separates an element's padding from its margin. You have many options when setting an element's border. You can specify a border's colour, style and width. You can specify an element's right, left, top and bottom border properties separately, or in one statement. You can also specify each side's border in one statement.

Table 11.5 Border CSS properties

Property	Function
border-left-colour	Specifies left border's colour.
border-left-style	Specifies left border's style.
border-left-width	Specifies left border's width.
border-left	Specifies left border's colour, style, width.
(the same for right, top, and bottom)	
border-colour	Specifies a border's colour.
border-style	Specifies a border's style.
border-width	Specifies a border's width.

Valid border colours are any valid colour name, RGB colour value or hexadecimal value. Valid width values are thin, medium, thick or a length. Valid styles are none, hidden, dotted, dashed, solid, double, groove, ridge, inset or outset.

Cross reference

See **tasks_css/task_css_border/borders.html** for completed example.

```
1 <html>
2 <header>
3 <title>Border Example</title>
4 <style>
5 body {background-color: black; color:
6 lime;}
```

◀ Setting element borders

Task steps

1 Open template.html and save with a different name.

2 For dramatic effect, make the background black. (5)

3 Create three paragraphs, make the first one have an orange colour, the second lime and the third red. (7, 11, 15)

4 Add a padding of 5 pixels. (7, 11, 15)

5 Give the first paragraph an orange, solid border, that is 2 pixels wide. Do this for the entire border using the border-style, border-width and border-colour declarations. (7–10)

6 Give the second paragraph a lime, dotted border, that is 2 pixels wide. Do this for the entire border. (11)

7 Set the third paragraph's right border as 8 pixels, solid and orange. (15)

8 Set the third paragraph's left border as 2 pixels, dashed and red. (15)

11

Setting element borders (cont.)

9 Set the third paragraph's top border as 1 pixel, grooved and orange. (15)

10 Set the third paragraph's bottom border as 5 pixels, red and ridged. (19)

11 Add an image to the HTML page and make it an image link. (25–26)

12 Save and display in your browser.

```
7 p#a {background-color: black; color:
8 orange; font-style: italic; border-
9 style: solid; border-width :2px;
10 border-color: orange; padding: 5px;}
11 p#b {background-color: black; color:
12 lime; border-style: dotted; border-width
13 : 2px;border-color: lime; padding: 5px;}
14 img#system { border-style: none;}
15 p#c {color: red; border-right: 8px solid
16 orange; border-left: 2px dashed red;
17 border-top: 1px groove orange; border-
18 bottom-width:5px; border-bottom-style:
19 ridge; border-bottom-color: red;
20 padding: 5px;}
21 </style>
22 </header>
23 <body>
24 <a id="apple_link"href="http://www.
25 apple.com"><img id="system" src="system.
26 png"/></a>
27 <p id="a">Solid</p>
28 </div>
29 <p id="b">Dashed</p>
30 </body>
31 <p id="c">Ugly</p>
32 </html>
```

CSS allows you to set an element's width and height. You declare an element's width by setting the width property. You declare an element's height by setting the height property. Both property's values can be auto, a length or a percentage.

How you set an element's width and height is important when determining a page's layout. So much so, that this task is divided into setting a relative width and height in this task, and setting a fixed width and height in the next task. When setting a relative width and height, the size of the element is determined in relationship to its containing parent. For example, if a div element is 50% of the width of a page, and the div element contains a paragraph with a 50% width, then the paragraph's width is 50% of the div element and 25% of the total page width. Absolute length values define the height and width of an element, regardless of the element's containing parent. Moreover, as you resized your browser, elements with a relative width and height resize themselves in relation to the browser; elements with a fixed height and width do not.

Cross reference

See **tasks_css/task_css_width_height/width_height.html** for completed example.

After completing the task view it in your browser. The two paragraphs inside the div element should be sized in relation to the div element. The paragraph you assigned a 50% width is 50% of its parent div element and 25% of the page's width. The other paragraph is its default size. Notice that the image was stretched to take 75% of the page.

```
1 <html>
2 <header>
3 <title>Width and Height</title>
4 <style>
5 body {background-color: whitesmoke;}
6 p#a {background-
7 color:white;color:red;border-
8 style:solid;border-color:red;border-
9 width:2px;width:15%;height:25%;}
```

Task steps

1. Save template.html using a new name.

2. Add three paragraphs. Assign each paragraph a solid border.

3. Assign the first paragraph a 15% width and a 25% height. (9)

4. Assign the second paragraph a 50% width and a 25% height. (12)

5. Leave the third paragraph as is.

6. Wrap the second and third paragraph in **<div></div>** tags. (27)

7. Assign the div element a 50% width and a 50% height. Give the tag a dotted, 2-pixel black border. (17)

8. Add an image to the page. In the style element, declare the image's width as 75%. (20)

9. Save and display in your browser. Resize your browser's window a few times.

11

Setting width and height (Percentage) (cont.)

```
10 p#b {background-color:white;color:blue;
11 border-style:solid;border-width:
12 2px;border-color:blue;width:50%;
13 height:25%}
14 p#c {background-color:white;color:green;
15 border-style:solid;border-width:2px;
16 border-color:green;}
17 div#d {width:50%;height:50%;border-
18 style:dotted;border-width:2px; border-
19 color:black;}
20 img {width:75%}
21 </style>
22 </header>
23 <body>
24 <img src="./system.png" width="128"
25 height="128"/>
26 <p id="a">Blue</p>
27 <div id="d">
28 <p id="b">Green</p>
29 <p id="c">Red</p>
30 <div>
31 </body>
32 </html>
```

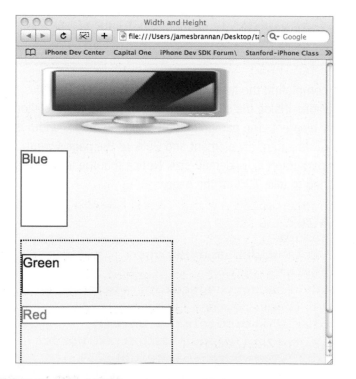

In the last task you set width and height using percentages. This made the element's width and height relational to its parent. When the page's dimensions changed, because the calculations were percentages, they changed too. When you set a width and height using a measurement, an element's width and height are no longer a relationship to its parent's dimensions. Instead, the element Is sized precisely to the specified width and height and remains at that width and height.

Cross reference
See **tasks css/task_css_width_height/width_height_abs.html** for completed example.

The first paragraph no longer resizes as the browser resizes. The div element and the first paragraph in the div element should no longer resize horizontally, but they should resize vertically. The image is now squeezed to a smaller size than its actual width, distorting the image.

```
1  <html>
2  <header>
3  <title>Width and Height Absolute</title>
4  <style>
5  body {background-color: whitesmoke;}
6  p#a {background-color: white; color:
7  red; border-style: solid; border-color:
8  red; border-width : 2px; width: 200px;
9  height:20px;}
10 p#b {background-color: white; color:
11 blue; border-style: solid; border-width
12 : 2px;
13 border-color: blue; width: 400px;
14 height: 25%}
15 p#c {background-color: white; color:
16 green; border-style: solid; border-width
17 : 2px; border-color: green; }
18 div#d {width: 500px; height:50%; border-
19 style:dotted; border-width: 2px; border-
20 color:black;}
21 img {width: 50px;}
```

Setting width and height (pixels)

Task steps

1. Save your work from the previous task with a different name.
2. Assign the image an absolute width that is smaller than the actual width of the image. (21)
3. Change the first paragraph's width and height to 200 pixels by 20 pixels. (8)
4. Change the second paragraph's width to 400 pixels. Leave its height as 25%. (13)
5. Change the division element to be 500 pixels wide. Leave its height as 50%. (18)
6. Save and view in your browser.

11

Setting width and height (pixels) (cont.)

```
22 </style>
23 </header>
24 <body>
25 <img src="./system.png" width="128"
26 height="128"/>
27 <p id="a">Blue</p>
28 <div id="d">
29 <p id="b">Green</p>
30 <p id="c">Red</p>
31 <div>
32 </body>
33 </html>
```

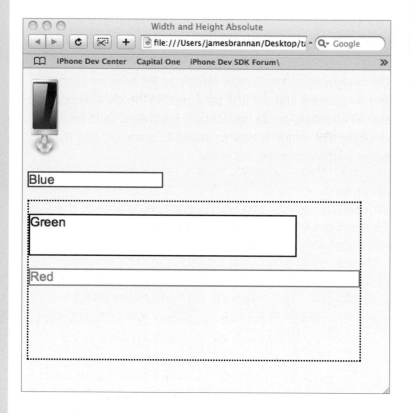

Positioning elements using CSS

Introduction

Web browsers normally position elements in the same order the elements appear in the source for an html page. In-line elements, such as the **** tags, are placed left to right, while block-level elements, such as the **\<p>\</p>** tags, are placed on a new line. This flow is the browser's normal layout flow and follows the natual flow that we read text in the West – the same flow as the flow on this page.

You can override a browser's normal flow using CSS to specify an element's positioning on a Web page. In this chapter you learn positioning elements using relative, absolute and fixed positioning. You also learn how to position an element to the left or right of other elements.

You have already learned that CSS views elements as a box, and this concept is called the box model. You have also learned the difference between block-level and in-line elements. Remember, in-line elements can only contain other in-line elements while block-level elements can contain both in-line and other block-level elements. Also remember that an element contains its opening tag, closing tag and everything in between the two tags. A **\<p>\</p>** tagset that contained text and an **\<img/>** tag also contains the **\<img/>** tag. If **\<div>\</div>** tags wrap the paragraph, than the div element contains the paragraph element. The div element also contains everything in the paragraph element; it's the grandfather of the paragraph's child elements.

What you'll do

Position elements using float and clear

Position elements using relative positioning

Position elements using absolute positioning

Position elements using fixed positioning

Table 12.1 Positioning concepts covered in this chapter	
Concept	**Function**
float	Specifies an element is aligned to the left or right of other normal flowing elements.
clear	Specifies no other normal flowing elements may float to the right, left, or both, of an element.
relative	Specifies an element is positioned relative to its default positioning by the browser.
absolute	Specifies an element is positioned in a user-specified position within the element's parent container (provided parent container's position is specified as relative, absolute or static).
static	Specifies an element is positioned in a user-specified position in a browser's viewport.

```
<div><p><img src="myimage.png"/>This is
my paragraph</p></div>
```

When positioning an element you position it within its containing block-level element, one of the element's ancestor block-level elements, or within a browser's display window (the viewport).

For your information

Browsers are often very forgiving, **<b><p>I'm illegal.</p></b>** will display perfectly well even though it is incorrect. You will also find that you can apply formatting to some in-line elements illegally.

```
<b style="float:left;">I make no
sense.</b>
```

Browsers turn the in-line element into a block-level element, but, in my humble opinion, you really should keep block-level elements block-level and in-line elements in-line. My advice is, if you want to display something as a block, then use a block-level tag.

```
<div style="float:left;"><b>I make
sense.</b></div>
```

Incidentally, you can do the same hack as your browser using the CSS display property. By assigning an element the CSS display property the value block forces a browser to treat the element as a block-level element. Conversely, assigning the property in-line forces a browser to treat an element as an in-line element.

```
<b style="display:block;float:left;
">I make no sense.</b>
```

12

Positioning elements using float and clear

You use the float property to move an element as far to the right or left as possible within the affected element's parent. Other normal flowing elements flow around the floated element to the right or to the left. Specifying an element floats right instructs browsers to place other normal flowing elements to the left of the floated element. Specifying an element floats left instructs browsers to place other normal flowing elements to the right of the floated element.

Remember how I admonished you to not use the HTML align property in the image tag because it's deprecated? I promised you that you would learn a better way using CSS. CSS float is that better way. If you want an image to float to the left of a paragraph you choose float:left. If you want an image to float right, you choose float:right;

Task steps

1. Save template.html with a new name.

2. Add a paragraph, make it a long one. (21)

3. Add two images just below the body tag. Give both a different id. (16, 18)

4. Declare that the image floats left. Format the image as desired. (8)

5. Declare that the second image floats right. (10)

6. Declare that no element can float left of the image. (11)

7. Add a small image three times just below the **<p>** tag. Assign the images the same class name. Give each image a different title attribute value. (22–24)

8. Add the same small image three times somewhere in the middle of the paragraph. Assign the images the same class name as in step 6. Give each image a different title attribute value. (30–35)

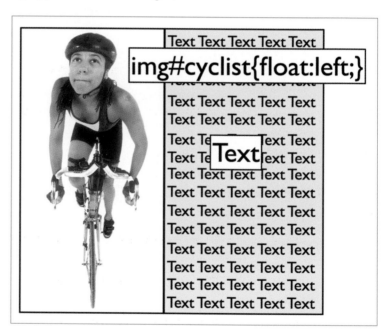

The CSS clear property is used the same as the HTML clear attribute in the **
** tag. The clear property specifies that an element is not allowed to have another floated element float to it's left, right or both.

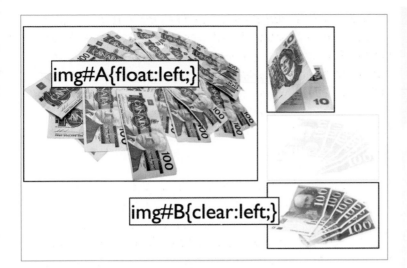

9 Declare that the small images are to float right. (30–35)

10 Save and view in your browser.

Table 12.2 Float and clear possible values	
Float	**Function**
left	Specifies an element floats left of other normal flowing elements.
right	Specifies an element floats right of other normal flowing elements.
none	Specifies an element doesn't float.
inherit	Specifies an element inherits its containing ancestor's float value.
Clear	**Function**
both	Specifies that no floated elements may float either left or right of an element.
left	Specifies that no floated elements may float left of an element.
right	Specifies that no floated element may float right of an element.
none	Allows other elements to float left, right or both left and right of this element.
inherit	Specifies the block-level element inherits its containing ancestor's clear value.

12

Positioning elements using float and clear (cont.)

Cross reference

See **tasks_css/css_positioning/float.html** for completed example.

The topmost image should float to the left of the text. The second image should float to the right of the text. The first image doesn't float to the left of the second image because the second image used the clear property to declare that nothing should float to its left. So the browser places the second image on the first line below the first image. The smaller images should each float to the right. Note that they float in the reverse order they are added to the page. Also notice if you resize your browser vertically, as the viewport shrinks the small images float to a new position.

```
1  <!DOCTYPE html PUBLIC "-//W3C//DTD HTML
2  4.01 Strict//EN"
3  "http://www.w3.org/TR/html4/strict.dtd">
4  <html>
5  <head>
6  <title>Float Example</title>
7  <style>
8  img#a {float:left; margin:5px; border:
9  dotted 1px black;}
10 img#b {float:right; margin: 5px;
11 border: dotted 1px black; clear:left;}
12 img.tux {float:right; margin:2px;}
13 </style>
14 </head>
15 <body>
16 <img id="a" src="./images/openbsd.png"
17 height="128" width="128" />
18 <img id="b" src="./images/
19 advancedsettings.png" height="128"
20 width="128"/>
21 <p>
22 <img class="tux" src="./images/tux.png"
23 title="1"/><img class="tux"
24 src="./images/tux.png" title="2"/><img
25 class="tux" src="./images/tux.png"
26 title="3"/>
```

```
27 This is a sentence. It has no meaning.
28 There is no context. ---snip--- This
29 paragraph is not meaningful and there
30 is no reason to read it. <img
31 class="tux" src="./images/tux.png"
32 title="1"/><img class="tux"
33 src="./images/tux.png" title="2"/><img
34 class="tux" src="./images/tux.png"
35 title="3"/>
36 This is a sentence. It has no meaning.
37 ---snip--- There is no context. This
38 paragraph is not meaningful and there
39 is no reason to read it.</p>
40 </body>
41 </html>
```

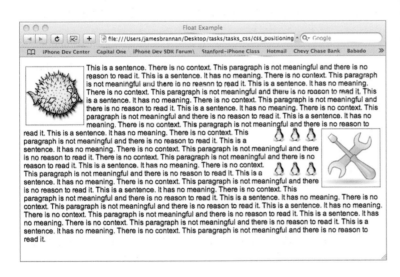

12

Positioning elements using float and clear (cont.)

Relative positioning allows you to position items relative to the item's normal position, as positioned by a browser. Relative positioning allows you to specifying how many pixels left, right, above or below an element's normal position using the left, right, top and bottom offsets. For instance, you might specify an image is 15 pixels down and 10 pixels right of its normal position.

```
img {position:relative; left:10px;
top:15px;}
```

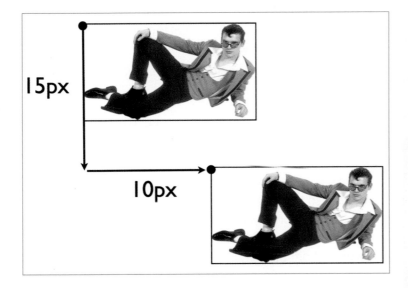

Cross reference

See **tasks_css/css_positioning/position_relative.html** for completed example.

Positioning elements using relative positioning

Task steps

1. Save template.html using a different name.

2. Add four **<div></div>** tags. Assign two different class names and two the same class name. Add some text in each div element. (27, 29, 31)

3. Wrap the four div tags in an outer div element. (24)

4. Assign one div a relative position and specify that it is −50 pixels from its normal left position. (14)

5. Assign one div a relative position and specify that it is 100 pixels from its normal left position and 50 pixels down from its normal position. (18)

6. Give all div elements different background colours and assign them all a border. (24, 27, 29, 31)

7. Save and view in your browser.

12

Positioning elements using relative positioning (cont.)

Table 12.3 Property covered in this task and its offsets	
Property	**Function**
position:relative	Specifies an element is positioned relative to the element's normal positioning by a browser.
left	Specifies an element is positioned to the right of its normal position.
right	Specifies an element is positioned to the left of its normal position.
top	Specifies an element is positioned down from its normal position.
bottom	Specifies an element is positioned up from its normal position.

The div you assigned a –50px value for the left property should be off your browser's viewing area on the left. That's because a browser would normally have positioned four block-level div elements one after another, each on a new line, aligned left. You instructed the browser to move the element 50 pixels to the left from its normal position. The div you assigned a 50px and 100px value should be 50 pixels to the right and 100 pixels down from the element's normal position.

```
 1 <!DOCTYPE html PUBLIC "-//W3C//DTD HTML
 2 4.01 Strict//EN"
 3 "http://www.w3.org/TR/html4/strict.dtd">
 4 <html>
 5 <head>
 6 <style type="text/css">
 7 span {margin 2px; padding: 5; }
 8 div.outer {height:50%; border: dotted
 9 1px black; margin-bottom:10px;
10 background: whitesmoke;}
11 div.normal{border: solid 1px black;
12 margin: 5px; background: tan;
13 width:400px;}
14 div.left{position:relative;left:
15 -50px;margin: 5px;background:
16 yellow;border: solid 1px
17 black;width:400px;}
```

```
18 div.right{position:relative;left:100px;
19 top:50px;margin: 5px; border: solid 1px
20 black;background: khaki;width:400px;}
21 </style>
22 </head>
23 <body>
24 <div class="outer">
25 <span>Div elements positioned
26 relative</span>
27 <div class="normal"><span>1. Normal
28 position.</span></div>
29 <div class="left"><span>2. Moved left
30 of normal position.</span></div>
31 <div class="right"><span>3. Moved right
32 and down from normal
33 position.</span></div>
34 <div class="normal"><span>4. Normal
35 position.</span></div>
36 </div>
37 </body>
38 </html>
```

Relative positioning is useful when you want to slightly modify an element's position. Without having to specify the element's exact position, you can slightly move the element relative to its normal position.

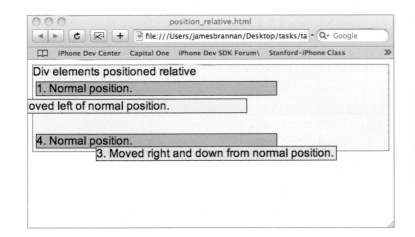

12

Positioning elements using absolute positioning

Task steps

1. Save template.html using a different name.

2. Add an image to the page five times. (27, 30, 33, 36, 40)

3. Wrap four images in **`<div></div>`** tags. Assign each div element a different id. (26, 29, 32, 35)

4. Add a border to all div elements.

5. Create styles for all four div elements. Assign them all an absolute position. (15, 17, 19, 21)

6. Position one div element right 5 pixels and down 250 pixels from the top left corner of your browser. (15)

7. Position one div element down 100 pixels and left 25 pixels from the top right corner of your browser. (17)

8. Position one div element up 20% and left 30% from the bottom left corner of your browser. (19)

This is a long but important task. If you want to create brilliant websites, you must understand absolute positioning. Absolute positioning is slightly confusing at first, but once it clicks it should prove easy. For me, the key is to think of my browser's – or parent block-level element's – four corners. After I realised that, absolute positioning became easy.

To position an element at a fixed location on the screen, you specify that it uses absolute positioning.

```
img#a {position:absolute;}
```

Specifying an element uses absolute positioning removes it from the normal browser layout flow. Your browser recognises that you wish to control where to position the element. The element's offset values determine the element's positioning within its containing element. But only if that containing element uses absolute, relative or fixed layout. If the containing element uses normal layout, or is unspecified, than the child element is positioned absolutely within the next parent container in the child element's parent container heirarchy (assuming the parent is absolute, relative or fixed). If no parent container in the heirarchy has absolute, relative or fixed positioning, the child is positioned within the browser's viewport window.

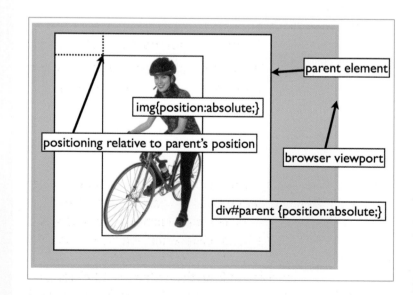

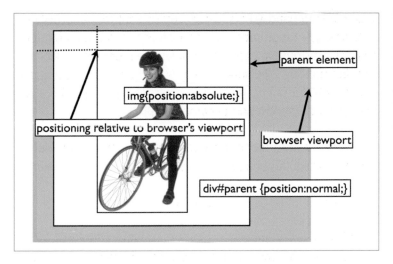

Consider the above image: If the containing element is body element, the image is positioned in relation to the browser's viewport. Offsets are left, right, top and bottom. What you do is specify how many measurement units (i.e. pixels), or what percentage of the parent container element, an element is positioned from the containing element's left, right, top and bottom edges. Typically you specify left/top, left/bottom, right/top, or right/bottom as your offset combination.

Table 12.4 Offset properties for positioning	
Property	**Function**
left	Specifies distance from containing element's left edge.
right	Specifies distance from containing element's right edge.
bottom	Specifies distance from containing element's bottom edge.
top	Specifies distance from containing element's top edge.

Think of the containing element's corners and where you wish to position the image in relation to the parent's corner. For instance, if you want to position an element 10 pixels up and 20 pixels right from the bottom left corner you would specify bottom:10px and left: 20px. You are specifying that your browser offsets the element from the bottom by 10 pixels and from the left by 20 pixels. If you wanted to position an element

Positioning elements using absolute positioning (cont.)

9 Position one div element up 10 pixels and left 10 pixels from your the right corner of your browser. (21)

10 Add some text to the left of each image, wrap in a span and format if you desire.

11 Wrap the fifth image in `<div></div>` tags. Assign the div tags relative positioning. (35)

12 Wrap the fifth image, but not its parent div element, in `<span></span>` tags. Assign the span element an id. (40)

13 Position the span using absolute positioning. Move the span right 60 pixels and up 30 pixels from its parent div element. (12)

14 Save and view in your browser. Resize your browser window several different sizes.

12

Positioning elements using absolute positioning (cont.)

20 pixels down and 20 pixels left from the top right corner you would specify top:20px and right:20px. You are specifying that your browser offsets the element from the top by 20 pixels and from the right by 20 pixels.

Let me provide some examples with supporting graphics. You could specify an image is positioned 5 pixels from the top and 10 pixels from the left. Or, position the image 10 pixels up and 5 pixels down from the top left corner of the containing element.

```
img#a {position:absolute;left:10px;
top:5px;}
```

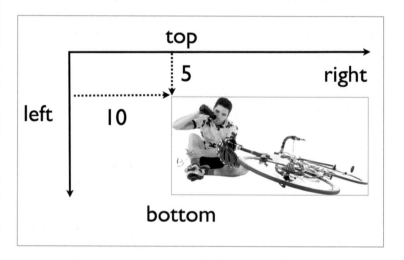

You could specify an image is positioned 5 pixels from the bottom and 10 pixels from the left. Or, position the image 5 pixels up and 10 pixels right of the containing element's bottom right corner.

```
img#a {position:absolute;left:10px;
bottom:5px;}
```

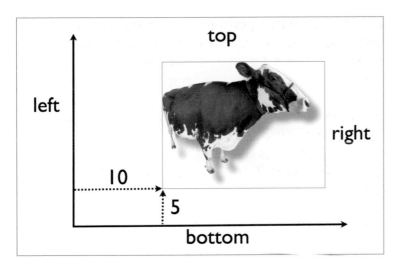

You could specify an image is positioned 10 pixels from the right and 5 pixels from the top. Or, position the image 5 pixels down and 10 pixels left from the top right corner of the containing element.

```
img#a {position:absolute;right:10;
top:5;}
```

You could specify an image is positioned 10 pixels from the right and 5 pixels from the bottom. Or, position the image 5 pixels up and 10 pixels left from the bottom right corner of the containing elements.

Positioning elements using absolute positioning (cont.)

```
img#a {position:absolute;right:10;
bottom:5;}
```

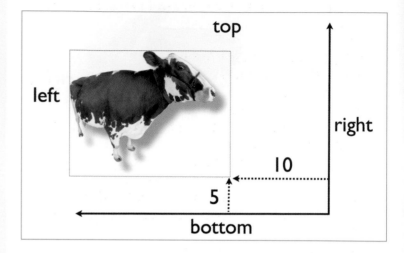

Cross reference

See **tasks_css/css_positioning/absolute_position_a.html** for completed example.

Upon completing this task you should see four div elements positioned exactly where you specified. The images and spans are each positioned within their respective parent using normal positioning. Note that one of the spans uses absolute positioning. I dislike hacks like this (span is an in-line element), but it illustrates the browser automatically making the span element a block-level element in order to position the span using your absolute positioning instructions.

The fifth image is positioned using normal flow within the span element. The span element is converted from an in-line to block-level element and is positioned absolutely within its parent div element. The parent div element uses relative positioning; however, no offset values are specified. Because no offsets are specified, the parent div remains in its default position. Specifying a relative position, but then assigning no offsets, is a common technique to lay out child element's within a parent element that you wish to flow naturally in a browser.

```
 1 <!DOCTYPE html PUBLIC "-//W3C//DTD HTML
 2 4.01 Strict//EN"
 3 "http://www.w3.org/TR/html4/strict.dtd">
 4 <html>
 5 <head>
 6 <style type="text/css">
 7 body {background:lightblue;}
 8 div{border-style:dotted; border-
 9 color:gray; padding:5px;}
10 span.b{vertical-align:top; color:red;
11 font-weight:bold;}
12 span#x{position:absolute; left:60px;
13 bottom:30px; color:purple; font-
14 weight:bold;border-style:dotted;}
15 div#a{position:absolute;left:5px;top:
16 250px;}
17 div#b{position:absolute;
18 top:100px;right:25px;}
19 div#c{position:absolute;bottom:20%;left
20 :30%;}
21 div#d{position:absolute;bottom:10px;
22 right:10px;}
23 </style>
24 </head>
25 <body>
26 <div id="a"><span class="b">(top:5px,
27 top:250px;)</span><img
28 src="./images/openbsd.png"/></div>
29 <div id="b"><span class="b">(top:100px,
30 right:25px)</span><img
31 src="./images/openbsd.png"/></div>
32 <div id="c"><span class="b">(bottom:20%,
33 left:30%)</span><img
34 src="./images/openbsd.png"/></div>
35 <div id="d"><span class="b">(top:10px,
36 right:10px)</span><img
37 src="./images/openbsd.png"/></div>
38 <div style="position:relative;border:
39 solid;width:50%;">
40 <span id="x"><img src="./images/openbsd.
```

12

Positioning elements using absolute positioning (cont.)

```
41 png"/></span><br/><br/><br/><br/><br/>
42 <br/><br/><br/><br/><br/><br/><br/><br/>
43 </div>
44 </body>
45 </html>
```

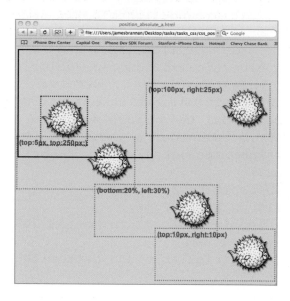

Important

Specifying that an element has absolute positioning removes the element from the browser's natural layout flow. However, elements occuring within that element (nested elements) are positioned by browsers using the natural layout flow within the parent element, unless you also specify the nested element's positioning. Positioning is not inherited.

For your information

You can also specify a negative value for positions. About 14 years ago, before CSS, there was a company (the company's name escapes me) that made a name for itself by exploiting a browser bug that allowed it to position images off the browser viewport's edge. This trick helped make the company famous, creating websites for companies such as Land Rover, and publishing two successful books on Web design. I forget the trick, but it was clever at the time. Today, however, CSS makes this trick easy using absolute positioning mixed with negative values.

```
body {background:black;}
img {position:absolute; left:-
120px;top:5px;z-index:1;}
span{position:absolute;
left:10%;top:40%; font-size:60px;
color:lime;z-index:2;}
```

You can also achieve the same effect if you float the image left and then assign it a negative margin.

Important

If overlapping elements are what you want, than be certain to specify the z-index of your elements. Think of elements as a stack of cards. The z-index property specifies the order the elements occur from front to back in a browser.

12

Positioning elements using fixed positioning

Fixed position is similar to absolute positioning except positioning is always relative to the browser window; parent containment is irrelevant. The element remains at the position regardless of the browser's size. Moreover, scrolling has no effect on the element, it remains in place. If you understand offsets for absolute positioning, you understand fixed positioning's offsets. The only difference is that the offset is always in relation to the browser's viewport.

Task steps

1. Save template.html with a different name.

2. Add three images to the page. (21, 22, 23)

3. Add a paragraph. Add enough text that your browser must scroll. (16)

4. Assign all three images a fixed position. (7, 8, 10)

5. Specify one image is 5 pixels right and 5 pixels down from the top left corner of your browser. (7)

6. Specify one image is 25 pixels left and 100 pixels down from the top right corner of your browser. (8)

7. Specify one image is 50 per cent left and 50 per cent down from the top right corner of your browser. (10)

8. Move one of the images to within the paragraph.

9. Save and view in your browser. Resize the window and scroll.

> **Cross reference**
>
> See **tasks_css/css_positioning/fixed.html** for completed example.

Once the task is complete, load it into your browser. The positions of the three images should remain fixed. The images are unaffected by scrolling. The image placed inside the paragraph element was unaffected by the placement, because fixed positioning always positions the element in relation to your browser's viewport.

```
1  <!DOCTYPE html PUBLIC "-//W3C//DTD HTML
2  4.01 Strict//EN"
3  "http://www.w3.org/TR/html4/strict.dtd">
4  <html>
5  <head>
6  <style type="text/css">
7  img#a{position:fixed;left:5px;top:5px;}
8  img#b{position:fixed;top:100px;right:
9  25px;}
10 img#c{position:fixed;top:50%;right:50%;}
11 p { position:relative; left:200px;
12 width:50%;}
13 </style>
14 </head>
15 <body>
16 <p>This is a paragraph about nothing.
17 This is a paragraph about ---snip---
18 This is a paragraph about nothing. This
19 is a paragraph about nothing.
```

```
20 </p>
21 <img is="a" src="./images/openbsd.png"/>
22 <img id="b" src="./images/openbsd.png"/>
23 <img id="c" src="./images/openbsd.png"/>
24 </body>
25 </html>
```

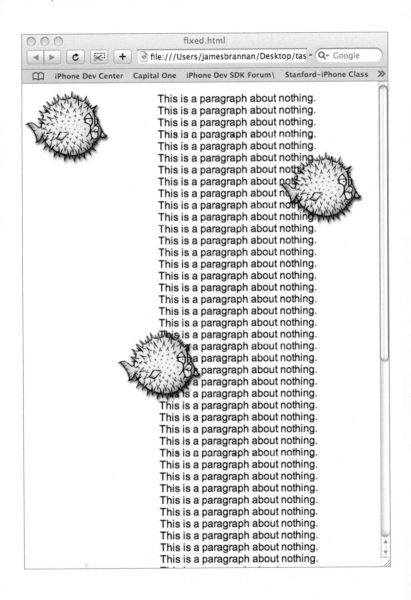

Exploring different page layout strategies

Introduction

In Chapter 12 you learned how to position elements on a web page This chapter expands on that knowledge by exploring a few popular layout styles. Layout styles fall into one of two larger layout strategies, fixed-width and liquid. When using a fixed-width layout, you define elements' widths using absolute values. Element width is independent of a browser's viewport. Conversely, when using a liquid layout, you define all elements' widths using percentages. The elements expand and contract depending on the browser's viewport size.

The most common elements used for these two layout strategies is the div element or the HTML table tag. To create a liquid layout using CSS, use a div element and assign its width a percentage. You can also set the div element's height. This allows the div element's size to expand and contract as the browser's viewport size changes.

```
<div id="pagecontent" style="width:90%;
height:90%; border-style:solid">
<p>This is a paragraph.</p>
</div>
```

To create a fixed-width layout using CSS, use a div element and assign its width a fixed value. This maintains the div element's dimension regardless of a browser's viewport size.

```
<div id="pagecontent"
style="width:500px; height:500px;
border-style:solid;">
<p>This is a paragraph.</p>
</div>
```

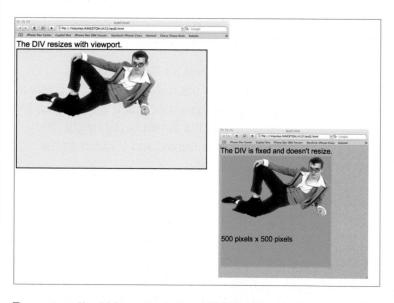

To create a liquid layout using an HTML table, assign the table's width as a percentage. This allows the table to expand and contract as the browser's viewport size changes. As with a div element, you can also specify a height when using a table.

```
<table width="90%" height="90%"
rules="all" frame="box">
<tr><td><p>This is a
paragraph.</p></td></tr>
</table>
```

To create a fixed-width layout using an HTML table, assign the table's width as a fixed value. This maintains the table's dimensions despite the browser's viewport size.

```
<table width="500px" height="500px"
rules="all" frame="box">
<tr><td><p>This is a
paragraph.</p></td></tr>
</table>
```

Using a liquid layout or a fixed width layout is a matter of personal preference. Both work equally well, and both have benefits and drawbacks. Liquid layouts fill a browser's window regardless of size. Moreover, the layout expands and contracts with the viewport. This dynamic resizing by a liquid layout accommodates users with small monitors.

You position elements to their precise position and width when using fixed layouts. This allows you complete control over an element's appearance in a browser's viewport. Moreover, as a browser's viewport becomes too small, because element size is independent of viewport size, elements do not reposition themselves and begin overlapping or forcing other elements onto new lines.

There is no law stating you must use one layout strategy or the other; you can mix them. For instance, one way you can deal with liquid layouts becoming too small is by specifying a fixed minimum width and fixed height as numeric values. Then the page is liquid, but only to the minimum sizes specified, at which point it becomes fixed-width and no longer resizes.

13

```
<div id="pagecontent"
style="width:90%;min-width:500px;min-
height:500px;height:90%;border-
style:solid;">
<p>This is a paragraph.</p>
</div>
```

Again, which style you use is a matter of personal preference. However, I feel comfortable making two sweeping generalisations. First, when creating an informational site containing considerable text and few graphics, use a liquid layout. Second, when creating an artistic site, containing less text and more graphics that require precise layout, use a fixed-width layout. Otherwise, sometimes the results might not be what you intended when a user resizes their browser.

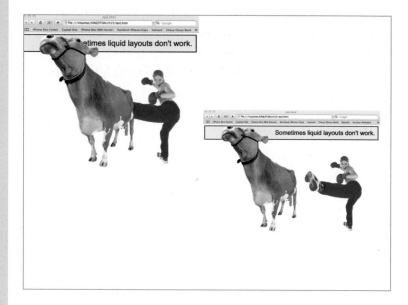

In this chapter you explore several different layouts. The layouts are fixed, liquid or a combination of the two strategies. The layouts covered are not exhaustive, but, rather, show you a sampling of different layouts. You can combine many different CSS styles and many different elements to achieve an endless combination of layouts. However, all layouts fall into three strategies: fixed-width, liquid or a combination of both.

A one column, fixed-width layout is so easy it almost doesn't warrant its own task. When using this layout, you should know the content and its rough dimensions beforehand. This layout is for precise control of a finite amount of content. A fixed-width, one column layout is most appropriate for a home page, or any page without a lot of content.

Cross reference

See **tasks/task_other/fluid_fixed/onecolumnfixed.html** for completed example.

The key to this task is using absolute positioning for the div and image element. In this task there is only one div element, so absolute positioning of the element is easy. The image is positioned absolutely so that it slightly overlaps the content div element. As an aside, note that I used a background image for the body. This background image is tiled vertically and horizontally.

```
1 <!DOCTYPE HTML PUBLIC "-//W3C//DTD HTML
2 4.01 Transitional//EN"
3 "http://www.w3.org/TR/html4/loose.dtd">
4 <html><head>
5 <style>
6 body{ font-family:serif;font-size:14pt;}
7 p{margin:20px 70px 10px 20px;}
8 h3 {margin:10px)
9 h1 {margin:10px 50px 10px 10px;
10 color:red;}
11 img { position:absolute; left: 650px;
12 top; 20px; z-index:1;} #content
13 { position:absolute; left:10px;
14 top:100px;
15 width:700px; height:580px;
16 background:whitesmoke;
17 border: 1px solid black;)
18 body{background-
19 image:url(./images/background.png);}
20 </style></head>
21 <body>
22 <img src="./images/large/cyclist26.tiff"
```

Using a fixed-width layout – one column

Task steps

1 Save template.html with a new name.

2 Copy an image to the same folder. Note, the image in this example is copyrighted, and is not provided in the example tasks. But you can always pick one of the 128 × 128 images available from this book's completed example.

3 Create a paragraph and add about five to ten sentences. (30)

4 Add **<h1></h1>** tags. This element is the page's header. (25–26)

5 Add **<h3></h3>** tags. This element is the paragraph's header. (27–29)

5 Wrap the paragraph and the two headers in **<div></div>** tags. Give the div element an id of content. (24)

6 Just above the **<div>** add the image. (22)

7 Add **<style></style>** tags to the HTML head element. (5, 20)

13

Using a fixed-width layout – one column (cont.)

8 Assign the paragraph and h3 elements margins. (6, 7)

9 Declare that the image use absolute positioning; 650 pixels from the left and 20 pixels from the top. Set the picture's z-index to 1 so it's the topmost object. (11)

10 Declare the div element use absolute positioning: 10 pixels from the left, 100 pixels from the top, and that it should be 700 pixels wide. Make the div's background whitesmoke and assign it a solid, black border. (13–17)

11 Assign the body a background image. You can get one from this task's completed example folder. (19)

12 Save and display in your browser.

```
23 alt="cyclist" width="179" height="486"/>
24 <div id="content">
25 <h1>Welcome to hell - The indoor
26 2x20</h1>
27 <h3>5 min warmup - 20 min work - 10 min
28 rest - 20 min work - 5 min
29 cooldown</h3>
30 <p>Do you want to be fast? Really fast?
31 Faster then you ever thought possible?
32 You do? Good, then maybe after doing
33 your first 2x20 you will come back
34 ---snip--- methodical and measurable as
35 weight-lifting.</p>
36 </div>
37 </body>
38 </html>
```

In this task you create another one column layout, only you make it liquid. Another key feature in this task is centring the page's content. This is a common layout technique that looks appealing.

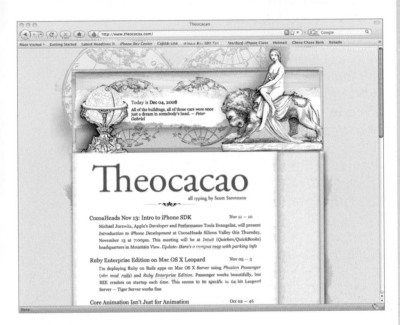

The easiest way to achieve a centred page is by wrapping all other elements within the body element in **<div></div>** tags and assigning the div element a zero top and bottom margin and an auto left and right margin.

```
<body>
<div style="margin: 0 auto"> --- page
content here ---</div>
</div>
</body>
```

Cross reference

See **tasks/task_other/fluid_fixed/onecol_liq_center.html** for completed example.

Using a liquid layout – one column, centred

Task steps

1. Save template.html using a different name.
2. Add **<div></div>** tags and assign it an id. (15)
3. Add some content to the page. Add an image if you wish.
4. Assign the body element a background colour. (7)
5. Assign the div element a border and background colour. (8)
6. Assign the top and bottom margin a zero border. Assign the left and right border an auto border. (10)
7. Add an image and make it float left. (16, 11)
8. Save the results and display in your browser. Resize the browser.

13

Using a liquid layout – one column, centred (cont.)

For your information

There is no inherent relationship between a liquid one column layout and centring the content. Centring content on a page is a common CSS layout technique that also works with a fixed-width layout.

The results of this task are straightforward. You should see a single column, centred on the page. As you resize your browser, the column's width should also resize.

```
1  <!DOCTYPE HTML PUBLIC "-//W3C//DTD HTML
2  4.01 Transitional//EN"
3  "http://www.w3.org/TR/html4/loose.dtd">
4  <html>
5  <head>
6  <style type="text/css">
7  body {background-color:tan;}
8  div#pagecontent { border-
9  style:solid;background-
10 color:khaki;width:80%;margin: 0 auto;}
11 img {float:left;}
12 </style>
13 </head>
14 <body>
15 <div id="pagecontent">
16 <img src="./images/vlc.png"/>
17 <p style="font-size:xx-large;">This is
18 an annoying under construction
19 message.</p>
20 </div>
21 </body>
22 </html>
```

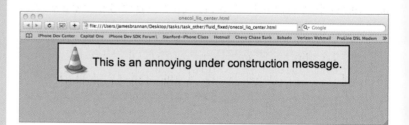

You achieve this layout by making one of two columns float left. The content added to the left div element floats to the left of the content added to the right div element.

```
<div id="left"
style="float:left;"></div>
<div id="right_column"></div>
```

You can vary the columns' widths as desired, just be certain to use relative widths. The important feature for this layout is that one of the two columns floats left and that neither uses absolute positioning. You could even get fancy if you wanted and use this layout to create more columns. For example, a four-column, liquid layout.

```
<div id="outer_left"
style="float:left;">
<div id="left"
style="float:left;"></div>
<div id="right_column"></div>
</div>
<div id = "outer_right">
<div id="left"
style="float:left;"></div>
<div id="right_column"></div>
</div>
```

Just remember, widths for box elements must not be fixed-width.

Cross reference

See **tasks/task_other/float_fixed/twocolumns.html** for completed example.

The results of this task are straightforward. You should see two columns, roughly the same width, that expand and contract as you resize your browser.

```
1 <!DOCTYPE HTML PUBLIC "-//W3C//DTD HTML
2 4.01 Transitional//EN"
3 "http://www.w3.org/TR/html4/loose.dtd">
```

◄ **Using a liquid layout – two columns**

Task steps

1 Save template.html with a different name.

2 Add two **<div></div>** tag sets. Assign the right div element the id of right and the left div element the id of left. (17, 24)

3 Add some HTML content to both div elements.

4 Declare the left div element floats left and has a width that's 40% of the page. Make its background yellow and border 1 pixel, solid black. (8)

5 Declare the right element floats left and takes 40 per cent of the page. Make its background tan and border 1 pixel, solid black. (11)

6 Save and view in your browser.

13

Using a liquid layout – two columns (cont.)

```
 4 <html>
 5 <head>
 6 <style type="text/css">
 7 h2, p {margin:0px 10px 10px 10px;}
 8 #left { float: left; width:40%;
 9 background:yellow; border: 1px solid
10 black;margin:2px;}
11 #right{background:tan; float: left;
12 width:40%; border: 1px solid
13 black;margin:2px;}
14 </style>
15 </head>
16 <body>
17 <div id="left">
18 <h2> Left &lt;div&gt; tag</h2>
19 <img src="./images/large/openbsd.png"/>
20 <p>This is the page's ---snip--- complex
21 layout.
22 </p>
23 </div>
24 <div id="right"><h2> Right &lt;div&gt;
25 tag</h2>
26 <p>This is the page's ---snip---
27 layout.</p>
28 </div>
29 </body>
30 </html>
```

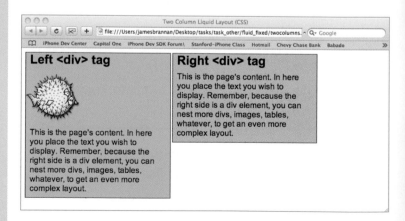

For your information

Note that you can use a fixed layout with this two column layout also. Modify the div element widths from percentages to fixed widths, and you have a two column, fixed-width layout.

```
#left { float: left; width:200px;
background:yellow; border: 1px
solid black;}
#right{background:tan; float: left;
width:200px; border: 1px solid
```

13

Using a liquid layout – three columns

Task steps

1 Save template.html with a different name.

2 Add three `<div></div>` tag sets. Assign the right div element the id of right, the centre div element the id of centre, and the left div element the id of left. (22, 29, 36)

3 Add some content to both div elements.

4 Declare all three elements float left. (10, 13, 16)

5 Assign all three div elements a 30% width. (10, 13, 16)

6 Add content to all three div elements and assign each div a different background colour.

7 Save and view in your browser.

This layout, like the two column layout, relies upon floating left. You create three div elements, floating each one left.

> **Cross reference**
>
> See **tasks/task_other/float_fixed/threecolumns.html** for completed example.

This task, like the previous task, relies upon the div elements floating left. The results are straightforward, you should see three columns of equal width.

```
 1 <!DOCTYPE HTML PUBLIC "-//W3C//DTD html
 2 4.01 Transitional//EN"
 3 "http://www.w3.org/TR/html4/loose.dtd">
 4 <html>
 5 <head>
 6 <title>Three Column Liquid Layout
 7 (CSS)</title>
 8 <style type="text/css">
 9 h2, p {margin:10px 10px 10px 10px;}
10 #left { float: left; width:30%;
11 background:yellow; border: 1px solid
12 black; }
13 #center{width:30%; float:left;
14 background:whitesmoke; border:1px solid
15 black; }
16 #right{width:30%; float: left;
17 background:tan; border: 1px solid
18 black;}
19 </style>
20 </head>
21 <body>
22 <div id="left"><h2> Left &lt;div&gt;
23 tag</h2>
24 <img src="./images/large/tux.png"
25 style="float:left;"/>
26 <p>This is the ---snip--- complex
27 layout.</p>
28 </div>
29 <div id="center"><h2> Centre &lt;div&gt;
```

```
30 tag</h2>
31 <img src="./images/vlc.png"
32 style="float:right;"/>
33 <p>This is the page's ---snip---
34 complex layout.</p>
35 </div>
36 <div id="right"><h2> Right &lt;div&gt;
37 tag</h2>
38 <p>This is the page's ---snip---
39 layout.</p>
40 </div>
41 </body>
42 </html>
```

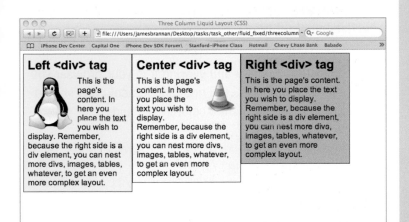

For your information

Replace the percentage values with fixed width values to make this task a three column, fixed width layout.

```
#left { float: left; width:200px;
background:yellow; border: 1px
solid black; }
#center{width:200px; float:left;
background:whitesmoke; border:1px
solid black; }
#right{width:200px; float: left;
background:tan; border: 1px solid
black;}
```

Using a combined layout – two columns liquid, one fixed

Task steps

1. Save template.html using a new name.

2. Add three `<div></div>` tags and assign each a different id. (26, 32, 42)

3. Assign the left div element an absolute position 10 pixels right and 60 pixels down from the top left corner. Assign the div a 200-pixel width. (12)

4. Assign the right div element an absolute position 10 pixels left and 60 pixels down from the top right corner. Assign the div a 200-pixel width. (15)

5. Assign the centre div element no border and no positioning. (19)

6. To make the div elements easier to distinguish, add images and formatting as desired. At a minimum you should add borders to the div elements and assign them each a margin.

7. Save and view in your browser.

Sometimes you might want, or need, a hybrid layout that combines liquid columns and fixed columns. For instance, perhaps you want a left and right fixed-width column and a variable-width column down the centre. Why would you want such a layout? I don't know, maybe you wish to put images on the left and right with a paragraph down the centre. Use your imagination. The point of this task is to illustrate, once you understand fixed-width and variable-width column layout, you can easily combine both on the same html page.

> ### Cross reference
>
> See **tasks/task_other/fluid_fixed/threecolumns_twofixedonefluid.ht**ml for completed example.

Upon completing this task and viewing it in your browser you should see three columns. The right and left columns should be fixed-width while the centre column is liquid.

```
1  <!DOCTYPE HTML PUBLIC "-//W3C//DTD HTML
2  4.01 Transitional//EN"
3  "http://www.w3.org/TR/html4/loose.dtd">
4  <html>
5  <head>
6  <meta http-equiv="Content-Type"
7  content="text/html; charset=UTF-8">
8  <title>Three Columns - two static one
9  liquid (CSS)</title>
10 <style type="text/css">
11 h2, p {margin:0px 10px 10px 10px;}
12 #left {position: absolute; left:10px;
13 top:60px;width:200px;background:tan;
14 border:1px solid black;   }
15 #right {position:
16 absolute;right:10px;top:60px;width:200px
17 ;background:yellow;border:1px solid
18 black;}
19 #center{background:whitesmoke;margin-
20 left: 205px;   margin-
21 right:205px;margin-top:60px;  border:1px
22 solid black;}
```

```
23  </style>
24  </head>
25  <body>
26  <div id="left">
27  <h2>Left div</h2>
28  <p><img
29  src="./images/large/ktip.png"/><img
30  src="./images/large/ktip.png"/></p>
31  </div>
32  <div id="center">
33  <h2>Center div</h2>
34  <p><img src="./images/large/tux.png"/>
35  This is the page's content. In here you
36  place the text you wish to display.
37  Remember, because the right side is a
38  div element, you can nest more divs,
39  images, tables, whatever, to get an
40  even more complex layout.</p>
41  </div>
42  <div id="right">
43  <h2>Right div</h2>
44  <p><img
45  src="./images/large/ktip.png"/><img
46  src="./images/large/ktip.png"/><img
47  src="./images/large/ktip.png"/><img
48  src="./images/large/ktip.png"/></p>
49  </div>
50  </body>
51  </html>
```

13

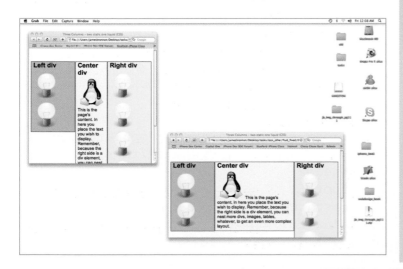

Creating a liquid layout using a table

Task steps

1. Save template.html using a different name.

2. Create a table and assign it an id. (18)

3. Create a table header and insert one row and one cell that has a column span of two columns. Add the title of the page to the table data cell. (20)

4. Create a table body and insert one row with two cells. (29)

5. Make the first cell's width 30% and add an unordered list as the content. (30)

6. Add several paragraphs to the second cell. (50)

7. Add a table footer. In the footer create one row with one cell. Assign the cell a columnspan of two. (24)

8. Add links to the cell. (26)

9. Apply CSS formatting to several of the page's elements. Try making backgrounds different colours.

You aren't restricted to using CSS for page layout. Tables, despite being considered old-fashioned, are still viable alternatives for page layout. You can put anything in a table data cell; use this fact to create HTML pages that use a table to provide structure rather than CSS and div elements.

> **Cross reference**
>
> See **tasks/task_other/fluid_fixed/tableliquid.html** for completed example.

The results are straightforward. The table provides a fluid page layout for the web page.

```
1 <!DOCTYPE HTML PUBLIC "-//W3C//DTD HTML
2 4.01 Transitional//EN"
3 "http://www.w3.org/TR/html4/loose.dtd">
4 <html>
5 <head>
6 <title>Table - Liquid Layout</title>
7 <style type="text/css">
8 body {background:tan;}
9 #tux {margin:5px; float:left;}
10 #navbar, li {font-size:large; }
11 h1, p {margin:10px;}
12 table#main{ background:tan; height:100%;
13 width:100%;}
14 tfoot, thead{background:whitesmoke;}
15 </style>
16 </head>
17 <body>
18 <table id="main" frame="box"
19 rules="all">
20 <thead>
21 <tr><td colspan="2"><h1>Popular Open-
22 Source Operating Systems</td></tr>
23 </thead>
24 <tfoot>
25 <tr><td colspan="2" align="center"><span
26 id="navbar">[Home | Link | Link | Link
27 | Link ]</span></td></tr>
```

```
28 </tfoot>
29 <tbody>
30 <tr><td width="30%">
31 <ul>
32 <li><img
33 src="./images/freebsd.png"/>Free
34 BSD</li>
35 <li><img
36 src="./images/openbsd.png"/>Open
37 BSD</li>
38 <li><img src="./images/suse.png"/>SUSE
39 Linux</li>
40 <li><img
41 src="./images/ubuntu.png"/>Ubuntu
42 Linux</li>
43 <li><img
44 src="./images/slackware.png"/>Slackware
45 Linux</li>
46 <li><img
47 src="./images/fedora.png"/>Fedora
48 Linux</li>
49 </ul></td>
50 <td><img id="tux"
51 src="./images/large/tux.png"/><p>This is
52 the page's content. ---snip--- even
53 more complex layout.</p>
54 <p>This is the page's ---snip---
55 complex layout.</p>
56 <p>This is the page's ---snip---
57 layout.</p>
58 <p>This is the page's ---snip---
59 layout.</p></td></tr>
60 </tbody>
61 </table>
62 </body>
63 </html>
```

Creating a liquid layout using a table (cont.)

i

For your information

To create a fixed-width table, set the table's width to a length value such as pixels.

13

Creating a liquid layout using a table (cont.)

For your information

Web designers who use CSS usually dislike using HTML layouts for design. When using CSS, all formatting rules are in one location, the CSS style sheet. When using tables, you must duplicate the table on every page. Want to slightly modify your site's layout? You must modify every page on your site. Although this book covers the use of tables for layout, for site maintainability, I recommend using CSS.

Site structure and navigation

Introduction

Now that you understand HTML and CSS, you need to understand a little about site structure and how to navigate that site structure. Organised simplicity is your goal. Think of site structure as an outline for an essay. When writing an outline for an essay, you want every paragraph to be cohesive and discuss one topic. You also want the paper's sections and subsections to have internal consistency. Websites are the same – you want cohesion and consistency.

Websites have an added dimension, though. You must also carefully weigh what information belongs on the same page and what information does not. Put too much information on a page, and users will be confused and have trouble digesting the information. Put too little infomation on a page – and many links to subtopic after subtopic – and users get tired of navigating through all the links. It's a balancing act between these two competing factors.

Start with a written outline when first creating a website. On finishing the outline, decide what information should be grouped on the same page. How you make information grouping decisions is a personal choice. There are two types of people – lumpers and splitters. If you're a lumper, you will probably have fewer pages in less folders. If you're a splitter, then you will probably have more pages in more folders. Both strategies are equally valid. But use some common sense – pages that are similar should be grouped together in the same

What you'll do

Understand a flat site structure

Understand a tiered site structure

Look at some websites' navigation strategies

Create a global top or bottom menu

Create a left floating site menu

Create a local menu

Create a breadcrumb trail

folder. This is good housekeeping, and will help you maintain your website because it will be more organised.

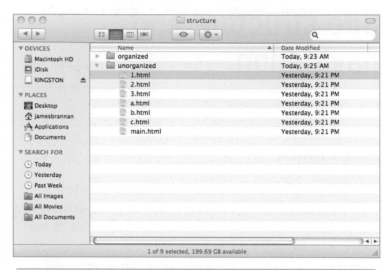

After determining your site's layout, you should plan the site's navigation. User navigation through your website is as important, if not more so, than your site's structure. Present important information so it is easily found. If the most important information on your website requires clicking through two or three pages to get to it, it's not going to seem that important to the user. Like site structure, there are no set rules you must follow. However, there are a few things you can do to make navigation easier for users.

Place a link back to your site's home page on every page. This gives a user an immediate way back home upon getting lost. The task 'Creating a breadcrumb trail' discusses a common technique called breadcrumb trails. A breadcrumb trail is a row of links showing the navigation path to the particular page the user is currently viewing. Usually, each step in the hierarchy is a separate link back to the relevant page.

home/operatingsystems/bsd/freebsd/
installation.html

Place main, global links along the top or bottom of a page. There are three common strategies for global links. You can keep the links restricted to information not within the flow of the rest of the site. For instance, on a site about computer operating systems, sponsored by Computers Inc., you might place links about Computers Inc. across the top of a page with only one link to the site's subject – operating systems.

[Operating Systems | About Computer
Inc. | Jobs | Contact | Links]

Another strategy is to place the site's top-level subjects across the top of a page. For instance, Computers Inc. might place the site's main topics along the top.

[Overview | UNIX | Linux | BSD]

Or, Computers Inc. might place a combination of top-level subjects, topics and unrelated topics. This combination is the strategy most websites seem to use.

[Overview | UNIX | Linux | BSD | About
| Contact | Join | Links]

14

As your site's main topics grow, placing too many links on a global menu across the top of a page, doesn't work well – the links no longer fit. But with a set number of links, placing a menu at the top or bottom of a page does work well.

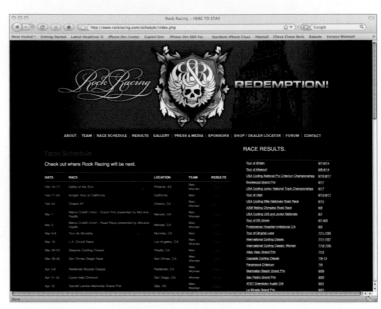

Important

I said there are no set rules. I lied. Consistency. Once you create your navigation, stick with it. Do not change link-ordering, names or appearance from page to page. You can modify which links are visible, but keep your navigation scheme consistent.

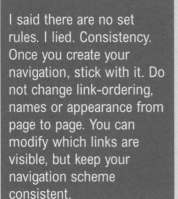

If you have a lot of links, either prune your main topics (lump more) or present your site's navigation as a menu along the left or right margins of your site's pages. This category menu contains the site's categories, or topics and subtopics, as a hierarchical menu. The menu can be placed absolutely, or float, depending on the page layout, and it can be simple or brilliant. Again, there are no set rules.

A flat site structure is the easiest site structure to maintain, provided your website is comprised of relatively few pages. All the files are in one folder, and you are only ever one click away from the home page.

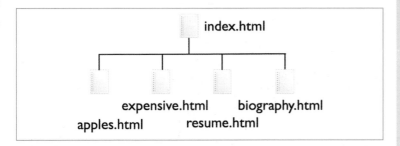

Cross reference

See **tasks_other/task_flat_site_structure/index.html** for completed example.

A flat website structure is straightforward and this task's example is no exception. Notice that all HTML pages are in the same folder. Also notice that you are never more then one page removed from index.html. It is a one-tier hierarchy. Pretty simple.

My Site:
1. My home page (index.html)
   a. about me (biography.html)
   b. my resume (resume.html)
   c. my love of apples (apples.html)
   d. too expensive (expensive.html)

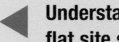

Understanding a flat site structure

14

Task steps

1 Open the example folder task_flat_site_structure. Notice that all the HTML pages are in the same folder.

2 Outline the website on paper.

3 Open index.html in your Web browser.

4 Click through the links. Note the links bar at the top of each page.

5 Pay special attention to expensive.html.

Understanding a flat site structure (cont.)

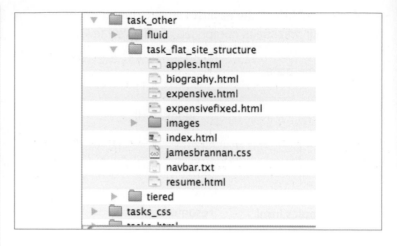

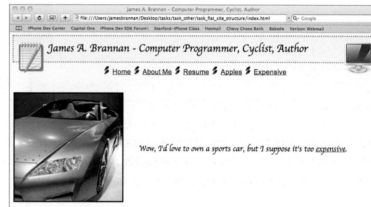

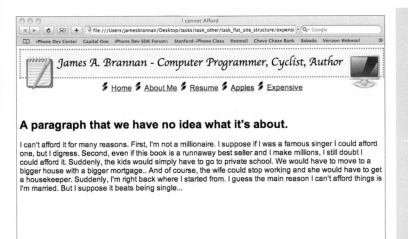

The navigation is equally simple, the site has few enough links that a top navigation bar works fine. But there is one problem with this simple site. Note the contextual link, expensive, in index.html. When you click on the link, you're taken to a page devoid of any context. What's too expensive – apples, my resume? And what if Google happened to have indexed this page and a user had come directly to the page? The user has no idea what is too expensive on expensive.html; every page should contain some contextual hints as to its content.

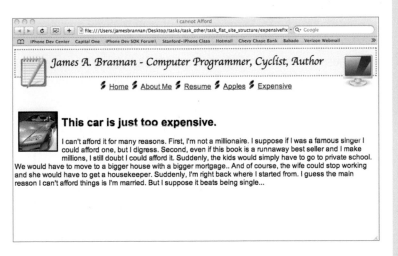

Understanding a tiered site structure

Task steps

1. Create an outline of your planned site on paper. It's okay if you don't know everything, I'm not trying to take away your spontenaity. But you should have a good idea of the main topics you wish covering.

2. Create a top-level folder for the project and then three subfolders entitled UNIX, Linux, and bsd. Add a subfolder entitled freeBSD in the BSD subfolder.

3. Save template.html as index.html and copy the file to each subfolder.

4. Copy index.html as solaris.html, aix.html and hp-ux.html in the UNIX subfolder.

5. Copy index.html as suse.html, ubuntu.html and fedora.html in the Linux subfolder.

6. Copy index.html as openbsd.html, freebsd.html and osx.html in the BSD subfolder.

If your site has depth to it, there is a good chance a flat structure might just make a mess of things. Imagine all your papers in one pile, without a filing cabinet. Finding something is difficult and applying any type of arrangement to the mess is more difficult, if not impossible. If I had all my papers filed in a filing cabinet, with each subject neatly labelled, researching a subject might take minutes instead of hours.

Websites of any depth need a little more organisation than a flat structure. Instead, they should be arranged in a heirarchy. A tiered website is a heirarchical structure much like an essay's outline. The top-level subjects are the top-level HTML pages. If you have many subtopics, then create HTML pages for each subtopic. If subtopics have further subtopics, create a folder for the subtopic, and place the subtopic's subtopics in the folder. You can leave the parent subtopic's HTML page in its parent folder or move the page to its subfolder. Repeat for each subtopic level. But, you probably shouldn't go more then two or three levels deep in folders.

Many books discuss site structure in depth but, in this book, I have said all I'm going to say on the subject. The chances are you will do what fits your personality. If you're a splitter/organiser, you're probably going to design a very organised, structured, tiered website. If your a lumper, or just plain disorganised (like the author), then a couple subfolders and a big mess are in order. Either way, both site structures work. Use your common sense is about the best advice I can give.

Cross reference

See **/tasks/task_other/tiered/WebContent/bsd** for completed example.

This task didn't have much results. All you did was create a skeleton for a website without any content. In the next few tasks you add menus to the site. Notice that every folder has a page entitled index.html. This is important. You want every folder to have either a default.html or index.html page. Remember, if you were to type:

```
http://www.mysite.com/unix
```

and there was no index.html or default.html, you see a directory listing.

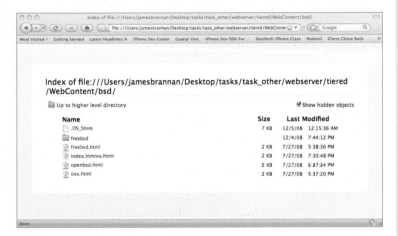

A directory listing is probably not what you want users to see, by adding index.html to each folder, you ensure the user sees that page if they just type a path to the folder.

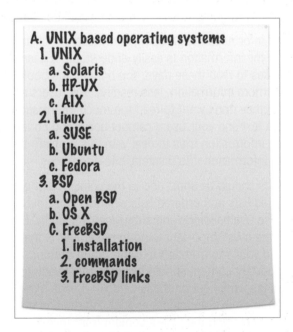

7 Copy index.html as installation.html, commands.html and links.html in the freeBSD subfolder.

8 Create a stylesheet entitled tiered.css and save it in the top-level folder.

Understanding a tiered site structure (cont.)

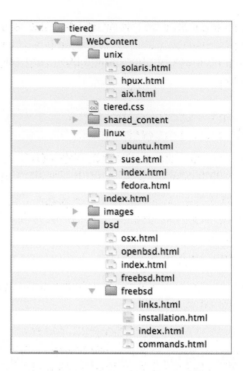

Before continuing with with this chapter's tasks, let's review several sites for navigation examples. Specifically, what you should look for are global navigation, category navigation and local navigation.

1. Open your browser and navigate to the **www.onlinebikecoach.com** website.

2. Move your mouse over the ONLINE BIKE COACH text in the top banner. Note that it's a link back to the site's main page.

3. Click on ONLINE COACHING. Note the page's information organisation. Also note that the ONLINE COACHING link is highlighted red.

4. Click on TECH CONSULTING.

5. Scroll to the bottom of the page, note the small menu in the bottom right corner.

This site illustrates several key concepts. You should put a link back to home, large and bold, on every page. Make the link stand out. This site uses a large image link on its banner. You should use a global menu on the top of the page. This site's global menu is a simple top menu of the site's main offerings. Using an appropriate grouping, the menu is short enough to fit in the page's margins. On the bottom of every page there is a second global menu.

Because the topics are limited, the site doesn't employ a category menu along its left or right side. Instead it just employs links in the body of the page and local menus.

1. Navigate to the **www.fixedgearfever.com** website.

2. Use the left menu to navigate to anywhere in the site.

3. Click the top banner.

This site uses a top global menu, just below the site's banner. The banner is a link to the site's homepage. The global links are housekeeping links and have nothing to do with the site's content. The site's primary navigation is in the category menu along the page's left margin.

Looking at some websites' navigation strategies (cont.)

1. Navigate to **www.rockracing.com**.

2. Click on TEAM.

This site is another example of a global menu where the site's topics are short enough to fit in a global menu. On the team page, notice the local menu along the top below the global menu. The links are anchors to locations further down the page. There is also a local menu along the right side of the page that allows you to jump directly to a subpage covering a particular rider.

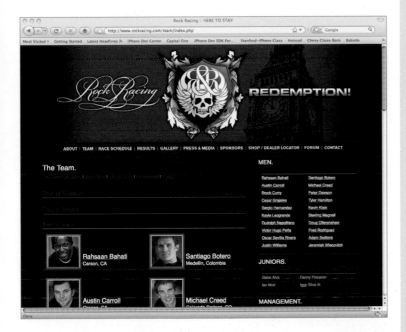

Creating a global top or bottom menu

Menus across the top or bottom of a page are typically reserved for top-level, global site links. Second- and third-level pages are usually excluded. Too many links in a top or bottom menu will not fit in the average Web page, so the links are limited to the site's most important. Housekeeping links, such as About Us and Contact Us are also typically on the top-level menu.

Task steps

1. Open the website created in the 'Understanding a tiered site structure' task.

2. Create a new folder called shared and a new page called header.html.

3. Add the appropriate links to the page. (15–22)

4. Add a base URL to the page's header. (9)

5. Test in your browser.

6. After ensuring the links work, remove all content below the outermost **</div>** closing tag.

7. Save as a file called header.inc.

8. Replace the top of every page with the header's code.

9. Save all pages and navigate through the site to ensure the links work correctly.

Cross reference

See **/tasks/task_other/tiered/WebContent/bsd** for completed example.

The task results are straightforward, if not repetitive. You added a header to every HTML page in the site. By creating a header that you include in other HTML pages, you ensure that all top-level menus are exactly the same. Notice that only the site's topmost links are included in the menu.

```
1 <!DOCTYPE HTML PUBLIC "-//W3C//DTD HTML
2 4.01 Transitional//EN"
3 "http://www.w3.org/TR/html4/loose.dtd">
4 <html>
5 <head>
6 <meta http-equiv="Content-Type"
7 content="text/html; charset=UTF-8">
8 <title>Tiered</title>
9 <base
10 href="file:///Users/brannanj/Desktop/
11 tasks/task_other/tiered/WebContent/">
12 </head>
13 <body>
14 <div id="global_nav_bar">
15 <span id="global_nav_span">
16 <!— Top level Global Navigation —>
17 [ <a
18 href="./bsd/index.html">BSD</a> |&n
19 bsp;<a href="./unix/index.html">UNIX</a>
20  | <a href="./linux/index.
21 html">Linux</a> ]
22 </span>
23 </div>
```

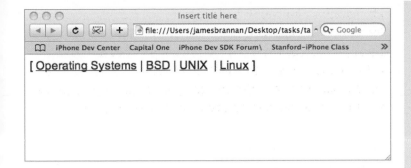

[Operating Systems | BSD | UNIX | Linux]

Timesaver tip

In this task and the remaining tasks in this chapter, there will be considerable repetition. For instance, in this task, you add a top menu to every page in the tiered site created earlier in this chapter. Typically, you would use a dynamic scripting language or CGI program to do this type of repetitive work for you. Before a Web page ever leaves the Web server, using programming, a program would dynamically build the Web page before returning it to a user.

```
<html>
<@myscripting language
include="./mysite/myheader.inc"/>
<p>...</p>
</html>
```

By the time the page made it to the user, the page would be HTML, with all the dynamically added content incorporated into the page.

Creating a global top or bottom menu (cont.)

```
<html>
<head>... content from the server-
side include ...</head>
<p>...</p>
</html>
```

The most common, free programming language is PHP. Using PHP, you could easily automate the inclusion of a top-level menu and a left-side menu.

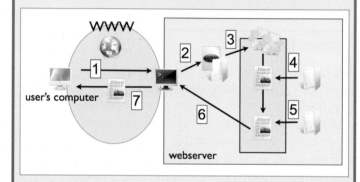

Processing steps

1. User requests a page with .php extension.

2. The Web server knows that the page is a PHP page and must be processed first.

3. The PHP module, or CGI program, gets the request for the page and gets the .php file.

4. The PHP processor replaces the PHP include statement with the top header.

5. The PHP processor replaces the PHP include statement with the left menu.

6. The complete HTML document is returned to the Web server.

7. The Web server returns the HTML document to the user.

Menus across the top or bottom of a page normally don't have enough space to include all a site's links if the site is of any substantial size. A common navigation technique is to include another menu along the left or right margin. By adding a menu along the side of the page, you create ample space to include all a site's links. There are many ways to create this side menu; the key is having at least one column along the left side of the page's left. In this task, assume a two column, floating layout, where the left column is the menu.

The results for this task, like the previous task, are straightforward, if not repetitive. Every page now has a left menu. The left menu has more detail than the top-level menu. Admittedly, the menu is spartan; however, because the CSS style sheet is external, you can easily format the list.

```
1  <div id="left_nav_bar">
2  <span id="left_nav_span"> <!-- note:
3  this is incorrect, as span is inline
4  while ul is block but is used in future
5  tasks so leave as is -->
6  <ul id="left_nav_li">
7  <li><a href="./index.html">Operating
8  Systems</a>
9  <ul>
10 <li><a href="./bsd/index.html">BSD</a>
11      <ul id="bsd_li">
12      <li><a href="./bsd/freebsd.html">
13      FreeBSD</a> </li>
14      <li><a href="./bsd/openbsd.html">
15      OpenBSD</a> </li>
16      <li><a href="./bsd/osx.html">OS
17      X</a></li>
18      </ul>
19 </li>
20 <li><a href="./unix/index.html">UNIX</a>
21      <ul id="unix_li">
22      <li><a href="./unix/solaris.html">
23      Solaris</a> </li>
24      <li><a href="./unix/hpux.html">HP-
25      UX</a></li>
26      <li><a href="./unix/aix.html">AIX
27      </a></li>
```

Creating a left floating site menu

14

Task steps

1. Open the website created in the previous task.

2. Create a new page called left_nav_menu.html.

3. Add the appropriate links to the page as an unordered list; make nested levels embedded unordered lists.

4. Wrap the outermost list in **<div></div>** tags. Assign the div element an id.

5. Add a base URL to the page.

6. Test in your browser.

7. After ensuring the links work, remove all content above and below the **<div></div>** tags.

8. Save as a file called left_nav_menu.inc.

9. Open every page and just after the top-level menu's **</div>** tag and before the page's **</body>** tag, add the content from left_nav_menu.inc to the page.

10. Save all pages and navigate through the site to ensure the links work correctly.

```
28        </ul>
29 </li>
30        <li><a href="./linux/index.html">
31        Linux</a>
32        <ul id="linux_li">
33        <li><a href="./linux/fedora.html">
34        Fedora</a></li>
35        <li><a href="./linux/suse.html">
36        SUSE</a></li>
37        <li><a href="./linux/ubuntu.html">
38        Ubuntu</a></li>
39        </ul>
40 </li>
41 </ul>
42 </li></ul>
43 </span>
44 </div>
```

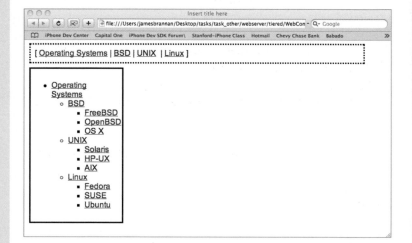

Depending on the complexity of your site, you might not want to place every link in the left navigation menu. Too many links might cause users to get confused by all the choices. A common strategy is to present smaller local menus. For instance, returning to the example from the previous couple of tasks, suppose for the freebsd operating system, you wished to present detailed installation instructions, detailed descriptions of every command and a comprehensive set of links for further information. Rather than placing the information in the left menu, you might wish to create a smaller menu for the freebsd operating system.

The results of this task are straightforward. A local navigation menu for the links in freeBSD is added to the pages within the freeBSD subdirectory.

```
<div id="free_bsd_nav">
<ul>
<li><a
href="./bsd/freebsd/installation.html">I
nstallation</a></li>
<li><a
href="./bsd/freebsd/commands.html">Comma
nds</a></li>
<li><a
href="./bsd/freebsd/links.html">Links</a
></li>
</ul>
</div>
```

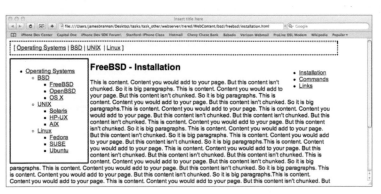

Task steps

1 Open the Web site from the previous task.

2 Create a new page entitled freebsd_nav.html.

3 Add the appropriate links to the page as an unordered list.

4 Wrap the list in **<div></div>** tags. Assign the div element an id.

5 Add a base URL to the page.

6 Test in your browser.

7 After ensuring the links work, remove all content above and below the **<div></div>** tags.

8 Save as a file called freebsd_nav.inc.

9 Open every page in the freeBSD subfolder and just after the before the page's **</body>** tag, add the content from freebsd_nav.inc to the page.

10 Save all pages and navigate through the site to ensure the links work correctly.

Creating a
breadcrumb trail

Task steps

1. Open installation.html in the freebsd subdirectory. If you completed the previous task, this file should have three menus in it.

2. Just below the local menu, type the path to installation.html.

3. For each section of the path, make a hyperlink to the section's corresponding page.

4. Wrap the path in **<div></div>** tags. Assign the div element an id.

5. Save and display in your browser.

As with inserting headers and global content, you would typically use a programming language such as PHP to dynamically create breadcrumb trails for you. However, to illustrate breadcrumbs, in this task you create one and add it by hand to a web page.

Breadcrumbs do exactly what their name implies: breadcrumbs provide a trail from a user's current location back to a site's home page.

Unless you apply CSS styles to the menus, the results appear spartan and unorganised. But it illustrates the concepts. A breadcrumb trail is a courtesy to users, allowing them always to know their location in the site, and providing them with an easy way back home.

```
<div id="breadcrumb">
<span id="bread">
<a href="./index.html">operatingsystems
</a>/
<a href="./bsd/index.html">bsd</a>/
<a href="./bsd/freebsd/index.html">
freebsd</a>/installation.html
</span>
</div>
```

Creating a breadcrumb trail (cont.)

For your information

Notice that the hyperlinks are linked to each folder's index.html page.

```
<a href="./bsd/index.html">
```

I instructed you to do this so you could click on the hyperlinks from your local directory. If this site was deployed on a Web server, you could leave off the index.html because the Web server would return the index page automatically.

```
<a href="./bsd">
```

For your information

In this chapter's examples, although the completed examples apply basic CSS styles to the results, the task explanations do not. If you only followed the task instructions, your results probably looked nothing like what you see in a modern web page. But that's okay; you created an external stylesheet (tiered.css) and you wrapped all the menus in div tags, each div with its own id. So you can easily format the menus globally for the site by modifying tiered.css.

A common layout for a website with menus such as we have created in this chapter is an inverted L layout. Global navigation links are across the top of the page and sometimes the bottom of the page. Often, a site has a banner, that banner usually appears above the global navigation links if the links are on the page's top. More in-depth category navigation links are usually along a page's left margin. Contextual links and local menus are usually displayed in the page content.

Creating a breadcrumb trail (cont.)

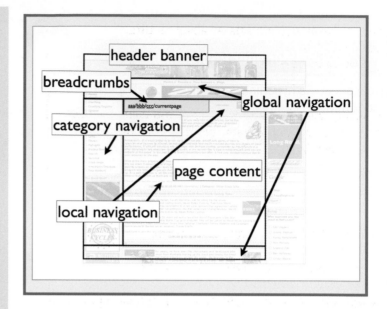

Timesaver tip

Specifying a complete path for every link can be tedious. You can use relative links, but what about common included content such as a top header? The included header might be in your site's top level, one level deed or further nested. You cannot use a relative hyperlink. When including common content by cutting and pasting, as we have done in this chapter, you can modify the links on every page. However, it is tedious and prone to error. Instead you could use an HTML base element.

The base element, specified by the **<base>** tag is placed in a document's head element and provides a common base URL for all links on a page. For instance,

```
<base href="www.mysite.com" />
```

causes your browser to prepend the base URL to every link in the page. When clicking the relative link

```
/sublevel_one/mypage.html
```

your browser would create an absolute URL.

```
www.mysite.com/./sublevel_one/
mypage.html
```

In reality, though, the probability of you using the base element is low. Why? Think about it. What happens if your page references an external website? Now the external link,

```
www.yahoo.uk
```

would be translated by your browser to,

```
www.mysite.comwww.yahoo.uk
```

which is not what you want. Note, it didn't even put in a slash for you, it literally prepended the base URL to the URL.

Validating and publishing your website

15

Introduction

If you've read through the entire book, congratulations, you've now reached the obligatory 'check your work and FTP your site to a free Web hosting service' chapter. Every beginners book on HTML and CSS has one, and this book is no different.

What you'll do

Validating your HTML and CSS

Uploading your website to a service provider

Validating your HTML and CSS

Task steps

1. Navigate to **validator.w3.org** and click on the **Validate by File Upload** tab.

2. Click **Choose File** and then select index.html from the tiered website created in Chapter 14.

3. Check **Verbose Output** and then click the **Check** button.

4. An error screen appears. The task in Chapter 14 was not valid; had our browser not been forgiving, the page never would have loaded.

5. Scroll down and review the error; the ul element is in an invalid location. Notice the list is enclosed in **<span></span>** tags.

   ```
   <span id="left_nav_
   span">
   ```

   Span elements are for in-line content; the ul element is block-level. What your browser did when rendering this page in previous tasks is automatically change the **left_nav_span** to a block-level element. It worked, but it isn't correct and is just plain sloppy.

Once you have written your HTML and CSS you should validate them. After all, by specifying the document type using

```
<!DOCTYPE HTML PUBLIC "-//W3C//DTD HTML
4.01 Transitional//EN"
"http://www.w3.org/TR/html4/loose.dtd">
```

your page is telling browsers that the page conforms to the html 4.01 transitional DTD.

The W3C, the standards body responsible for the HTML specifications, provides a free online HTML validation service at the **http://validator.w3.org** website. It also provides a free CSS validation service at the **http://jigsaw.w3.org/css-validator/** website.

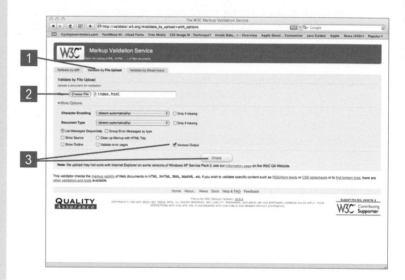

6 Remove the `<span></span>` tags, save and revalidate. The page passes.

7 Now check the stylesheet, tiered.css, from the tiered task.

8 Navigate to **jigsaw.w3.org/css-validator/** and click on the By file upload tab.

9 Upload tiered.css and click the Check button. It passes the first time.

15

For your information

You can also enter snippets of CSS directly into the validator by using the By direct input tab. That is how I validated the CSS in this book. But note, some of this book's CSS doesn't validate because I insisted on using more than the 17 valid colour names. For instance, whitesmoke is not a valid CSS colour name.

Uploading your website to a service provider

File transport protocol (FTP) is how you transfer files from your local computer to your web host. I'm assuming you have a service provider. If you don't, check with your Internet Service Provider (ISP), chances are you have free space allotted to you. Otherwise, go on Google, find one of the numerous pay Web hosts, and select one. In this task I use a free Web hosting provider called Tripod. You can use this service for free too if you can stand the advertisements. If you don't want the advertisements, you can pay for space with Tripod. It's a pretty reliable service that has been around since the Web's early days. But before you do, remember, you probably have free space, sans advertisements, on your ISP's Web server. Navigate to your ISP's customer service or FAQ section and search for free Web hosting.

After you obtain space on a Web server, this task illustrates just how easy it is to upload your files to your Web host.

The results are straightforward, you uploaded your pages to your Web host. Using an FTP program is not difficult. The page is pretty ugly, it has ads above and below it, and a popup appears when you navigate to the page, but it *is* free. For a small cost, Tripod provides hosting services without the advertisements.

Task steps

1 If you haven't already, find a Web host. Find out their FTP server's name so you can FTP. For this task I created an account on Tripod. By the time you read this book, though, I will have deleted that site.

2 Download an FTP program. For this task, I use FireFTP, a Firefox add-on. You can download FireFTP by going to the Tools menu, selecting Add-ons, and then finding FireFTP. There is only so much a GUI FTP program can do, so they are all pretty similar, and the steps, though in this task specific for FireFTP, apply to any FTP program.

3 After installing FireFTP, select FireFTP from the Tools menu. After FireFTP loads, select Create an account . . .

4 Assign the site an Account name, add the FTP server to Host, add your username and password. Click the Ok button when completed.

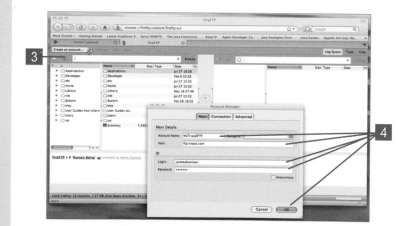

Uploading your website to a service provider (cont.)

5 Before continuing you need to modify the tiered website from the previous chapter.

6 If you haven't already done so, find out the base URL to your website on the server. Mine is

`http://jamesabrannan.tripod.com/`

on Tripod. (This site was deleted after completing this task.)

7 Change the base tag href to your site's base URL plus

`/tiered/WebContent/`

which for my site is

`http://jamesabrannan.tripod.com/tiered/WebContent/`

8 After completing, return to FireFTP and login to the FTP site.

9 Transfer the files to your server. Usually you can just click on the top-level folder and transfer all the files and sub-folders at once. Note that Tripod only allows sites with three subdirectory levels.

15

Uploading your website to a service provider (cont.)

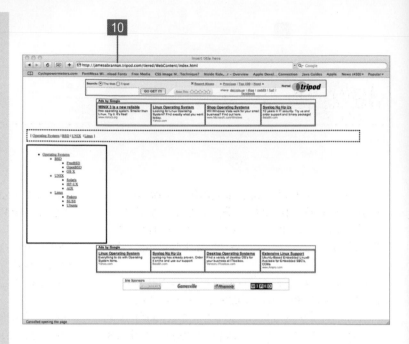

10 After uploading, navigate to your site and you should see it on your Web host's server.

Jargon buster

Aspect ratio – An image's proportion expressed as width divided by height. For instance, a 100 pixel × 100 pixel image has a 1:1 aspect ratio. A 300 pixel × 100 pixel image has a 3:1 aspect ratio.

Bookmark – A Web address that you can save so your browser remembers. Later you can navigate to the bookmarked page by selecting its bookmark rather than typing the page's address.

BSD – Berkeley Software Distribution: UNIX version developed at the University of California.

Code – Computer instructions, short for source code. Source code is written computer instructions.

Deprecated – Replaced software features that should no longer be used. A replaced element or attribute that is outdated by a newer element, attribute, or construct. For instance, most HTML formatting features were replaced by CSS, so these HTML formatting features are deprecated.

DreamWeaver – Web development software maintained and sold by Adobe.

Extension – Letter following a filename's period . that indicates the information type of file. For instance, .html is an extension that indicates the file contains HTML.

Favicon – An icon that preceeds a favorites link. Displays in the browser's address bar before the address. Also displays in the favorites list before the hyperlink.

Favorites – See bookmark. Bookmarks are also called favorites because often users bookmark his or her favourite site.

GNU – General Public Licenses an organisation started in 1984 to promote a free operating system similar to Unix. The GNU software was ultimately combined with Linux. GNU now exists for a much broader purpose of promoting open-source software. GNU wrote both the LGPL and GPL licensing schemes and is active in ensuring others follow the licenses.

Google it – In Web vernacular 'googling it' is looking up something online using the Search engine Google.

Hexadecimal – A base-16 numbering system used to represent binary data (zeros and ones) in a more human friendly way. Used extensively in computer science and electronics field.

Integer – A whole number.

iWeb – A graphical Web development tool made by Apple. iWeb is a very easy to use program for end-users with little to no HTML or CSS experience.

Linux – A free UNIX-like operating system developed by Linus Torvalds.

Maintainability – How easy it is to find problems in a program, fix a program and modify the program.

Object-oriented programming – A programming style where programming constructs are treated as objects.

Pixel – Individual dot in an image. All images on your monitor are composed of pixels.

Plug-in – Additions you can install on your computer that allow playing multimedia content not otherwise supported by a browser. For instance, Adobe Flash is a plug-in you must install separately from your browser.

Safari – Web browser which comes standard on all Apple computers.

Tabular data – Data that typically can be represented in a spreadsheet.

Template – A pattern. In this book it is an HTML or CSS document that's used as your starting point, so you're not required to recreate common HTML or CSS code each time you create a new document.

Thumbnail – A smaller version of a graphic, designed to allow your browser to download and view a graphic quickly, by downloading the thumbnail rather than the full-sized image.

UNIX – An operating system created by Bell Labs in the 1970s. The most popular operating system for large-scale Web providers or servers that have to support heavy usage.

Viral video – Video shared over the Internet. This sharing leads to the video becoming popular.

Viewport – A browser's viewing area.

Z-index – The CSS property for z-order. Z-order is the front to back order of elements in a page. Elements with a higher z-index are displayed in front of elements with a lower z-order.

Appendix A: HTML tags used in this book

Element	Description
<!--...-->	Specifies a comment.
<!DOCTYPE>	Specifies the document type.
<a></a>	Specifies an anchor.
<abbr></abbr>	Specifies an abbreviation.
<area></area>	Specifies an area inside an image map.
<b></b>	Specifies bold text.
<base></base>	Specifies a base URL for all a page's links.
<big></big>	Specifies big text.
<blockquote> </blockquote>	Specifies a long quotation.
<body></body>	Specifies the body element.
 	Inserts a single line break.
<caption></caption>	Specifies a table caption.
<cite></cite>	Specifies a citation.
<code></code>	Specifies computer code text.
<col></col>	Specifies table column attributes.
<colgroup></colgroup>	Specifies table column group.
<dd></dd>	Specifies a definition description.
<del></del>	Specifies deleted text.
<div></div>	Specifies a document's section.
<dfn></dfn>	Specifies a definition term.
<dl></dl>	Specifies a definition list.
<dt></dt>	Specifies a definition term.
<em></em>	Specifies emphasised text.
<fieldset></fieldset>	Specifies a fieldset.

Element	Description
<form></form>	Specifies a form.
<h1></h1> ...	Specifies header 1 to header 6.
<head></head>	Specifies document's information.
<hr/>	Specifies a horizontal rule.
<html></html>	Specifies an HTML document.
<i></i>	Specifies italic text.
<img/>	Specifies an image.
<input></input>	Specifies an input field.
<ins></ins>	Specifies inserted text.
<kbd></kbd>	Specifies keyboard text.
<label></label>	Specifies a form control label.
<legend></legend>	Specifies a fieldset title.
<li></li>	Specifies a list item.
<link></link>	Specifies a resource reference.
<map></map>	Specifies an image map.
<meta></meta>	Specifies meta information.
<ol></ol>	Specifies an ordered list.
<optgroup></optgroup>	Specifies an option group.
<option></option>	Specifies a drop-down list option.
<p></p>	Specifies a paragraph.
<pre></pre>	Specifies pre-formatted text.
<q></q>	Specifies a short quotation.
<samp></samp>	Specifies sample computer code.
<select></select>	Specifies a selectable list.
<small></small>	Specifies small text.
<span></span>	Specifies document section.
<strong></strong>	Specifies strong text.
<style></style>	Specifies a style definition.
	Specifies subscripted text.
	Specifies superscripted text.
<table></table>	Specifies a table.
<tbody></tbody>	Specifies a table body.

Element	Description
<td></td>	Specifies a table cell.
<textarea></textarea>	Specifies a text area.
<tfoot></tfoot>	Specifies a table footer.
<th></th>	Specifies a table header.
<thead></thead>	Specifies a table header.
<title></title>	Specifies the document title.
<tr></tr>	Specifies a table row.
<tt></tt>	Specifies teletype text.
<ul></ul>	Specifies an unordered list.
<var></var>	Specifies a variable.

Appendix B: CSS properties covered in this book

Background properties		
Property	**Description**	**Valid values**
background	Specifies element's background	background-attachment value, properties in one declaration. background-colour value, background-image value, background-repeat value, background-position value
background-attachment	Specifies image is fixed or scrolls as page scrolls.	fixed, scroll
background-color	Specifies element's background colour.	colour (hexadecimal, name, rgb), transparent
background-image	Specifies element's background image.	none, url
background-position	Specifies background image's starting position.	top centre, top left, top right, centre left, centre centre, centre right, bottom left, bottom centre, bottom right, x% y%, x-position y-position
background-repeat	Specifies background image repetition.	repeat, repeat-x, repeat-y, no-repeat

Border properties

Property	Description	Valid values
border	Specifies element's borders in one declaration.	border-colour value, border-width value, border-style value
border-bottom	Specifies element's bottom border properties in one declaration	border-bottom-width value, border-style value, border-colour value
border-bottom-color	Specifies element's bottom border colour.	border-colour value
border-bottom-style	Specifies element's bottom	border-style value border style.
border-bottom-width	Specifies element's bottom border width.	thin, medium, thick, numeric length value
border-color	Specifies element's four borders.	colourname, rgb, hexadecimal (one to four values)
border-left	Specifies element's left border properties.	border-left-width value, border-style value, border-colour value
border-left-color	Specifies element's left border colour.	border-colour value
border-left-style	Specifies element's left border style.	border-style value
border-left-width	Specifies element's left border width.	thin, medium, thick, numeric length value
border-right	Specifies element's right border properties.	border-right-width value, border-style value, border-colour value
border-right-color	Specifies element's right border colour.	border-colour value
border-right-style	Specifies element's right border style.	border-style value
border-right-width	Specifies element's right border width.	thin, medium, thick, numeric length value
border-style	Specifies element's border style (one to four values).	none, hidden, dotted, dashed, solid, double, groove, ridge, inset, outset
border-top	Specifies element's top border properties.	border-top-width value, border-style value, border-colour value
border-top-color	Specifies element's top border colour.	border-colour value
border-top-style	Specifies element's top border style.	border-style value
border-top-width	Specifies element's top border width.	thin, medium, thick, numeric length value
border-width	Specifies element's border width (one to four values).	thin, medium, thick, numeric length value

Element dimension properties

Property	Description	Valid values
height	Specifies element's height	auto, numeric length value, %
line-height	Specifies element's distance between lines.	normal, numeric length value, %
max-height	Specifies element's maximum height.	none, numeric length value, %
max-width	Specifies element's maximum width.	none, numeric length value, %
min-height	Specifies element's minimum height.	numeric length value, %
min-width	Specifies element's minimum width.	numeric length value, %
width	Specifies element's width.	auto, numeric length value, %

Font properties

Property	Description	Valid values
font	Specifies font properties.	font-style value, font-variant value, font-weight value, font-size/line-height value, font-family value
font-family	Specifies font-family names.	family-name value, generic-family name value
font-size	Specifies font size.	xx-small, x-small, small, medium, large, x-large, xx-large, smaller, larger, numeric value, %
font-style	Specifies font style.	normal, italic, oblique
font-weight	Specifies font weight.	normal, bold, bolder, lighter, 100, 200, 300, 400, 500, 600, 700, 800, 900

List properties

Property	Description	Valid values
list-style	Specifies list properties.	list-style-type value, list-style-position value, list-style-image
list-style-image	Specifies list item marker uses image.	none, url
list-style-position	Specifies list item marker placement.	inside, outside
list-style-type	Specifies list item marker type.	none, disc, circle, square, decimal, decimal-leading-zero, lower-roman, upper-roman, lower-alpha, upper-alpha, lower-greek, lower-latin, upper-latin, hebrew, armenian, georgian, cjk-ideographic, hiragana, katakana, hiragana-iroha, katakana-iroha

Margin properties

Property	Description	Valid values
margin	Specifies element's margin properties.	margin-top value, margin-right value, margin-bottom value, margin-left value
margin-bottom	Specifies element's bottom margin.	auto, numeric length value, %
margin-left	Specifies element's left margin.	auto, numeric length value, %
margin-right	Specifies element's right margin.	auto, numeric length value, %
margin-top	Specifies element's top margin.	auto, numeric length value, %

Padding properties

Property	Description	Valid values
padding	Specifies element's padding	padding-top value, padding-right value, padding-bottom value, padding-left value
padding-bottom	Specifies element's bottom padding.	numeric length value, %
padding-left	Specifies element's left padding.	numeric length value, %
padding-right	Specifies element's right padding.	numeric length value, %
padding-top	Specifies element's top padding.	numeric length value, %

Positioning properties

Property	Description	Valid values
float	Specifies if an element is to the left or right.	left, right, none of other elements.
position	Specifies element's position.	static, relative, absolute, fixed
clear	Specifies no element can float left or right of element.	left, right, both, none
bottom	Specifies element's distance from parent bottom.	auto, %, numeric length value
left	Specifies element's distance from parent left.	auto, %, numeric length value
overflow	Specifies element's behaviour if content goes beyond element's bounds.	visible, hidden, scroll, auto
position	Specifies element's position.	static, relative, absolute, fixed
right	Specifies element's distance from parent right.	auto, %, numeric length value
top	Specifies element's distance from parent top.	auto, %, numeric length value
vertical-align	Specifies element's vertical alignment.	baseline, sub, super, top, text-top, middle, bottom, text-bottom, numeric length value, %
z-index	Specifies element's stack order on page.	auto, numeric value

Text properties

Property	Description	Values
color	Specifies text colour.	colour name, rgb, hexadecimal
letter-spacing	Specifies space between letters.	normal, numeric length value
text-align	Specifies element's text alignment.	left, right, centre, justify
text-decoration	Specifies text decoration.	none, underline, overline, line-through, blink
text-indent	Specifies element's first text line indentation.	numeric length value, %
text-transform	Specifies element's text transformation.	none, capitalise, uppercase, lowercase
white-space	Specifies element's white space handling.	normal, pre, nowrap
word-spacing	Specifies space between words.	normal, numeric length value

Pseudo-classes

Pseudo-class	Purpose
:active	Specifies style for active element.
:focus	Specifies style for element with focus.
:hover	Specifies style for element moused-over.
:link	Specifies style for unvisited link.
:visited	Specifies style for visited link.
:first-child	Specifies style for element that is first child of another element.

Pseudo-elements

Pseudo-element	Purpose
:first-letter	Specifies style for first letter in text.
:first-line	Specifies style for first line in text.

Appendix C: CSS colour name, hexadecimal value and RGB value

Colour name	Hexadecimal value	RGB value
indianred	CD 5C 5C	205 92 92
lightcoral	F0 80 80	240 128 128
salmon	FA 80 72	250 128 114
darksalmon	E9 96 7A	233 150 122
lightsalmon	FF A0 7A	255 160 122
crimson	DC 14 3C	220 20 60
red	FF 00 00	255 0 0
firebrick	B2 22 22	178 34 34
darkred	8B 00 00	139 0 0
pink	FF C0 CB	255 192 203
lightpink	FF B6 C1	255 182 193
hotpink	FF 69 B4	255 105 180
deeppink	FF 14 93	255 20 147
mediumvioletred	C7 15 85	199 21 133
palevioletred	DB 70 93	219 112 147
lightsalmon	FF A0 7A	255 160 122
coral	FF 7F 50	255 127 80
tomato	FF 63 47	255 99 71
orangered	FF 45 00	255 69 0
darkorange	FF 8C 00	255 140 0
orange	FF A5 00	255 165 0
gold	FF D7 00	255 215 0
yellow	FF FF 00	255 255 0
lightyellow	FF FF E0	255 255 224

Colour name	Hexadecimal value	RGB value
lemonchiffon	FF FA CD	255 250 205
lightgoldenrodyellow	FA FA D2	250 250 210
papayawhip	FF EF D5	255 239 213
moccasin	FF E4 B5	255 228 181
peachpuff	FF DA B9	255 218 185
palegoldenrod	EE E8 AA	238 232 170
khaki	F0 E6 8C	240 230 140
darkkhaki	BD B7 6B	189 183 107
lavender	E6 E6 FA	230 230 250
thistle	D8 BF D8	216 191 216
plum	DD A0 DD	221 160 221
violet	EE 82 EE	238 130 238
orchid	DA 70 D6	218 112 214
fuchsia	FF 00 FF	255 0 255
magenta	FF 00 FF	255 0 255
mediumorchid	BA 55 D3	186 85 211
mediumpurple	93 70 DB	147 112 219
blueviolet	8A 2B E2	138 43 226
darkviolet	94 00 D3	148 0 211
darkorchid	99 32 CC	153 50 204
darkmagenta	8B 00 8B	139 0 139
purple	80 00 80	128 0 128
indigo	4B 00 82	75 0 130
slateblue	6A 5A CD	106 90 205
darkslateblue	48 3D 8B	72 61 139
mediumslateblue	7B 68 EE	123 104 238
greenyellow	AD FF 2F	173 255 47
chartreuse	7F FF 00	127 255 0
lawngreen	7C FC 00	124 252 0
lime	00 FF 00	0 255 0
limegreen	32 CD 32	50 205 50
palegreen	98 FB 98	152 251 152

Appendix C: CSS colour name, hexadecimal value and RGB value 285

Colour name	Hexadecimal value	RGB value
lightgreen	90 EE 90	144 238 144
mediumspringgreen	00 FA 9A	0 250 154
springgreen	00 FF 7F	0 255 127
mediumseagreen	3C B3 71	60 179 113
seagreen	2E 8B 57	46 139 87
forestgreen	22 8B 22	34 139 34
green	00 80 00	0 128 0
darkgreen	00 64 00	0 100 0
yellowgreen	9A CD 32	154 205 50
olivedrab	6B 8E 23	107 142 35
olive	80 80 00	128 128 0
darkolivegreen	55 6B 2F	85 107 47
mediumaquamarine	66 CD AA	102 205 170
darkseagreen	8F BC 8F	143 188 143
lightseagreen	20 B2 AA	32 178 170
darkcyan	00 8B 8B	0 139 139
teal	00 80 80	0 128 128
aqua	00 FF FF	0 255 255
cyan	00 FF FF	0 255 255
lightcyan	E0 FF FF	224 255 255
paleturquoise	AF EE EE	175 238 238
aquamarine	7F FF D4	127 255 212
turquoise	40 E0 D0	64 224 208
mediumturquoise	48 D1 CC	72 209 204
darkturquoise	00 CE D1	0 206 209
cadetblue	5F 9E A0	95 158 160
steelblue	46 82 B4	70 130 180
lightsteelblue	B0 C4 DE	176 196 222
purwablue	9B E1 FF	155 225 255
powderblue	B0 E0 E6	176 224 230
lightblue	AD D8 E6	173 216 230
skyblue	87 CE EB	135 206 235

Colour name	Hexadecimal value	RGB value
lightskyblue	87 CE FA	135 206 250
deepskyblue	00 BF FF	0 191 255
dodgerblue	1E 90 FF	30 144 255
cornflowerblue	64 95 ED	100 149 237
royalblue	41 69 E1	65 105 225
blue	00 00 FF	0 0 255
mediumblue	00 00 CD	0 0 205
darkblue	00 00 8B	0 0 139
navy	00 00 80	0 0 128
midnightblue	19 19 70	25 25 112
cornsilk	FF F8 DC	255 248 220
blanchedalmond	FF EB CD	255 235 205
bisque	FF E4 C4	255 228 196
navajowhite	FF DE AD	255 222 173
wheat	F5 DE B3	245 222 179
burlywood	DE B8 87	222 184 135
tan	D2 B4 8C	210 180 140
rosybrown	BC 8F 8F	188 143 143
sandybrown	F4 A4 60	244 164 96
goldenrod	DA A5 20	218 165 32
darkgoldenrod	B8 86 0B	184 134 11
peru	CD 85 3F	205 133 63
chocolate	D2 69 1E	210 105 30
saddlebrown	8B 45 13	139 69 19
sienna	A0 52 2D	160 82 45
brown	A5 2A 2A	165 42 42
maroon	80 00 00	128 0 0
white	FF FF FF	255 255 255
snow	FF FA FA	255 250 250
honeydew	F0 FF F0	240 255 240
mintcream	F5 FF FA	245 255 250
azure	F0 FF FF	240 255 255

Colour name	Hexadecimal value	RGB value
aliceblue	F0 F8 FF	240 248 255
ghostwhite	F8 F8 FF	248 248 255
whitesmoke	F5 F5 F5	245 245 245
seashell	FF F5 EE	255 245 238
beige	F5 F5 DC	245 245 220
oldlace	FD F5 E6	253 245 230
floralwhite	FF FA F0	255 250 240
ivory	FF FF F0	255 255 240
antiquewhite	FA EB D7	250 235 215
linen	FA F0 E6	250 240 230
lavenderblush	FF F0 F5	255 240 245
mistyrose	FF E4 E1	255 228 225
gainsboro	DC DC DC	220 220 220
lightgrey	D3 D3 D3	211 211 211
silver	C0 C0 C0	192 192 192
darkgray	A9 A9 A9	169 169 169
gray	80 80 80	128 128 128
dimgray	69 69 69	105 105 105
lightslategray	77 88 99	119 136 153
slategray	70 80 90	112 128 144
darkslategray	2F 4F 4F	47 79 79
black	00 00 00	0 0 0

Troubleshooting guide

HTML basics

If you wish to create an HTML document, and you don't know how, see Creating a basic document: document declaration, header, metadata and body, pg. 12.

If you wish to add a comment to your HTML, see Creating HTML comments, pg. 14.

If you wish to create an HTML paragraph, see Creating HTML paragraphs, pg. 18.

If you wish to create headings, see Adding headings to your document, pg. 20.

If you wish to add a list of items to your document, see Creating ordered and unordered lists, pg. 22; see also: Creating a definition list, pg. 26.

If you wish to change a list to use letters or Roman numerals, see Formatting ordered and unordered lists, pg. 28.

If you wish to add quotation marks, see Formatting quotations, pg. 30.

If you wish to format your HTML, see Marking up other text elements, pg. 33.

If you wish to add special characters to your HTML, see Inserting special characters, pg. 37.

Understanding hyperlinks

If you wish to add a URL to your document, see Using hyperlinks – absolute URLs, pg. 45; see also: Using hyperlinks: relative URLs, pg. 47.

If you wish to have a linked page open in a new browser window, see Adding targets to hyperlinks, pg. 50.

If you wish to link from one location in a document to another location in the document, see Creating anchors, pg. 53.

If you wish to link to an email address, see Linking to an email address, pg. 55.

If you wish to change a hyperlink's appearance or colour, see Formatting hyperlinks: color, pg. 180; see also: Formatting hyperlinks – lines, borders, background color, pg. 182.

If you wish to create an image link, see Formatting hyperlinks – image links, pg. 184.

Adding and editing images with HTML

If you wish to add an image to your page, see Adding images to a Web page, pg. 59.

If you wish to add a favicon to your site, see How to display a custom icon in a browser (a favicon), pg. 65.

If you wish to use an image as a hyperlink, see Creating image links, pg. 66.

If you wish to use thumbnails, see Creating image links, thumbnails, pg. 68.

If you wish to create an image map, see Creating an image map, pg. 70.

If you wish to create an image link, see Formatting hyperlinks – image links, pg. 184.

Working with tables

If you wish to create a basic HTML table, see Creating table rows and data cells, pg. 75; see also: Adding padding and spacing to table cells, pg. 78; Adding headings to tables, pg. 81; and Specifying column spans and row spans, pg. 88.

If you wish to add a caption to a table, see Adding a caption to a table, pg. 83.

If you wish to add advanced formatting to a table, see Adding frame attributes to tables, pg. 85; see also: Specifying a table's header, body, and footer, pg. 90; and Adding table dividing lines using rules, pg. 92.

Creating forms

If you wish to add a form to your HTML page, see Building a simple form, pg. 97.

If you wish to add a checkbox to your form, see Adding a check box, pg. 101.

If you wish to add a radio button to your form, see Adding radio buttons, pg. 104.

If you wish to create a form for users to upload a file, see Adding file fields, pg. 106.

If you wish to create a form where users can enter paragraphs of text, see Adding a text area, pg. 108.

If you wish to add a drop-down choice to a form, see Adding select elements (lists and menus), pg. 110.

If you wish to add a legend to your form or grouping several form elements, see Adding a fieldset and legend, pg. 114.

Formatting text

If you wish to set an element's font, see Setting and element's font family, pg 144.

If you wish to set an element's font size, see Setting an element's font weight and size, pg. 152.

If you wish to align text, see Aligning text, pg. 159.

If you wish to change word spacing or line spacing, see Formatting text using word and letter spacing, pg. 161.

Working with colours

If you wish to create a colour palette for your site, see Understanding Web colours – choosing a palette, pg. 165.

If you wish to change an element's colour, see Specifying a colour four different ways, pg. 168.

If you wish to change an element's background colour, or adding a background image, see Setting background colour, pg. 170.

If you wish to change an element's text colour, see Setting foreground colour, pg. 175.

If you wish to change a hyperlink's colour, see Formatting hyperlinks: color, pg. 180

Borders and padding

If you wish to add padding to an element, see Setting element padding, pg. 191.

If you wish to set an element's margin, see Setting element margins, pg. 194.

If you wish to add a border to an element, see Setting element borders, pg. 197.

If you wish to set an element's width and height, see Setting width and height (percentage), pg. 199; see also: Setting width and height (pixels), pg. 201.

Positioning elements

If you wish to position an image within a paragraph, so the paragraph flows around the image, see Positioning Elements using float and clear, pg. 206.

If you wish to position an element, see Positioning elements using relative positioning, pg. 211; see also: Positioning elements using absolute positioning, pg. 214; or, Positioning elements using fixed positioning, pg. 222.

If you wish to create a single-column page, see Using a fixed width layout: one column, pg. 229; see also: Using a liquid layout: one column, centred, pg. 231.

If you wish to create a two-column page, see Using a liquid layout: two columns, pg. 233. Note: this topic also discusses fixed layouts.

If you wish to create a three-column page, see Using a liquid layout: three columns, pg. 236. Note: this topic also discusses fixed layouts.

Building a website

If you wish to create a website, with structure and navigation. See Understanding a flat site structure, pg. 247; see also: understanding a tiered site structure, pg 250.

If you wish to create menus for your website, see Creating a global top or bottom menu, pg. 256; see also: Creating a left floating site menu, pg. 259; and Creating a local navigation menu, pg. 261.

If you wish to create a breadcrumb trail, see Creating a breadcrumb trail, pg. 262.

If you wish to validate your site's HTML or CSS, see Validating your HTML and CSS, pg. 268.

If you wish to upload your site to a service provider, see Uploading your website to a service provider, pg. 270.